Private Armed Forces and Global Security

Private Armed Forces and Global Security

A Guide to the Issues

Carlos Ortiz

Contemporary Military, Strategic, and Security Issues

PRAEGER

AN IMPRINT OF ABC-CLIO, LLC
Santa Barbara, California • Denver, Colorado • Oxford, England

Library of Congress Cataloging-in-Publication Data
Ortiz, Carlos.
    Private armed forces and global security : a guide to the issues / Carlos Ortiz.
        p. cm. — (Contemporary military, strategic, and security issues)
    Includes bibliographical references and index.
    ISBN 978-0-313-35592-9 (print : alk. paper) — ISBN 978-0-313-35593-6
(ebook) 1. Private military companies—History—21st century. 2. Private military
companies—History—20th century. 3. Security, International—History—
21st century. 4. Security, International—History—20th century. I. Title.
    U240.O785 2010
    355.3'5—dc22   2009046663

ISBN: 978-0-313-35592-9
EISBN: 978-0-313-35593-6

14 13 12 11 10   1 2 3 4 5

This book is also available on the World Wide Web as an eBook.
Visit www.abc-clio.com for details.

Praeger
An Imprint of ABC-CLIO, LLC

ABC-CLIO, LLC
130 Cremona Drive, P.O. Box 1911
Santa Barbara, California 93116-1911

This book is printed on acid-free paper ∞

Manufactured in the United States of America

For
my parents

Contents

Preface

Private military companies (PMCs) and global trends toward the privatization of security first attracted my attention in the early 1990s. Back then, I used to mention PMCs and people thought I was maybe an arms dealer disguised as an academic. Times have changed. Now almost everyone has a view about private personnel working in conflict zones. By 1996 I was formally researching the subject, which eventually led to a PhD and various related presentations and publications. I cite some of my earlier work here and take forward previous arguments.

Throughout this journey, the need for easily accessible material on the subject has been made patent to me time and again. Moreover, during numerous conversations held with people of different backgrounds and ages, people's desire to learn about all the different types of private armed forces typical of contemporary conflict has been made obvious as well. There is also a renewed impetus to the historical analysis of the private exercise of force. Discussions have additionally been directed toward the outlining of paths to the study of PMCs. This rich dialogue engendered my desire to write this book and informed the structure of its contents.

In the course of my research, I have become indebted to countless people. Some of them are cited in the book. In a field of scholarly inquiry that has exploded since the onset of the Iraq conflict, however, the views of many other relevant sources have fallen outside the scope of the analysis. Nevertheless, I believe the book plants the seeds for any interested reader to pursue alternative avenues of study and discover the many fascinating titles documenting the study of PMCs and adverse private forces. I sincerely hope this will make up for my failure to acknowledge specific works and exchanges I have sustained over the years with many authors.

In covering such a wide area and providing abundant empirical grounding, I might have produced some inconsistencies. While I hope any such instances would not undermine the narrative contained here, I take full responsibility for them.

Finally, I would like to thank my family. It was reassuring for me to have their unconditional support in undertaking this project.

Abbreviations

17N	Revolutionary Organization 17 November
9/11	Terrorist attacks of September 11, 2001, in the United States
AA	Asbat al-Ansar (Band of Partisans)
AECA	Arms Exports Control Act
AFDL	Alliance of Democratic Forces for the Liberation of Congo-Zaire (Alliance des forces démocratiques pour la libération du Congo-Zaïre)
AI	Ansar al-Islam (Supporters of Islam)
AIDS	Acquired immune deficiency syndrome
AJ	Al-Jihad
AMB	Al-Aqsa Martyrs Brigade
AMISOM	African Union Mission in Somalia
ANC	Armée Nationale Congolaise (Congolese National Army)
ANO	Abu Nidal Organization
AQ	Al-Qaeda (The Base)
AQI	Al-Qaeda in Iraq
AQIM	Al-Qaeda in the Islamic Maghreb
AS	Al-Shabaab (The Youth)
ASG	Abu Sayyaf Group
AU	African Union
AUC	Autodefensas Unidas de Colombia (United Self-Defense Forces of Colombia)
Aum	Aum Shinrikyo
CALEA	Communications Assistance for Law Enforcement Act
CEO	Chief executive officer

CFR	Code of Federal Regulations
CGPCS	Contact Group on Piracy off the Coast of Somalia
CIA	Central Intelligence Agency
CICA	Competition in Contracting Act
CIO	Compagnie des Indes Orientales (French East Indies Company)
CIRA	Continuity Irish Republican Army
CivPol	Civilian police mission
CMPR	Civil-military-private military relations
CMR	Civil-military relations
CPA	Coalition Provisional Authority (Iraq)
CPP/NPA	Communist Party of the Philippines/ New People's Army
CSC	Computer Sciences Corporation
DDTC	Directorate of Defense Trade Controls
DEA	Drug Enforcement Administration
DHKP/C	Revolutionary People's Liberation Party/Front
DHS	Department of Homeland Security
DOD	Department of Defense
DOS	Department of State
DRC	Democratic Republic of the Congo
DS&T	Directorate of Science and Technology
DSL	Defence Systems Ltd.
EIA	Energy Information Administration
EIC	English East India Company
ELN	Ejercito de Liberacion Nacional (National Liberation Army)
EO	Executive Outcomes
ETA	Euzkadi Ta Askatasuna (Basque Fatherland and Liberty)
EU	European Union
EUFOR	EU Forces
FAA	Forças Armadas Angolanas (Angolan Armed Forces)
FAO	Food and Agriculture Organization
FARC	Fuerzas Armadas Revolucionarias de Colombia (Revolutionary Armed Forces of Colombia)
FATA	Federally Administered Tribal Areas (Pakistan)
FBI	Federal Bureau of Investigation
FCO	Foreign and Commonwealth Office (UK)
FCPA	Foreign Corrupt Practices Act
FedBizOpps	Federal Business Opportunities
FNLA	Frente Nacional de Libertação de Angola (National Front for the Liberation of Angola)

FOCI	Foreign Ownership, Control, or Influence
FOMUC	Force multinationale en Centrafrique (Multinational Force in the Central African Republic)
FY	Fiscal year
GAO	Government Accountability Office
GIA	Groupement Islamique Armé (Armed Islamic Group)
GICM	Groupe Islamique Combattant Marocain (Moroccan Islamic Combatant Group)
GSA	General Services Administration
HAMAS	Harakat al-Muqawama al-Islamiya (Islamic Resistance Movement)
HHD	High human development
HIV	Human immunodeficiency virus
HSC	Homeland Security Corporation
HUJI-B	Harakat ul-Jihad-i-Islami/Bangladesh
HUM	Harakat ul-Mujahadeen
IED	Improvised explosive device
IFOR	Implementation Force (Bosnia and Herzegovina)
IG	Gama'a al-Islamiyya
IJU	Islamic Jihad Union
IMF	International Monetary Fund
IMO	International Maritime Organization
IMU	Islamic Movement of Uzbekistan
IOs	International organizations
IPOA	International Peace Operations Association
IPTF	International Police Task Force (Bosnia and Herzegovina)
ISDS	International Security & Defence Systems
ISPS	International Ship and Port Facility Security
IT	Information technology
ITAR	International Traffic in Arms Regulations
JEM	Jaish-e-Mohammed (Army of Muhammad)
JI	Jemaah Islamiya
KADEK	Freedom and Democracy Congress of Kurdistan
KBR	Kellogg Brown & Root
KC	Kahane Chai
KGB	Komitet Gosudarstvennoi Bezopasnosti (Committee for State Security, Soviet Union)
KGK/PKK	Kongra-Gel/Kurdistan Workers' Party
KH	Kata'ib Hizballah
KPCS	Kimberley Process Certification Scheme
LHD	Low human development

LICUS	Low-income countries under stress
LIFG	Libyan Islamic Fighting Group
LJ	Lashkar i Jhangvi (Army of Punjab)
LOGCAP	Logistics Civil Augmentation Program
LSD	Lysergic acid diethylamide
LT	Lashkar-e Tayyiba (Army of the Righteous)
LTTE	Liberation Tigers of Tamil Eelam
MCC	Millennium Challenge Corporation
MEJA	Military Extraterritorial Jurisdiction Act
MEK	Mujahedin-e Khalq Organization
MEND	Movement for the Emancipation of the Niger Delta
MEO	Most efficient organization
MHD	Medium human development
MI6	UK intelligence agency
MINURCA	UN Mission in the Central African Republic
MINURCAT	UN Mission in the Central African Republic and Chad
MNCs	Multinational corporations
MPLA	Movimento Popular de Libertação de Angola (Popular Movement for the Liberation of Angola)
MPRI	Military Professional Resources, Inc.
MTI	Monitoring the Internet
NATO	North Atlantic Treaty Organisation
NCC	National Counterterrorism Center
NGOs	Nongovernmental organizations
NPM	New public management
OECD	Organisation for Economic Co-operation and Development
ONUC	Opération des Nations Unies au Congo (UN Operation in the Congo)
OPEC	Organization of the Petroleum Exporting Countries
OSCE	Organization for Security and Co-operation in Europe
PAE	Pacific Architects and Engineers
PCP	Phencyclidine
PFI	Private Finance Initiative
PFLP	Popular Front for the Liberation of Palestine
PFLP–GC	Popular Front for the Liberation of Palestine–General Command
PIJ	Palestinian Islamic Jihad–Shaqaqi Faction
PLF	Palestine Liberation Front–Abu Abbas Faction
PMCs	Private military companies
PMSCs	Private military and security companies
PPCs	Public-private comparators

PPF	Participating Police Force (Solomon Islands)
PPPs	Public-private partnerships
PSCs	Private security companies/Public service comparators
R&D	Research and development
RAMSI	Regional Assistance Mission to Solomon Islands
RCA	Republic of Central Africa
RDD	Radiological dispersal device
RIRA	Real IRA
RN	Revolutionary Nuclei
RS	Revolutionary Struggle
RUF	Revolutionary United Front
SADF	South African Defence Force (during apartheid)
SAIC	Science Applications International Corporation
SANDF	South African National Defence Force (post-apartheid)
SAS	Special Air Services
SFOR	Stabilization Force (Bosnia and Herzegovina)
SIEDO	Subprocuraduría de Investigación Especializada contra la Delincuencia Organizada (Deputy Attorney's Office of Specialized Investigation of Organized Crime)
SL	Sendero Luminoso (Shining Path)
SSR	Security sector reform
SSSI	Strategic Security Solutions International Ltd.
SUA PROT 1988	Protocol for the Suppression of Unlawful Acts against the Safety of Fixed Platforms Located on the Continental Shelf
SUA PROT 2005	Protocol to the Convention for the Suppression of Unlawful Acts against the Safety of Maritime Navigation
TA2000	Terrorism Act 2000 (UK)
TEP	Train-and-Equip Program
TIDE	Terrorist Identities Datamart Environment
UCMJ	Uniform Code of Military Justice
UK	United Kingdom
UN	United Nations
UNAMIR	UN Assistance Mission for Rwanda
UNAMSIL	UN Mission in Sierra Leone
UNAVEM	UN Angola Verification Mission
UNCLOS	UN Convention on the Law of the Sea
UNCRO	UN Confidence Restoration Operation (Croatia)
UNDP	UN Development Programme
UNICEF	UN Children's Fund

UNITA	União Naçional para a Independência Total de Angola (National Union for the Total Independence of Angola)
UNMIBH	UN Mission in Bosnia and Herzegovina
UNMOP	UN Mission of Observers in Prevlaka
UNOCI	UN Operation in Côte d'Ivoire
UNODC	UN Office on Drugs and Crime
UNOMIG	UN Observer Mission in Georgia
UNOMSIL	UN Observer Mission in Sierra Leone
UNOSOM	UN Operation in Somalia
UNPD	UN Procurement Division
UNPREDEP	UN Preventive Deployment Force (Macedonia)
UNPROFOR	UN Protection Force (former Yugoslavia)
UNPSG	UN Police Support Group (Croatia)
UNTAES	UN Transitional Administration in Eastern Slavonia, Baranja and Western Sirmium
USAID	US Agency for International Development
USA PATRIOT	Uniting and Strengthening America by Providing Appropriate Tools Required to Intercept and Obstruct Terrorism
USIS	U.S. Investigations Services, Inc.
USML	U.S. Munitions List
USS	U.S. Ship
USSG	U.S. Sentencing Guidelines
UXO	Unexploded ordnance
VOC	Verenigde Oostindische Compagnie (United Dutch East Indies Company)
WIC	Geoctroyeerde West-Indische Compagnie (Dutch West Indies Company)
WPPS	Worldwide Personal Protective Services
WSI	Wackenhut Services, Inc.
WWII	Second World War

CHAPTER 1

Introduction

In the wake of the terrorist attacks of September 11, 2001 (9/11), our interest in terrorism and conflict grew significantly. The subsequent incursions into Afghanistan and Iraq by the United States and its allies have fostered wider awareness of the role private armed forces play in contemporary conflict. Intense coverage by the news media, together with the explosion of second generation Internet-based communications and social networking, has resulted in enhanced exposure and a manifold debate about the private exercise of lethal violence. In addition to terrorists, rebels, insurgents, and organized crime, various types of security contractors populate the unfolding narrative about global instability in the 21st century. We are in the middle of an inescapable debate, for even the most peripheral film, television program, magazine title, or ordinary conversation seems to converge nowadays on Iraq or any other field of battle, real or imaginary.

There is some realization, both in popular and in expert circles, that we appear to have entered a new era of conflicts characterized by the extensive use of private force. At the same time, our perceptions are being fed by our overexposure to the events and actors that have dominated the airwaves and cyberspace since 2001 and will continue to do so for the foreseeable future. Shootings and bombings in Iraq, the Taliban insurgency in Afghanistan, the systematic killing of civilians in Sudan's Darfur region, piracy attacks off Somalia's coast, drug-trafficking, and the latest actual or alleged terrorist attempts are among the issues and places providing vivid imagery of the current state of world affairs and private armed forces within our world. We also need to think about the deteriorating global financial outlook and the emerging struggle over natural resources, as they are also sources of instability. Deep and widespread anxiety is palpable.

The newer generations, which this book aspires to count as part of its audience, are perplexed about the faltering peace. Humanity was seemingly progressing to a point that allowed us to imagine we were close to turning the page on large-scale warfare and global turmoil. Moreover, because we have learned to accept that most forms of private violence are deemed illegitimate, the use of private contractors by governments in arenas of conflict is necessarily a matter of concern. Appearances can be deceiving. In addition to 9/11 and its aftermath, history has not unfolded in synchronization with the best-laid plans and hopes.

This book does not purport to answer all the challenging questions these developments give rise to. It attempts to offer neither another account about the wrongs of the world nor another account of what we could have done to avert them. Its aims are modest yet inspiring. It seeks to inform the reader about the myriad of private armed forces typical of contemporary conflict, their history, the environments in which they operate, and how we are studying them. In other words, the book introduces a critical theme: private armed forces and global security. The theme's mainstream qualities highlight its influence on contemporary debate. However, it also denotes a phenomenon with a profound impact on the fabric of international politics and security.

Private Armed Forces and Global Security

The events of the last few years have brought into sharper focus new facets of conflict. Not only have new schisms been integrated into protracted struggles, but they also easily transcend their focal point of origin and are exported or internationalized. This is the darkest side of globalization. In the endless webs of connections established, private armed forces crystallize into one form or another, mutate, and release or counteract waves of criminality and irregular warfare.

In Afghanistan, for example, the Taliban insurgency continues to dislocate international reconstruction efforts. Since the ousting of the Taliban regime from power in 2001, opium production has grown to make the country the largest illicit world supplier.[1] The United Nations Office on Drugs and Crime (UNODC) estimated in 2008 that it accounts for over 90 percent of the total global output. Inasmuch as the Taliban exploits the illegal trade, Afghanistan's drug economy projects to Iran to the west, to Pakistan and China to the east, and to the central Asian republics of Turkmenistan, Uzbekistan, and Tajikistan to the north. From there, opiates enter the global traffic and transit networks. Concurrently, various private firms are engaged in diverse activities including counter-narcotics, law-enforcement training, and armed protection. There are many other hubs where private armed forces concentrate. Since 2003, Iraq has been one of the densest and a focal point of the debate about private armed forces' role in contemporary conflict.

Let us imagine global security as a delicate and flexible membrane encompassing our planet. The effects of conflicts would show as depressions descending into the affected areas. There would be black hole–like cavities, corrugated areas, capricious indentations, and depletions indicating proclivity to armed struggle. As a living membrane, each depression would cause ripples and even send shockwaves across the surface. The formation of each depression would be dependent on its own conflict origins together with the mutually reinforcing effects of other faults in the system. A glimpse into the problem comes from conflict data since the end of the Second World War, which shows that the numbers of conflicts between and within states peaked in the 1980s. They appear to have leveled but are not significantly lower than the average seen during the upheavals of the Cold War.[2] Private armed forces such as those of insurgents and guerrillas and actors such as warlords and child soldiers are typical of these conflicts.

Beyond the state as the unit of analysis, the superimposition of the increasingly transnational and pervasive character of organized crime and terrorism adds further complexity to the problem. For instance, the border region between Afghanistan and the Federally Administered Tribal Areas of Pakistan is known to harbor extremist factions, including the Taliban and al-Qaeda. Together with Pakistan, Afghanistan is also an important producer of cannabis resin (hashish). There are reasons to suspect links between the illicit profits from the drug trade and terrorist activities originating in the region. After 9/11, it seems belated but necessary to stress that the opportunistic puncture of our imaginary global security membrane by terrorist or criminal networks can be catalytic and potentially explosive.

Private armed forces thus command commensurable attention from governments and international and nongovernmental organizations (IOs and NGOs). Whether they are communicating policy, the status of peace and reconstruction missions, or reactions to the latest incidents recorded by the news media, allusions to particular armed groups are commonplace. The desire to understand the current problem also finds an answer in academia. Since the turn of the century, the university curriculum has been expanding to cover the study of the private exercise of force and its implications.

The present book contributes to this knowledge base by satisfying a demand for comprehensive information about private armed forces. A multidisciplinary framework underpins the narrative and guides its empirical character. I draw upon theories and concepts originating from various disciplines such as international studies, security, development, public management, and military history. This approach reflects the variable angles from which the subject can be approached and the interests of a diverse and inquisitive audience. For the general public, it offers a reference handbook on a complex and polarizing subject. For scholars and security practitioners, the methodology used facilitates the dissection of trends and actors characteristic of conflict environments. The abundant highly anecdotal or theoretical accounts sometimes fail to arrive at this broader picture. From this picture, the book unravels novel links between the state and private force interlacing the global security dynamic of the 21st century.

The State and Lethal Force

We need to understand private armed forces in the context of the state. It is traditionally accepted that the exercise and overseeing of the legitimate uses of force are state prerogatives. The use and management of constabulary and military forces are their most recognizable articulations. In the influential words of the late Max Weber, the state is "a human community that (successfully) claims the monopoly of the legitimate use of physical force within a given territory."[3]

Private armed forces appear to either challenge the state monopoly of force (or violence) or circumvent its application. Hence, we generally perceive their activities as illegitimate. This is undoubtedly the case with regard to acts perpetrated by criminal, insurgent, and terrorist organizations. Nonetheless, applying this logic to the types of private forces in effect working alongside the state, namely security and military contractors, is problematic. Such forces tend to access the state monopoly with the sanctioning and acquiescence of the state.

Notwithstanding the close relationship between the state and force, it has to be acknowledged that the state has never fully achieved a total monopoly over legitimate violence. History documents the monopoly as an important principle guiding the evolution and definition of the modern state. However, it is not an immutable quality.

Without the need to go further afield for now, we can see that the superpowers and their allies made extensive use of firms and mercenary groups to achieve their goals during the Cold War, albeit frequently away from the spotlight. With the thawing of the Cold War and its subsequent end, the neoliberal turn of the world economy has resulted in the widespread adoption of policies favoring private sector participation in spheres of government, including sovereign spheres such as defense and security.

At the same time, partly due to patterns of military downsizing over the last two decades but also due to budgetary constraints, the reinvention of military forces as leaner and more specialized machines has fostered greater dependence on commercial firms. In particular, the state now relies heavily on them for performance of the functions no longer carried out by members of the armed services. The private sector has also traditionally been heavily involved in the development and maintenance of weaponry and military hardware.

Two trends appear from this trajectory. On the one hand, to variable extents, states have always resorted to private actors to enhance the means of coercion at their disposal. On the other hand, this has been more evident since the 1990s than during the last century or more.

The use of private companies is now overt, often publicly tendered, and highly competitive. In terms of U.S. military mobilizations, for instance, the ratio of contractor to military personnel had gone up from approximately 1 to 5 in the Vietnam War to 1 to 1 in the Balkans conflict in the 1990s.[4] The Iraq conflict showed the same 1 to 1 ratio of contractor to military personnel in 2008. My own database numbers over 300 mostly Western corporate identities offering a wide range of private military and security services. About a third of these firms has deployed to Iraq at some point since the onset of the conflict. The West, particularly the United States and the United Kingdom (UK), leads the supply of these firms and the policy shift toward a greater reliance on them. The question arises: can we still think about a state monopoly of violence?

To answer this question, it is pertinent to recall the second part of Weber's definition, which is seldom quoted. Weber noted that "the right to use physical force is ascribed to other institutions or to individuals only to the extent to which the state permits it."[5] Therefore, while remaining the ultimate arbiter of the legitimate uses of force, the state increasingly assigns defense and security functions to private commercial firms.

This is not far-fetched. In the United States, the Second Amendment grants individuals the right to keep and bear arms. In the UK, the 1976 Diplock Report set a precedent with the view that the "personal freedom" of British citizens to accept service as mercenaries would be justified only if it did not run against the "public interest."[6] The broader framework this volume offers further corroborates the tendency.

Against this backdrop, an important distinction emerges between the types of private armed forces working alongside the state and the international community to reinforce peace and stability and those posing a challenge to the state and the international community. I largely regard contractors rendering military and security services as the former type. One thesis propounded in this book is that the relationship between the public and private sectors with regard to the legitimate exercise of force has irreversibly changed. We need to move forward from the one-dimensional perception of the monopoly of force to a model that incorporates private sector collaboration in its articulation and management. Private military companies (PMCs) are key players in the emergent strategy.

Private Military Companies

I use the term "PMCs" to refer to the firms profiting from the offering of military and security-related expertise that until recently was considered the preserve of the state and provided by military, police, and intelligence forces. The services on offer are wide ranging and cover tasks in the areas of combat, training, support, security, intelligence, and reconstruction. Whereas some tasks might involve the possibility of exercising force, as in the case of armed protection, a large proportion of them, such as the provision of risk advice and intelligence support, are not intrinsically lethal. Even so, all private military services involve knowledge of the use of lethal force and belong to the hybrid public-private culture now permeating the state monopoly of violence.

PMCs are organized like commercial firms in more conventional business areas. They are formally incorporated, and although not exactly paragons of transparency, they produce corporate literature, attend international conferences, maintain Web sites, and tend to be affiliated to defense or security professional associations. It is common for PMCs to be headquartered close to centers of power such as Washington. DC, and London, but to maintain offices in strategic locations throughout the world. Whether articulated as units within large corporations, as subsidiaries, or as independent firms, PMCs are part of a growing and fast expanding private military industry that became increasingly visible in the early 1990s.

"Security contractors" is another term used loosely to refer to PMCs. It is possible that the extensive reporting on them in Iraq by the news media has contributed to readers' interest in the topic. The protection of assets and personnel in dangerous locations is perhaps the most common service PMCs offer. In Iraq, it has covered static security, personal security details, security escorts, convoy security, and advice and planning.[7] However, besides conveying a narrow view of the business based only on protection, the term has been also applied indiscriminately to contractors that have nothing to do with security or the military, which can lead to confusion.

Some commentators and firms prefer the term "private security companies" (PSCs). I use this term sparingly in this book in order to avoid comparison with conventional security firms engaged in, for example, the guarding of shopping malls or private estates.

Many share the view of PMCs as business entities pursuing genuine commercial goals. However, investigating what PMCs are and do is also a terrain inviting controversy. The activities of a relative minority of firms have contributed to conjure up an image of reckless behavior on the public. Moyock,

North Carolina–based Xe (formerly Blackwater Worldwide) and London-based Aegis Defence Services are among the latest high-profile additions to the list. Media reports on the March 31, 2004, Fallujah incident that resulted in the ambushing and killing of four Blackwater employees and the shootings both firms have allegedly been involved in come to mind here.[8]

Even though industry-wide force is not generally deployed with the regularity and intensity portrayed, the fact that PMCs prosper where conflict is ripe and employ former soldiers does not help to soften perceptions. Thus, PMCs are on occasions also depicted as mercenaries. In this light, it should be noted that the "company" part of the term PMC derives from business tradition and does not, properly, imply a military unit, as new audiences sometimes read it and derive conclusions from it.

The alternative terminology used, including a more recent term, private military and security companies (PMSCs), provides a contextual perspective on the complexities surrounding the conceptualization of PMCs. Nevertheless, the reader should be aware that all these terms and images point to the same phenomenon.

The Debate about PMCs

The debate about PMCs bifurcates along the lines of the two views outlined: PMCs as genuine and legitimate commercial enterprises or PMCs as mercenaries or profiteers of the worst kind. Supporters see them as flexible and cost-effective alternatives to state soldiers and police, facilitating commercial activity into otherwise unviable markets, and even as prospective peacekeepers. Critics, conversely, approach them as agents undermining state authority, intending to capture the natural riches of the developing world for the benefit of multinational corporations (MNCs), and ultimately fostering underdevelopment and conflict.

In this field of scholarly inquiry, which was until recently in its infancy, academic output has largely drawn from established traditions. Because the inclusion of PMCs in the management of the monopoly of violence runs against this orthodoxy, the views of critics of this inclusion dominate the debate. However, it is peculiar that, in many of the orthodox analyses, PMCs are examined in isolation from the insecure environment encouraging their use.

Sub-Saharan Africa in the 1990s, for example, was particularly conducive to the rise of PMCs and their study as a distinct academic subject. Pervasive low-intensity conflict rendered their services essential to allow public, private, and humanitarian organizations to operate. Nonetheless, one predominant focus was on the killings, mutilations, and forced recruitment of child soldiers by rebels in countries such as Sierra Leone and Angola. The other major strand of the debate dealt with human rights and economic abuses ascribed to PMCs, which on occasions read as if the analysis was meant for the rebels behind the atrocities and not the firms attempting to counter-act them. In Iraq and Afghanistan we have the daily reports on suicide and road bombings and broader sectarian violence, which appear somehow not to have any bearing upon analyses of the reasons behind the contracting of PMCs and their actions on the ground. It is like imagining war and conflict with only one belligerent side in mind, often PMCs.

To put it bluntly, we rarely reflect that PMCs are contracted out to help reengineer a regime of security lost to the pillage and predatory advances of all sorts of armed factions.

Evidently, PMCs do not always achieve the goals sought when they are contracted. To start with, high-risk environments make it difficult to oversee all the eventualities involved in service delivery when formalizing contracts. Contractual incompleteness, overbilling, and abuses of force do sometimes occur. There is also the issue that the rendering of services might result in human loss and it is done for a profit. Indeed, some would judge it controversial that I do not issue an outright condemnation of PMCs. However, the security field is evolving so rapidly that I find there is some relevance in providing the reader with a text casting PMCs in a different light.

Therefore, the analysis of private armed forces can move in a direction that, first, identifies PMCs as opposite to the adverse private forces foster-ing instability, and secondly, superimposes private military services into the conflict environments that make them attractive security solutions. This comparative standpoint does not condone the abuses of force some PMCs perpetrate, which naturally worry critics, nor does it justify the use of PMCs as the most innovative solution to deal with conflict, as their support-ers like to argue. However, it takes into consideration the realities of opera-tions on the ground, the coexistence of good and adverse private forces, and a reconfigured monopoly of violence featuring PMCs in its management.

Challenges and Opportunities

The proposed approach is relevant for at least three reasons. The first relates to globalization, the second to the management of government, and the third to the private use of force in historical perspective.

Globalization analysts argue that as non-state actors multiply and en-croach upon state ambits, sovereignty is being systematically eroded. PMCs together with, for example, IOs, lobbying groups, MNCs, and NGOs, belong here. Governments generally work toward the reconciliation and accommo-dation of the external influence. There are consultations, joint committees, and partnerships involving non-state actors, as well as sudden policy shifts in response to global issues such as terrorism, climate change, and financial crises. For globalization involves a multitude of actors affecting one another and processes unfolding simultaneously and globally.

At the same time, whereas world culture, economics, and politics converge in shared values and concerns, some social groups oppose change and express it violently. Considering the challenge they pose to democracy, freedom, and law and order, it is possible to catalogue organized crime and insurgent and terrorist forces as such groups. The revolution in the means of communications and the ease of international travel have facilitated globalization and engendered many positive developments. Regrettably, the adverse private forces take undue advantage of social mobility and the expediency of financial and information flows.

There is little room to manipulate globalization. Yet embracing positive outcomes while working to ameliorate or contain undesirable ones is a possibility. A key task is finding an accommodation that is mutually beneficial to all the parties engaged in the strengthening of global security. In this respect, PMCs are part of an established commercial sector. The need to counteract the advances of adverse private forces already shapes the supply of and demand for private military services. Out of this logic, governments have hired PMCs to enhance homeland security, MNCs to safeguard operations, and relief agencies and NGOs to facilitate humanitarian missions. Consequently, this role should not be overlooked. By distinguishing it from that played by adverse private forces we would be able to outline more constructively its scope and limitations.

As the reader may infer, globalization has inevitably contributed to more networked styles of governance and security. Nevertheless, the periodic renewal of the institution of government is also behind this diffusion. Every few decades new approaches to public management displace or complement preceding models. The present stage bears the hallmarks of neoliberalism. The market orientation inherent in neoliberal policies has favored private sector input in all spheres of the public sector. PMCs are certainly required in arenas of conflict and contracted by both state and non-state clients. However, their use also implies the inclusion of PMCs in state defense and security. This shift is consequential and effectively reflects the reconfiguration of the monopoly of violence.

The integration of PMCs into policy and strategy is more advanced in the West than elsewhere, though the transformation is far from complete. The monopoly of violence currently amalgamates old principles with the emerging paradigm involving PMCs and, broadly, contractors. Further, although the trend toward the privatization of security is global in scope, countries converge with it in various ways. It is important to look at all these connections in order to understand global security in the 21st century.

Even though the separation between the public and private realms in the legitimate exercise of force is increasingly diffuse, copious scholarship continues to reaffirm this separation rather than work on its reexamination, which is overdue. It is challenging to depart from familiar terrain. This is particularly the case if we take a path calling for the reassessment of PMCs. The novel nature of the privatization of security makes necessary the contextualization of the phenomenon in modern history.

This historical exploration documents the gradual emergence of the monopoly of violence, its consolidation, and its recrystallization into the new security architecture during the second half of the 20th century. PMCs might not be the highest point of this historical journey. However, they represent the latest link humanity has forged. Hence, we need to identify and embrace the distinctive challenges and opportunities it possesses. It is in this spirit that the present volume has been conceived.

Organization of the Book

The book is divided into two parts. The first part comprises the main narrative and is organized around four themes and chapters: the history of private military forces, the types of private armed forces, the conflict environments in which private forces operate, and approaches to the study of the privatization of security. In the concluding chapter, I reflect on the book's themes and outline emerging security challenges. The second part of the book, contained in appendixes, provides lists of PMCs, profiles of international terrorist and drug-trafficking organizations, extracts from important legal documents dealing with the sanctioning and regulation of PMCs, and summaries of counterterrorism conventions.

The reader would derive the greatest benefit from covering all the ground. Nevertheless, the book has been compiled in such a way as to permit accessing particular chapters as though they were free standing. Additionally, numerous examples, case studies, figures, and tables are provided to help familiarize the reader with the actors and issues at hand.

Because some elements of the proposed analysis do not conform to the normative and critical strands typical of the literature on this topic, debate should be forthcoming. In light of the book's relevance to the way we think about security, this debate is desirable. Above all, I sincerely hope the book will assist anyone in accessing a fascinating and multifaceted subject.

Notes

1. United Nations Office on Drugs and Crime, *World Drug Report 2008* (New York: United Nations, June 2008), 7.

2. See Figure 3 in Center for Systemic Peace, "Global Trends in Armed Conflict, 1946–2008," Severn, MD, http://www.systemicpeace.org/CTfig03.htm (accessed June 1, 2009).

3. Max Weber, "Politics as a Vocation," in *From Max Weber: Essays in Sociology*, ed. and trans. H. H. Gerth and C. Wright Mills (London: Routledge, 1997), 78.

4. See Table 2 in Congressional Budget Office, *Contractor Support of U.S. Operations in Iraq* (Washington, DC: Congress of the United States, August 2008), 13.

5. Weber, "Politics as a Vocation," 78.

6. Diplock Committee, *Report of the Committee of Privy Counsellors Appointed to Inquire into the Recruitment of Mercenaries*, Cmnd 6569 (London: Stationery Office, August 1976), para. 52(3).

7. Government Accountability Office, *Rebuilding Iraq: Actions Still Needed to Improve the Use of Private Security Providers* (Washington, DC: Government Accountability Office, 2006), 5.

8. See, for example, Channel 4, "Aegis Close Down Website," *Channel 4 News*, April 7, 2006; and Committee on Oversight and Government Reform, "Hearing on Private Security Contracting in Iraq and Afghanistan," Washington, DC, October 2, 2007.

CHAPTER 2

Private Forces in Historical Perspective

In November 2007, the exhibition "Albrecht of Waldstein and his Era" opened in the city of Prague, in the Czech Republic. Albrecht of Waldstein (also spelled Wallenstein) was the most prominent private military general of early modern times and came close to establishing his own European state. The president of the Czech Senate called combatants like him "adventurers with a sword in their hands." The city of Poole, in Somerset, England, celebrates yearly the Harry Paye Charity Fun Day. Paye was a notorious English pirate. Around 1400, his crew burnt the Spanish port of Finisterre and stole a cherished cross from a local church. After over 600 years, in 2008 a wooden cross was given to the people of Finisterre as a gesture of goodwill.

In March 2009, the Dutch promised to hand back to the people of Ghana something slightly more haunting than a cross: the severed head of King Badu Bonsu II. The head has been kept in formaldehyde since it was taken by Dutch forces early in the 19th century. Some of the most important overseas trading companies of early modern times were Dutch, and Ghana was one of their trading posts. Overseas trading companies, pirates, and privateers are experiencing a renaissance in academic writing and popular culture. American privateers were prolific from the War of Independence onward and figured in the recent "Pirates, Privateers and Freebooters" exhibition at the Montreal Museum of Archaeology and History.

Examples abound showing that the private exercise of force is clearly not a recent historical development. However, the farther away we move in time, the more we tend to see private military actors with bemusement, even a hinted-at sense of veneration. However, some people see such actors in a very different light. Hence, the "Mercenary" series of paintings by the late Leon Golub (1922–2004) engender a sense of immediate apprehension. In a widely cited 1981 interview with Matthew Baigell, Golub noted that the mercenaries portrayed were not specifically American, Cuban, South African, or Soviet, but were intended as a representation of "intentions, implications of violence, threat, of irregular means, [and] the way they inflict themselves upon us." Beyond these depictions of mercenaries around the time of the Cold War, some people have suggested a parallel between Golub's "Interrogation" series of paintings and the photos behind the Abu Ghraib prison scandal. Unlike Golub's mercenaries and interrogators, the private military companies (PMCs) linked to the latest outpourings of popular condemnation are legal and overt commercial entities.

Indeed, the world has changed dramatically since mercenary armies, pirates, and mercantile armed forces were a regular feature of life; and even since European mercenaries converged on the postcolonial African wars of the 1960s and 1970s and terrorism became a global phenomenon. Today, PMCs collaborate with the state in the management of its monopoly of violence. Therefore, we need to see what has changed in order to determine to what extent these contrasting perceptions about different types of private armed forces are justifiable. The historical exploration undertaken below, spanning the period from the late Middle Ages to the 20th century, will help us form a critical and comparative view of the contemporary dynamic.

Medieval and Early Modern Private Forces

In spite of the problem of international terrorism and many protracted conflicts, our generation knows the difference between war and peace. Likewise, despite the widespread use of contractors by governments in arenas of state defense and security, we have grown up in a system that allows us to differentiate between the public and private uses of force.

Back in the late Middle Ages (1300–1500) and in early modern times (1600–1800), however, these distinctions were very fluid. Long periods of peace appeared to be anomalous and there was no clear separation between state and private forces. Moreover, the notions of being national or foreign with regard to a conflict had not yet fully developed. In this light, we see that the typical patterns of military organization of these eras predominantly involved mercenary groups, or the incorporation of foreign soldiery.

The most prominent groups were the mercenary companies of the late Middle Ages, the armies of rulers, the military entrepreneurs that proliferated in the 17th century, the militias, the forces maintained by the companies chartered for overseas exploration and trade, and pirates and privateers. Militias are the only group I examine here that should not be categorized as mercenary in character. Nonetheless, they constitute an important link in the historical evolution of state forces that needs to be acknowledged. As we proceed to deconstruct the forces of the period, Europe takes center stage.

Mercenary Companies

During the late Middle Ages, the "great" and the "free" companies emerged.

The Hundred Years War (1337–1453), an intermittent series of wars between the English and French royal houses fighting for the throne of France, resulted in the mobilization of numerous combatants fighting over the contested dominions. In 1360 the Treaty (or Peace) of Brétigny resulted in nine years of peace. With the Peace, most of the deployed soldiery was released from duty and left unemployed. Some of these soldiers organized themselves in large groups and went on to offer their services to medieval rulers. These formations, known to period chroniclers and posterity as the "great companies," were active in France, Italy, and Spain. The legendary White Company (La Compagnie Blanche), for example, came to employ some 5,000 or 6,000 war veterans and enjoyed notoriety in Italy. In Spain, the Castilian Civil War (1366–1369), an offshoot of the Hundred Years War, became one of the theaters of operation for these mercenaries (called at the time *routiers*).

Although the Peace of Brétigny provides a rationale for arguing the origin of the great companies, similar formations predate it. Byzantine Emperor Andronicus II Paleologus, for instance, hired the Catalan Grand Company (Universitas Catalanorum) in 1302 for service in Greece. Between 1353 and 1363 the Great Company of Fra Moriale employed about 10,000 soldiers and operated in Italy.

The great companies were part of the wider phenomenon of the "free companies." They were bands of mercenaries that originated in the soldiery demobilized when conflicts ended and numbered anything from a few hundred to a few thousand soldiers. Among the first recorded free companies, we find those belonging to the Catalonians William della Torre and Diego de Rat at the turn of the thirteenth and fourteenth centuries. The Cerruglio Company, composed of over 800 Germanic soldiers who deserted the army of Louis of Bavaria, subdued the City of Lucca and sold it to Genoa during its 1329–1330 campaign.

In fact, the great companies were formed by amalgamating a number of free companies, each headed by an elected captain. The decade after the Peace of Brétigny, some 91 of 166 captains who were known to have led free companies into or out of France were also documented at some point as leaders of great companies.[1]

As the ad hoc hiring of mercenaries increasingly became outmoded, Renaissance Italy became the epicenter of the free company phenomenon.

Mercenaries started to be raised through *condotte* (contracts), formalized between the *condottieri* (contractors) supplying and commanding the mercenary companies and the flourishing Italian city-states. These mercenary companies were no longer transient mercenary bands but more permanent and disciplined organizations formally employed over defined periods.

Besides the fact that rivalry between the city-states motivated the hiring of the *condottieri*, affluence in the Italian peninsula also encouraged this private military system. The commonality of the practice resulted in the term *condottieri* transcending its specific use and becoming an alternative means of reference to conventional mercenaries. Inevitably, some commentators have argued historical parallels between PMCs and the free companies and *condottieri*.

The mercenary trade became a common practice and an important source of income for the masses. Whereas peace in one corner of Europe produced a fresh supply of willing recruits, armed conflict in another corner motivated a demand for them. At the same time, in the transition from feudal to modern times, warfare progressively fed off this market instead of remaining largely a prerogative of the noble classes.

It is during this belligerent period that the modern state started to take shape. An emerging notion, if not yet of the nation or state, of transcending locality, was increasingly accompanied by the motivation for rulers to engage in war to achieve political or economic goals rather than simply to solve religious or royal quarrels. The armies that fought these wars were the armies of rulers.

The Armies of Rulers

During early modern times, armies in Europe were robust military instruments at the disposal of their rulers. In other words, they were monarchical or governmental possessions rather than institutions designed to safeguard the integrity of the nation-state, as we understand them now.

The resources needed to raise and maintain these armies were significant, particularly considering the endemic nature of conflict in Europe and the large contingents that fought wars. In 1650, for example, France had an army of about 125,000 people, Spain an army of 100,000, Great Britain an army of 70,000, Sweden-Finland an army of 50,000, Austria an army of 33,000, and the Dutch Republic an army of 30,000. By 1760, while the Spanish army had shrunk to 59,000, the French army had grown to 347,000, the British army to 99,000, the Swedish-Finnish army to 53,000, the Austrian army to 201,000, and the Dutch army to 36,000.[2] These figures are contrasted in Table 2.1 with the current size of these armies. In order to imagine the fortitude of these

Table 2.1 European armies 1650–2009

	1650	% of 2009 Number	1750	% of 2009 Number	2009
Austrian	33,000	94.6	201,000	575.9	34,900
British	70,000	43.7	99,000	61.8	160,280
Dutch	30,000	74.0	36,000	88.8	40,537
French	125,000	35.4	347,000	98.4	352,771
Spanish	100,000	45.1	59,000	26.6	221,750
Swedish	50,000	108.2	53,000	114.7	16,900
Finnish					29,300

The table is designed simply to illustrate the large size of early modern European armies; as the changing political boundaries of Europe are not taken into consideration. For example, it was only in 1707 that England and Scotland became part of the same country (Great Britain). Figures for 1650 and 1750 are taken from Figure 3.1 in Peter Wilson, "Warfare in the Old Regime 1648–1789," in *European Warfare 1453–1815*, ed. Jeremy Black (London: Macmillan Press, 1999). Figures for 2009 are taken from the International Institute for Strategic Studies, *The Military Balance 2009* (London: Routledge, 2009).

17th- and 18th-century armies, the reader should keep in mind the smaller size of populations three centuries ago.

Raising such large contingents meant that any army under one flag would effectively have a significant foreign composition, making it from our present standpoint a mercenary force. Whereas these mercenary armies were essentially a projection of a ruler's economic and political power, warfare became a multinational endeavor.

Mercenaries were hired on an individual basis or in military units. Armies often embedded troops of Germanic, Scandinavian, Scottish, and Swiss origin, who on many occasions engaged in combat against their own kind.

The Swiss cantons distinguished themselves as the prime suppliers of mercenaries. Not only were Swiss mercenaries considered the best warriors, but they also attracted the highest wages. From the Middle Ages to modern times, their footprint is found in all the European armies. The French, in particular, were proud of their Swiss regiments. Estimates fluctuate, but during the 16th century, French kings employed between 270,000 and 350,000 Swiss nationals.[3] The Papal Guard, now mainly a ceremonial force, has been staffed by Swiss soldiers since its foundation in 1506.

By submitting themselves to the allegiance of rulers, however, mercenaries became part of something bigger. Besides fighting for motivations other than their own, they became functionally involved in military endeavors consistent with the evolving and consolidating nature of the army of the state and the public uses of force.

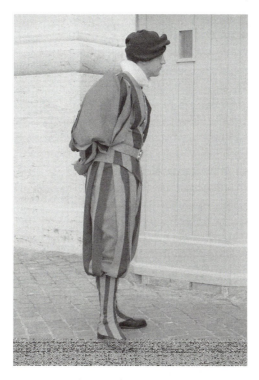

The Papal Swiss Guard
Although it now plays a largely ceremonial role, the Papal Swiss Guard was once the private armed force protecting the Pope and the Vatican. The guards still wear the same colorful uniforms as they did centuries ago. Photo: Author's collection.

Military Entrepreneurs

Every European country involved in wars requiring large armies found itself in financial difficulties. Spain, for instance, was technically bankrupted as a result of war in 1607, 1627, and 1647, with its army stationed in the Netherlands mutinying over lack of pay in over 50 instances between 1570 and 1607.[4] Military expenditure could be anything up to 60 or 70 percent of a government budget, and could even bankrupt the government. The resources needed to pay soldiers regularly were not entirely at the disposal of rulers, and this moved them to rely on noblemen willing to share the financial risks and potential spoils of war. In military history, these noblemen are commonly referred to as "military enterprisers" or "military entrepreneurs."

Military entrepreneurs acted as military brokers. A ruler in need of military labor would enter into a formal agreement with a military entrepreneur to supply a number of soldiers for a particular period and at agreed wages. Typically, rulers would engage entrepreneurs who were noblemen and had attained high military rank. These entrepreneur generals would then delegate recruiting to lower-ranking military entrepreneurs, who on many occasions already commanded their own regiments or companies, a legacy of the free company system. Therefore, there were military entrepreneurs of different ranks, and the system allowed for the transfer of ownership of regiments and companies as dictated by transactions.

Military entrepreneurship was typical of the Thirty Years War (1618–1648), a conflict that originated in the Germanic states but spread to most of Europe. In France, royal muster rolls referred to the men as, for example, "soldat du sieur (X), capitaine au régiment de (Y)."[5] Fritz Redlich estimates the total number of military entrepreneurs of different ranks that operated during the Thirty Years War at about 1,500.[6]

Some military entrepreneurs such as Albrecht E. W. von Wallenstein and Bernhard of Saxe-Weimar achieved great fame. Wallenstein became not only the most successful entrepreneur of the age but also the wealthiest man in Europe. In 1625, Ferdinand II, ruler of the Holy Roman Empire, created him duke of Friedland in gratitude for his services, notably for raising a force in excess of 20,000 combatants at his own expense. Wallenstein became the commander of the Imperial Army, controlling a force of over 60,000 soldiers. On a smaller scale, Bernhard of Saxe-Weimar also exerted political influence and was a capable recruiter. In 1635, he entered into French service and remained there until his death in 1639. France took over his army and put it under the command of Jean-Baptiste Budes, comte de Guébriant.

Evidently, rulers did not exert direct control over the lower ranks fighting on their behalf. Nevertheless, the system functioned because of the economies of scale this form of recruitment achieved and the abundance of entrepreneurs and soldiers willing to sell their services for a price.

Militias and Civilian Self-Defense

An exploration of the literature on the period would commonly suggest that civilians in arms did not figure prominently in warfare. However, military life was not just a matter of the armies of rulers, mercenaries, and military entrepreneurs, as militias populated conflict fields as well.

Militias were forces recruited by authorities from the civilian population at times of crisis or of shortage of military labor. If it were not for the service obligation imposed upon them, militiamen would otherwise be engaged on their daily trades. Commonly recruited at the level of parishes, militias carried out a self-defense function, often of a local character. By the time the

Spanish Armada was launched in 1588 with the intention of invading England and overthrowing Elizabeth I, for example, the General or National Levy was composed of militias mustered by the country's landowners and placed under the command of the English Crown.

It is relevant to emphasize the local character of militias. At a time when citizenship had not acquired its modern meaning and the means of mass transportation were very limited, the civilian's prime allegiance was to the community to which he belonged. Consequently, rulers seeking to enlist militias for extracommunal service met with resentment and opposition.

The local character of militia undertakings also signified that sometimes civilians organized themselves to fight the forces commissioned by their rulers, such as forces of transiting mercenaries on campaign.

Militias, constituting complementary forces used to perform a duty at times of crisis, can be regarded as antecedent to territorial armies and national guards. On the other hand, given the armed challenge they on occasions posed to their own rulers, whether this challenge was justified or not, one could also see militias as insurgents or rebels of some sort.

Private Maritime Forces in the Age of Empire

Civilians claimed their natural self-defense prerogative and took to arms to fight foreign rulers, their own rulers, or mercenaries. Mercenaries exercised lethal force in both the public and private realms. They shifted roles between those of footloose soldiers in arms and state-sanctioned soldiers, employed directly by rulers or subcontracted by entrepreneurs on rulers' behalf. This fluidity and diffuse definition of the legitimate use of violence was projected overseas by the forces maintained by the companies licensed for distant trade, as well as pirates and privateers. Unlike the patterns of military organization so far outlined, these private forces were not bound to Europe. With the seas as their conduit, they projected their belligerence on a global scale.

The International Charter System

Companies chartered for overseas exploration and trade proliferated in the seventeenth and eighteenth centuries. A chief motivation for their creation was the exploitation of the profitable trade in spices, sugar, tea, silk, china, and other goods from the Indies. The Indies was a term used initially to designate remote lands away from Europe, predominantly in the East. Subsequently, a distinction between the East Indies (the Middle East, Asia, and Oceania) and the West Indies (South America and the Caribbean) emerged. Europeans have consumed exotic commodities for centuries. However, before the advent of the international charter system, they did not control the supply of these commodities.

Governments sanctioned these companies through "charters." A charter specified the rules for the constitution and governance of a company and granted a trade monopoly over particular goods and geographical areas of trade. This nascent form of commerce introduced the idea of incorporation, with stockholders supplying the capital needed for companies to operate. Companies assumed a unified identity, which was frequently managed by courts or boards of directors and investors.

Nearly all of the European nations with maritime capabilities established companies for trade in the Indies, East and West, and Africa. History documents companies established at least in Denmark, England, France, Portugal, Scotland, Sweden, and the United Provinces (the Netherlands). Nonetheless, in terms of scale, innovation, and sophistication, the overseas enterprise of the English and the Dutch in the East Indies stands out from the attempts undertaken by other countries in the region and their national counterparts elsewhere. For the Dutch, trade matured in the form of the United Dutch East Indies Company (Verenigde Oostindische Compagnie or VOC) and for the English in the form of the English East India Company (EIC). These two companies traded in the East Indies for over two centuries.

The company model adopted by the English and the Dutch, which approximates to that of modern listed multinational corporations (MNCs), set a standard for European merchants in general. The proliferation of such companies resulted in the creation of a European charter system of global reach.

Despite the business ingenuity displayed by companies, monopoly rights and the private use of force to protect them were two defining characteristics (and prerogatives) of the charter system. To enact the latter prerogative, also granted by public charter, the forces commanded by the companies developed into sophisticated instruments of warfare. They were part of larger commercial enterprises. However, their distinctive organization allows them to be characterized as private armed forces in their own right.[7]

Overseas Private Armies

The forces of the trading companies comprised both army and navy complements. In the early ventures overseas, the forces were ad hoc groups of individuals of diverse backgrounds. As these were voyages of adventure, with high mortality rates and uncertain outcome, many of the recruits lacked proven military skills. With the maturation of the charter system, however, the forces grew in size and sophistication.

Private armies were raised in Europe by the companies' recruiters and exported overseas. Yet, on occasions, the direct transfer of military personnel from the state facilitated the task. In 1668, for example, control of Bombay (today's Mumbai) was passed to the EIC by King Charles II, after it was ceded by Portugal to him. In the transition, Crown troops were offered service with the company. The garrison complement in Bombay then numbered about five officers, 139 noncommissioned officers and men, two gunners, and 54 "Topasses."[8]

The EIC army, as well as those of other leading East Indies companies, grew systematically to incorporate a larger European core diluted within a native majority. By the 18th century, Asia was perhaps as militarized as Europe. In Bombay, the army grew from 2,550 individuals in 1763 to 26,500 by 1805.[9]

The rising number of European soldiers in Asia resulted in the transfer of recruitment and service practices from Europe. The VOC, for example, hired the regiment of Colonel Charles Daniel de Meuron, a military entrepreneur from Switzerland, to provide services in the Cape of Good Hope and Ceylon (present-day Sri Lanka). Upon British forces taking control of Sri Lanka in 1796, most of the soldiers in De Meuron's regiment entered into British service. The EIC and the French East Indies Company (Compagnie des Indes Orientales or CIO) were also known to employ Swiss mercenaries.

While the mobility of private soldiers between rival companies to some extent matched the workings of the military in Europe, the vastness of Asia imposed certain natural limits on military entrepreneurship and private soldiers' ambitions. However, before commercial imperatives fully gave way to colonial empires controlled by governments, the option of serving local Asian rulers in addition to chartered companies remained.

Private Navies

Alongside the companies' armies, their maritime forces had a parallel evolution. In assessing this trajectory, it seems reasonable to assume some correlation between the numbers of vessels sent overseas and the size of the maritime forces. Between 1600 and 1795, the VOC sent many more ships to the East Indies than did the EIC, with about 4,720 ships sent by the VOC as opposed to 2,676 by the EIC; the CIO trailed with 1,455.[10] The numbers of ships sent by these three companies gives us some idea of the large number of combatants that took to the seas in their vessels.

The EIC also established the Bombay Marine, a local naval force to protect the regional trade; this force evolved into the basis for the Indian Navy. However, the company-wide naval crews were organized around the EIC Maritime Service. In the development of this service, a division of labor was instituted, together with minimum requirements for service and parameters for advancement in rank.

Pay in the Maritime Service was not significant, but in economic terms, attraction to the job was found in the form of "encouragements" and "indulgences."[11] Encouragements included rewards for any sailor who prevented damage to EIC property or for the loss of limbs during duty. Indulgences, on the other hand, represented the business that sailors were permitted to conduct overseas on their own account.

Arguably, the Maritime Service evolved into a elite force and was considered by many contemporaries as superior to the British Royal Navy. Technological innovations and naval tactics pioneered by the Maritime Service considerably enhanced the Royal Navy upon the Maritime Service's assimilation into the Royal Navy in the 19th century.

The VOC also commanded an admirable naval force, followed by the CIO. Minor maritime nations maintained naval complements too, and on occasions worked alongside the English, the Dutch, and the French.

In exercising force in a private capacity, it is clear that the overseas companies assigned themselves functions now more closely associated with the institution of the modern state, notably the right to raise and maintain armed forces. Besides facilitating the control of commercial routes, they also worked to counteract the threats posed by pirates and privateers.

Pirates

Pirates were seafaring plunderers of maritime holdings under any flag. Contrary to the romanticized depictions in films and novels, early modern piracy involved acts of lethal violence and barbarism. It was not uncommon for pirates to torture and murder crews and leave survivors marooned on the seas without any means of survival. Merchant vessels on the seas or anchored in ports and bays, in the overseas companies' depots and factories, and in coastal towns were all piracy targets. Most pirate ships were former merchant transports reinforced as instruments of warfare, having been either taken as a prize or traded in exchange for looted cargoes. Thus, they posed a robust challenge to anyone the pirates chose to attack.

Piracy acquired distinctive regional meanings, in practice and folklore. The terms "corsairs" and "buccaneers" transcended their historical origins to become alternative ways to allude to pirates.

Although the term "corsair" has been used with some latitude to refer to the pirates that operated in seas adjacent to Europe, it is more specifically applied to those who were based on the Barbary Coast. The Barbary Coast was the North African seaboard of Morocco, Algeria, Tunisia, and Libya. The Barbary corsairs were largely Muslim pirates preying on Christian vessels. Venetian shipping and trade from the Levant, the coastal region of present-day Syria, Lebanon, and Israel, offered lucrative opportunities. The Maltese corsairs were also notorious predators.

"Buccaneers," in contrast, were pirates active during the 17th century in the Caribbean and on adjacent coasts. The term originally referred to men of

French origin living on the island of Hispaniola (the present-day Dominican Republic and Haiti). The chief focus of their attacks was Spanish shipping on the "Spanish Main," a term used in that period for the coastal waters of the Spanish Empire in the Caribbean. The most famous buccaneer was Henry Morgan (1635–1688), a Welshman who arrived in Hispaniola sometime after 1650. Together with plundering off the coast of Cuba and Yucatan, Mexico, history documents the ransacking of Portobello, Panama, in 1668 by a force of a few hundred soldiers commanded by Morgan.

Pirate bases and communities were established in strategic maritime spots. For the buccaneers, the small island of Tortuga, northwest of Hispaniola, was a prime haunt. Toward the end of the 17th century, the bulk of the buccaneer community relocated to Port Royal, Jamaica, which was awash with drinking and vice. From New Providence, in the Bahamas, pirates tackled the lucrative merchant route to and from the North American colonies. Pirates frequented various harbors in the Thirteen Colonies too. On the other side of the world, Madagascar, an island off the southeast coast of Africa, larger than Florida, became an important pirate hub. From there, pirates frequently preyed upon the convoys of the East Indies companies en route to Europe.

These geographical demarcations convey the international and mobile character of piracy, and thus they implicitly denote the multinational character of pirate crews, which integrated able seamen such as former merchant or navy sailors lured to the activity for private gain or the lifestyle involved. Captured slaves were also sometimes retained as crew members.

Privateers

Privateers, in contrast, were private vessels or captains licensed by governments to carry out armed hostilities and seize the transports and cargoes of rival nations during periods of war. During early modern times, privateering was a regular feature of warfare. It was endemic among the leading maritime nations (the English, the French, the Dutch, the Portuguese, and the Spanish). It took place in European waters, the maritime routes connecting Europe to its colonies and merchant settlements, and distant seas.

From the War of Independence onwards, the Americans became important privateers. By the War of 1812, while the U.S. Navy had 23 vessels in open waters armed with 556 guns, there were 517 privateers armed with 2,893 guns.[12]

Letters of marque or reprisal were the legal documents issued by governments to sanction the practice of privateering. Letters of marque would commonly specify the prize privateers were allowed to take in addition to the terms for its retrieval and delivery. Rules were also established for the distribution of the goods between crews, investors, and authorities, for the rewards for captured prisoners, and for whether neutral ships were to be targeted in the search for belligerent nations' cargoes. The conditions dictated by letters of reprisal, granted to merchants seeking retaliation for attacks on their sea holdings, could be more specific and restrict retribution to the equivalent of the lost or damaged property.

The letters were binding. To ensure compliance, privateers were often required to post bonds and allow for the inspection of the seized cargos. Clearly, the farther away that privateering took place from the authority that issued the letters of marque or reprisal, the higher the likelihood that the agreed-upon terms would not be fully observed. Common problems were the ransoming of captured crews and the trading of seized goods before inspection.

At times, broader empowerments or blanket arrangements, including unlimited looting and permission to damage or destroy the enemy's properties, were also granted by the letters of marque. In other words, privateers were allowed to engage in acts of war. Seamen willing to engage in privateering could be hired for single voyages or whole campaigns. Sailing from well-established ports such as Boston and New York in the United States, Liverpool and Bristol in England, and Dunkirk and Saint Malo in France, opportunities for privateering were publicly advertised and abundant. If allowed, seamen could be privateers one season and merchant sailors the next, and even retain their army or navy ranks while on private duty.

To some extent, it was the letter of marque or reprisal that distinguished privateers from pirates, as in theory the former were publicly sanctioned while the latter could be prosecuted and hanged. Whereas Henry Morgan is often portrayed as a buccaneer, he was actually empowered by a commission of war against Spain from the English governor of Jamaica.

On occasion, a royal charter could distinguish overseas trade from what otherwise could be regarded as acts of piracy or privateering. Piet Pieterszoon Hein was a pirate to many, a privateer to some, but certainly a vice admiral of the WIC. Under whatever title, in the late 1620s he was welcomed as a hero in the Netherlands after capturing the Spanish treasure fleet. Clearly, the boundaries between the various patterns of military organization on the seas were as ill defined as those on land.

The Rise of the State and the Decline of Private Forces

Between the seventeenth and the twentieth centuries, the rise of the institution of the modern state accompanied the establishment of distinctions between public and private violence. The use of force originating outside the public realm was gradually narrowed down, eventually rendered illegitimate, and on many occasions criminalized. The patterns of military organization that have been examined and three major armed conflicts contributed to this transformation.

The Thirty Years War

The Thirty Years War had profound significance for the political transformation of Europe, as during its course a close relationship between the evolving state and its mutating army developed.

The dynastic ambitions of the House of Habsburg with regard to the throne of the Holy Roman Empire triggered the Thirty Years War. The empire comprised a number of territories in central Europe with what now occupies Germany at its heart. In 1617, Emperor Matthias placed Archduke Ferdinand II of Styria on the throne of Bohemia. Bohemia was a largely Protestant principality and Ferdinand II was a devout Catholic. The move was intended to ensure Ferdinand's succession to the imperial title upon Matthias's death. In a Europe polarized by Catholicism and Protestantism, his zealous attitude sparked Protestant unrest. Seeking to reassert their control, the Habsburgs launched a war against Bohemia. The pan-European conflict unleashed by this war went on for three decades.

As war raged and the associated costs escalated, rulers were forced to reassess their strategies for the raising and maintenance of armies. In particular, loyal, full-time troops became desirable. Many rulers attempted some form of conscription, primarily through the maintenance of militia rosters. In addition, prospective soldiers were forcibly drawn from convicted criminals, the destitute, and the unemployed. However, unlike civilians who lacked the motivation to fight and required training, mercenaries were abundant, they were versed in the arts of war, and many of them already owned weaponry. Yet they represented an expensive and temporary solution to a permanent problem.

These paradoxes reflected the shifting organization, deployment, and legitimatization of the use of force that had to be overcome in the transition from the mercenary to the standing army of the state. If not yet completely and rationally, the end of the Thirty Years War offered part of the solution to the problem.

The enormity of the economic and human loss caused by the Thirty Years War contributed to its end. Today it would be difficult to imagine a large segment of the Western world ravaged by famine, suffering from mass unemployment, and with countless towns destroyed or empty. Yet this is the picture of many parts of Europe at the end of the conflict. In 1648, the Treaties (or Peace) of Westphalia formalized its conclusion. The Peace resulted in a clear partition of Europe. The still largely mercenary armies that emerged after the war became instruments promoting the absolute power enjoyed by monarchs.

In the process, the centralization of power resulted in rulers assuming total control over the means of coercion.

War thus came to play an important role mediating the affairs of states in the reconfigured map of Europe. Armies controlled by states, for their part, were conceived as providing the ideal forces. However, the wealth generated by the merchant class was needed to pay for wars and soldiers. As a result, rulers had to accommodate in their mandates the interests of this growing and buoyant social group. In this nascent culture, the capacity to maintain political power at home became intertwined with the fortunes of the distant trade, and with the overseas trading companies and their forces.

At the same time, the confluence of the profits enjoyed by the growing middle classes and the ideas originating in the Enlightenment began to erode the principles of absolutism, the absolute and apparently inalienable rule by monarchs. The conflict reached a climax toward the end of the 18th century.

The American War of Independence

If the Thirty Years War had had an important impact on the creation of the political foundations of the modern state, the American War of Independence (1775–1783) and the French Revolution (1789–1799) accelerated the transformation of its social base and the relationship between the state and its citizenry.

By the end of the Seven Years War (1756–1763), which was fought in central Europe, the Indian subcontinent, and North America, France had lost its colonies in Canada and Louisiana to Britain. Additionally, with the handing over of Florida by Spain, which had sided with France during the war, Britain had consolidated its hold over North America. The costs incurred during the war and those associated with maintaining garrisons in North America persuaded Britain to levy a series of taxes on its colonial settlements. Popular contempt for the taxation system led to disturbances, uprising, and eventually war.

On July 4, 1776, the thirteen British colonies proclaimed their independence. In the European courts, France provided credibility to the proclamation by offering military support. The Dutch and other European maritime nations trading with the colonies followed suit.

As in the case of other conflicts away from Europe, the involvement of Europeans resulted in varying exportation of their military practices. Notably, during the war a contingent of some 19,000 auxiliaries of Germanic origin were hired by the British to fight on their side.[13] The recruits mainly originated from the area of Hessen-Kassel; hence they are referred to as Hessian mercenaries.

The Americans, for their part, became important privateers. Testifying to this development, during the conflict the number of American private armed vessels showed a noticeable increase: 136 in 1776, 73 in 1777, 115 in 1778, 167 in 1779, 228 in 1780, 449 in 1781, and 323 in 1782.[14] If historians have argued that for Great Britain its merchant fleets constituted an important link in the evolution of the Royal Navy, similar arguments have been advanced with regard to American privateers and the consolidation of the U.S. Navy.

On September 3, 1783, the Treaty of Paris formally ended the war and recognized the independence of the United States of America. Undoubtedly, the French took into account the events in North America and their outcome on the eve of the French Revolution a few years later.

Contractors

The United States of America gradually transformed its militia forces into a patriotic national army. Nevertheless, during the War of Independence the estimated ratio of contractor to military personnel was about one to six.[15]

Halfway between the beginning of our historical exploration and the present day, this is a reminder that contractors have always played a role in support of warfare.

The Company of Fra Moriale had been a great company. However, about 20,000 camp followers were part of this medieval operation, including women.[16] Wallenstein was indeed the most famous military entrepreneur. Yet, from his own estates, he also produced armaments for his own regiments and the European rulers employing them.

The overseas trading companies employed civilian support in the supply and equipment of their convoys at ports and shipyards, as well as in the running of their remote forts and trading posts. Figure 2.1 illustrates variations in the use of contractors by the United States from the War of Independence onward. In France, during the French Revolution, any valuable skill was assimilated into the state-run revolutionary campaign. Afterward, military supply gradually reverted to contractors, the ostentatious "new rich" of the nascent Republic.[17] Rather than being a destabilizing component or an exception to the rule, contractor support appears to be a thread intertwined with the modern development of warfare.

The French Revolution

In July 1789, the Bastille was stormed by a Parisian mob, signaling the start of the French Revolution. The Bastille, a medieval fortress erected during the reign of Charles V (1338–1380), was a prison. Its fall was symbolic

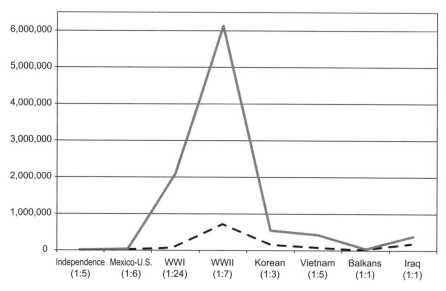

Figure 2.1   Ratio of Contractors to U.S. Military Personnel

The chart compares total U.S. military personnel (solid line) with an estimate of
the number of contractors employed during major wars and international conflicts
since 1775 (dashed line): the American War of Independence (1775–1783), the
Mexican-American War (1846–1848), the Civil War (1861–1865), the First World
War (1914–1918), the Second World War (1939–1945), the Korean War (1950–
1953), the Vietnam War (1959–1975), the Balkans conflict (1995–2000), and the
Iraq conflict (2003–). The estimated ratio of contractors to U.S. military personnel
is given in parentheses. The chart uses data from the Congressional Budget Office's
2008 report, *Contractor Support of U.S. Operations in Iraq* (Washington, DC: Congress
of the United States, August 2008).

of the passing of royal authority, as well as a powerful propaganda icon for
the revolutionary movement. The uprising sent shockwaves throughout
Europe.

The resulting wars between revolutionary France and kingdoms seeking to
reinstate monarchical rule irreversibly eroded the principles of absolutism. In
question was the idea of the state as a God-given princely and dynastic possession as against the ideas born out of social notions such as *liberté, égalité,
fraternité* (liberty, equality, fraternity). The social upheaval associated with
the French Revolution made European rulers wary of their own people.

The need to defend the new regime was evident to the revolutionary leaders before Louis XVI, the dethroned king of France, was guillotined in January 1793. On August 23, 1793, the Comité de salut public (Committee of
Public Safety), effectively the new executive government, decreed that all

French people were to be permanently available for military service until all enemies of the Republic were expelled from the country. This mass conscription, the *levée en masse*, created an unprecedented national militia of about one million people. Thereafter, the principle of the army as a national body started to gain credence.

The American and French revolutionary experiences reinforced one another and changed forever the European political landscape. In Latin America, wars of independence were fought early in the 19th century.

State Terror and Rebellion

An altogether different legacy of the French Revolution is that associated with the emergence of modern "state terror" and the use of the term "terrorism."

Conflict between revolutionary factions gave way in 1793–1794 to the Reign of Terror. By October 1793, when Marie-Antoinette was guillotined, the Revolutionary Tribunal had become established as the institution charged with purging France of counterrevolutionaries and traitors.

The Terror was a state-sponsored campaign using acts of organized violence with the intention of creating a climate of fear, of "terror." The ultimate goal was for fear to become instrumental in the attainment of political goals. Pejoratively and associated with the abuse of public office and state power, this is how terrorism was characterized and remembered for some generations after the French Revolution. Edmund Burke, the leading critic of the French Revolution in England, thus wrote in a polemic essay of "thousands of hell-hounds called Terrorists...let loose on the people."

Further adding to the civilian unease, the *levée en masse* forcibly integrated men, women, children, and the elderly into the war effort. In a period in which citizens turned in practice into combatants or victims, thousands died during the terror campaign.

The execution of Maximilien Robespierre in July 1794 marked the end of the Terror. He was one of the most dominant figures behind the Revolution, the Committee of Public Safety, and the bloodshed.

Other forms of terrorism more familiar to our contemporary understanding of the term emerged over the next century. In Russia, the Narodnaya Volya (People's Will) was a terrorist organization that targeted members of the royal family and succeeded in assassinating Czar Alexander II in March 1881. The method used was a bomb. While the czar and his attacker perished, about two dozen bystanders were injured in the attack. Similarly, on June 28, 1914, a young Serb nationalist shot and killed Archduke Franz Ferdinand of Austria and his wife, an attack that set in motion the chain of events leading to the First World War. The killer was linked to Mlada Bosna (Young Bosnians) and

Robespierre: Political cartoon
This is a political cartoon from the period of the
French Revolution, depicting the threatening at-
titude of Robespierre as seen by ordinary people.
Photo: Author's collection.

the Black Hand, two among various terrorist groups active in the Balkans and
inspired by anarchism, secessionism, and nationalism.

Police Forces and Mafia Crime

After the Congress of Vienna (1814–1815), a diplomatic council convened by the leading European nations to settle boundary disputes upon the
end of the Napoleonic Wars, the last thing governments wanted to give people was arms. Just the opposite: "they attempted to deprive them of the arms
they already had."[18]

Together with the move to defuse the civilian population, policing was
emerging as a distinctive profession. Among early examples of centralized,
professional, and civilianized constabularies, the Metropolitan Police of London was established in 1829, the New York City Police in 1844, and the

Boston Police in 1854. With paramilitary roots, the French Gendarmerie, the Italian Carabinieri, and the Spanish Guardia Civil provide important historical precedents too.

It became the responsibility of police forces to deal with crime, such as the growing problems that terrorism and mafias posed for the authorities and society alike. The secret police of Czarist Russia successfully dismantled Narodnaya Volya, which had been behind the assassination of Czar Alexander II. In England, the bombing campaign of 1883–1887 by the Irish Republican Brotherhood led to the creation of the London Metropolitan Police's Special (Irish) Branch, generally regarded as the first counterterrorism police unit in the world.

In New Orleans, Police Superintendent David C. Hennessey was charged with dealing with the growing crime problem affecting the city in the late 19th century. His righteous zeal appears to have been behind his murder on October 15, 1890. Scores of Sicilians were arrested and eventually 19 of them were charged with murder. They were part of the broader mafia phenomenon penetrating the American underworld.

At that time the U.S. Department of Justice was already conducting investigations at the federal level, often employing private detectives, but it was in 1908 that the (Federal) Bureau of Investigation (FBI) was formally created. This early force comprised 34 agents.

However corruptible, fallible, and brutal the early stages of civilian law enforcement sometimes were, Boston learned the alternative of life without the police. Shortly after its police force went on strike in 1919, the city became a major riot and crime scene.

As well as projecting force outward, toward belligerent states, authorities were increasingly projecting force inward, toward criminals, rebels, and terrorists. All of this was part of the process of the state assuming control over the legitimate use of force.

Monopolizing Force

In the 18th century, the patterns of military organization with a private element were already fading away, mutating, or being effectively integrated into the public realm.

Military entrepreneurs were still around. However, the role of the officer as a military broker began to be narrowed down after the Peace of Westphalia. Further contributing to the demise of the entrepreneur system, the smaller states, particularly Germanic ones, increasingly supplied auxiliaries to the leading European powers in return for subsidies.

The end of the companies chartered for overseas trade had different origins. These ranged from mismanagement and corruption to the dismantling of the monopoly rights that guaranteed their profitability. Practically bankrupt, the WIC was liquidated in 1674, the CIO in 1769, and the VOC in 1795. The EIC, terminated in 1874, gradually lost trading privileges until it only retained a monopoly over British trade with China, a country not a single company was able to subjugate. Toward its end, however, rather than a commercial company, the EIC had become the colonial administrator of India. Niels Steensgaard comments that the North American companies were successful colonizing vehicles, though "as business ventures, they were all failures."[19] When colonial empire and industrialization superseded the charter system, the armies and navies maintained by the larger companies were assimilated by the state.

It was after the Crimean War (1853–1856), fought between the Russian Empire and a coalition that included France, the UK, and the Ottoman Empire (Turkey), that privateering was formally wound up. During the Congress of Paris (February–April 1856), convened to formalize the peace, a declaration aimed at abolishing privateering was issued. Only seven states originally signed the Paris Declaration Respecting Maritime Law. Nonetheless, over time it became universally accepted, turning into customary international law.

Together with the phasing out of privateers and the rise of state navies, piracy was progressively subdued. While remaining a perennial feature of troubled waters, it became a manageable crime.

In the 19th century, it increasingly became accepted that security forces should be national bodies drawn from the citizenry. Along with the nationalization of warfare, Adam Smith wrote in 1776 in *The Wealth of Nations* about the necessity for the art of war to "become the sole or principal occupation of a particular class of citizens." The last time a European state raised a mercenary army was in 1854, when Britain hired German, Italian, and Swiss mercenaries for the Crimean War, though the war finished before they were deployed.[20] Further reasserting the norm and setting ordinary civilians apart from regular forces, the 1868 Saint Petersburg Declaration established that "the only legitimate object which States should endeavor to accomplish during war is to weaken the *military forces* of the enemy." The European colonies in Asia and Africa would need to wait until their independence in the 20th century before commanding their own national forces.

The foreign soldier would not entirely disappear from state forces but would gain new credentials carefully articulated around quasi-citizenship paradigms. For example, the traditional Swiss regiments maintained by the French Army were disbanded in 1830, but only to give way for the establishment of the French Foreign Legion the following year. Another relevant example comes from the regular hiring of Gurkhas (individuals of Nepalese origin) by the British Army. This practice was initiated by the EIC, subsequently inherited by the British Indian Army (the UK-led colonial force), and finally transferred to the British Army. Broader flexibility in the recruitment of soldiers across members of the Commonwealth, composed of countries formerly part of the British Empire, exists to the present day. Because of the need for fresh recruits due to the Afghanistan and Iraq conflicts, the United States has offered a route to nationhood to foreign nationals through military service, and so on.

It would be easy to say that previous models for the raising and maintenance of state forces were unsteady, as they were cobbled together by disparate public and private arrangements. Nonetheless, there is no agreement about the central reason for the shift from the mercenary army to the regular army of the state. It is only certain that, against a belligerent historical background, political, economic, and social factors converged to produce the regular army. The overarching result was that the modern state achieved a monopoly over legitimate violence and largely neutralized or criminalized its (illegitimate) use outside this comparatively recent and novel framework.

The New Age of Private Forces

The two world wars of the 20th century further tested the institutional framework established by the state to sanction the legitimate use of force. Clearly, mercenaries did not disappear, but they played a much more attenuated role in warfare. From the 1960s onward, however, the old profession presented itself anew. A succession of wars linked to the independence of countries in Africa, the Middle East, and Southeast Asia from their European masters was accompanied by a rise in insurgent and rebel movements. Together with insurgency and rebellion, mercenary activity proliferated once more.

Postcolonial Mercenaries in Africa

Mercenaries of the new era first became notorious in the Belgian Congo. The Congo (subsequently Zaïre and now the Democratic Republic of the Congo or DRC) gained independence from Belgium in 1960. Within days of independence, Moïse Tshombe proclaimed the secession of Katanga, a province in the southern part of the country.

Belgium, which retained control of important mining interests in the province under the umbrella of the mining corporation l'Union Minière du Haut-Katanga, backed Tshombe and seconded some 200 officers to the new Katangese Gendarmes. In addition, mercenaries were hired by Tshombe to assist with the consolidation of his regime and to repel the threat posed by the Congolese Army (Armée Nationale Congolaise or ANC) and tribal rivals; subsequently, UN troops were added to his concerns.

A peacekeeping force under the United Nations Operation in the Congo (ONUC, 1960–1964) ended the secession in January 1963. Thereafter, UN international peacekeeping forces, the Blue Helmets, would become a regular feature in conflict theaters.

The secession of Katanga dominated the headlines and Moïse Tshombe made the cover of *Time* magazine on December 22, 1961. The accompanying article highlighted the composition of the forces during the secession: U.S. Air Force transports carried Ethiopian, Gurkha, Indian, and Swedish soldiers under a UN mandate (the peacekeepers) to fight the Belgians, British, and French serving with the Katanga forces (the auxiliaries and the mercenaries). Although the distinction between auxiliaries and mercenaries was sometimes unclear, during the secession some 500 foreign soldiers were in service in Katanga. The number probably rose to over 1,000 the following year, when Tshombe, returning from exile to become the prime minister of the Congo, hired foreign combatants to quash the Simba rebellion (1964–1965) in the eastern part of the country.

Angola, to the east of the Congo, was divided into the supporters of three fronts after independence from Portugal in November 1975. It was to the Marxist-oriented Popular Movement for the Liberation of Angola (Movimento Popular de Libertação de Angola or MPLA) that the Portuguese passed power at independence. As it was customary for regimes embracing Communism at the time, the MPLA proclaimed a people's republic. The National Front for the Liberation of Angola (Frente Nacional de Libertação de Angola or FNLA) and the Union for the Total Independence of Angola (União Nacional para a Independência Total de Angola or UNITA) challenged the MPLA's rule. Mercenaries and foreign advisors supported each side of the conflict. The FNLA dwindled, leaving the MPLA and UNITA to continue the fight through the rest of the decade, during the 1980s, and into the 1990s.

During the Nigerian Civil War (1967–1970), sparked by the Biafran secessionist movement, mercenaries fought on both sides of the conflict. In Katanga, the mercenary leader Jean Schramme led a new uprising in 1967. In the Comoro Islands, Bob Denard staged successful coups in 1975 and 1978. From 1975 onward, South African mercenaries fought against the guerrillas threatening white minority rule in Rhodesia (now Zimbabwe). In 1977, a mercenary group led by Mike Hoare attempted to overthrow the Marxist government of Ahmed Kérékou in Benin. The exploits of Denard, Schramme, and Hoare entered the literature on this subject and nicknames associated with them, such as *les affreux* (the horrible ones), became part of mercenary folklore.

Adding to the multiethnic pot, in a continent where state borders seldom match tribal boundaries, tribal groups fought one another. From the viewpoint of the inhabitants of the involved territories, a rival tribal group was as mercenary as the Europeans or the African-born whites who joined the fighting. In the DRC alone, a country roughly the size of Western Europe, there are over 200 different ethnic groups.

The Rise of Guerrillas and Terrorists

Onto the anticolonial movements sweeping the world, we need to superimpose the Cold War logic in order to understand the violent turn that world affairs suddenly took.

In the enlarged postcolonial international system (from 51 states joining the UN upon its creation in 1945 to 152 states by 1979), the United States and the Soviet Union sought to win the allegiance of the newly independent territories. The process resulted in state rulers aligning with either the West or the Communist bloc in exchange for support for their contested regimes. The other side in the Cold War, in turn, backed the rebel groups that were challenging the ruling governments.

Thus, while Cuba provided support to the MPLA in Angola, the United States, through the CIA and via Zaïre, assisted the FNLA; and South Africa backed UNITA. In the Nigerian Civil War (1967–1970), the UK and British mercenaries supported the Nigerian forces while France and French mercenaries supported the Biafrans. This Cold War logic that was reshaping the world fueled instability everywhere in the Third World.

In Latin America, where countries had attained independence in the previous century, the struggle was ideological. Throughout the region, insurgents rose up to fight against the governments that did not embrace Marxism. In the hope of igniting a peasant revolt, guerrilla fighting in the rural areas of Latin America became the preferred tactic. The strategy worked for Fidel Castro and Ernesto "Che" Guevara in Cuba. After Cuba, Guevara found himself out of his depth in attempting the same in the Congo. After leaving the Congo, and with support from Cuba, he led a small guerrilla group in Bolivia called the National Liberation Army of Bolivia (Ejército de Liberación Nacional de Bolivia). He was captured and executed in 1967.

In Argentina, the conflict between the military regime of Jorge Rafael Videla Redondo and leftist groups (or anyone who questioned his rule) was very violent. In Chile, General Augusto Pinochet overthrew the leftist government of Salvador Allende in 1973 and unleashed a similar purging campaign. To some analysts, the events in Chile and Argentina were new instances of state terror.

Meanwhile, the Middle East and Europe saw the hijacking of commercial airliners and other terrorist attacks by Palestinian militants. The September 1972 killing of Israeli athletes and coaches attending the Munich

Olympic Games signaled the escalation of the conflict between Palestinians and Israelis, which continues unabated. A mercenary front also opened in the Middle East.

Contractors in the Arabian Peninsula

The Middle Eastern governments turned to the UK, the United States, and France for military assistance, official, mercenary, or otherwise, to strengthen their regimes.

After a coup in North Yemen. in September 1962, the faction of the army that carried it out proclaimed North Yemen as the Yemen Arab Republic. In the ensuing civil war (1962–1970), the UK and Saudi Arabia went on to support the royalist tribes in their fight against the Egypt-backed (under Gamal Abdel Nasser's Marxist rule) republican forces. Some of the mercenaries who were active in the Congo went on to serve in North Yemen and subsequently Oman.

The Dhofar Rebellion (1963–1975) against the sultan of Oman provided another fertile mercenary ground. South Yemen, renamed the People's Republic of Southern Yemen after independence from Great Britain in 1967, assisted the Dhofar rebels, while the UK backed the sultan's forces.

The confluence of the Cold War and postcolonial conflict dynamics is identifiable in these conflicts. However, the dense foreign military presence in Oman also offers a good case study for the analysis of the rapid evolution of mercenary practices during the second half of the 20th century.

Fred Halliday classified mercenaries in Oman in the 1970s into the following five categories:

1. Mercenaries backed by the UK government and engaged in training, specialized offensive operations, and communications.
2. Individual soldiers offering their services to foreign governments.
3. Officers seconded by the British military to other armed forces.
4. British personnel training and operating exported military equipment as part of arms contracts.
5. Peasants from countries in the region pouring into adjacent conflicts.[21]

This typology demystifies the stereotypical views of the mercenaries of the new era as belonging to a single undifferentiated category. The composition of foreign forces in Katanga already offered us a glimpse into the issue. Halliday inadvertently identifies the legitimate penetration of the monopoly of violence by private military actors. Category 1 covers embryonic forms of PMCs; category 2 covers foreign military personnel assimilated by the state; category 3 covers auxiliaries; and category 4 covers defense contractors.

North of Oman and Yemen, the Kingdom of Saudi Arabia found an important ally in the United States. American defense corporations, which commonly offer training services linked to arms contracts, were in the process of establishing a stronghold in Saudi Arabia and other countries in the Middle East, Africa, and the developing world in general.

To recapitulate, during the Cold War, public interests in international relations were frequently projected covertly or semiofficially by the leading powers. On occasion, it was possible for governments to abandon this ambiguous terrain. The United States drew support from soldiers from Australia, New Zealand, the Philippines, South Korea, and Thailand during the Vietnam War. However, mercenary or quasi-mercenary practices became a medium for the realization of foreign policy goals. Within this resurgence of private armed forces, the evolution of a strand of the mercenary trade into corporate entities would give rise to PMCs and gradually distinguish them from conventional forms of mercenaries.

Cold War PMCs and Beyond

Most of the PMCs of the Cold War era originated in the United States and the UK. The two countries continue to be the main suppliers of PMCs.

The most recognizable forerunner of the contemporary PMCs was perhaps Watchguard International Ltd., a British firm launched in 1967 by the late Lieutenant-Colonel Sir David Stirling. Stirling is better known for establishing an elite military unit during the Second World War (L Detachment SAS brigade), which set the basis for what later became the Special Air Services (SAS). The SAS together with the Special Boat Service comprise the British equivalent of the U.S. Special Operations Forces.

Stirling was involved in the military campaign in North Yemen. Like Stirling, numerous experienced former British soldiers were engaged in the provision of military training and advice. Watchguard was created as a private firm seeking to employ this type of personnel and satisfy commercially the demand for these services. Besides military instruction, the firm also found a niche in the offering of programs designed to counteract military coups, a widespread malaise of the period. This involved anticoup drills, the training of a force to provide protection against assassination attempts, the setting up of emergency headquarters, and the establishment of an independent communications network through which rulers could try to reassert their control.[22] The firm was reported as operating in various African and Arab countries.

Among other British corporate identities that surfaced in the 1970s, we find Control Risks and Security Advisory Services Ltd. In 1975, managers from the kidnap and ransom segment of Hogg Robinson Insurance and Travel

Group established Control Risks. Control Risks (now Control Risks Group) turned into a lasting and successful enterprise. Security Advisory Services (or SAS Ltd.), on the other hand, was a transient enterprise of ill repute set up by a certain John Banks in an attempt to continue his mercenary career through a corporate front. More than a PMC, the front was used for the recruitment of mercenaries for "interesting work abroad," as the advertisement read, namely, to fight alongside the FNLA in Angola.

In the case of the United States, early PMCs can be traced back to their involvement in the Vietnam War (1959–1975). Steven Zamparelli argues that during the war the use of civilian contractors began to change, as they were no longer strangers to the sound of battle.[23] Often cited in the literature are the cases of Booz Allen, which was involved in diverse defense tasks, including the designing of a training program for Vietnamese officers,[24] Air America, which was the covertly owned wing of the CIA in Asia, and Vinnell Corporation, which was engaged in the running of military bases and ad hoc frontline duties. By the end of the Vietnam War, Vinnell had secured a lucrative long-term contract to train the Saudi Arabian National Guard. Vinnell continues to be engaged in Saudi Arabia.

As the examples suggest, PMCs originating in the United States were aspects of or units within corporations. Indeed, the relationship between defense corporations and the U.S. government goes further back than the Vietnam War. In 1941, Bechtel people were working on the upgrading of an airbase and building an airfield in the Philippines when the Japanese attacked Pearl Harbor, prompting the United States to enter the Second World War (WWII). In 1961, in his farewell address, President Dwight D. Eisenhower had issued his famous warning about the emergence of a military-industrial complex. This was largely due to military expansion during WWII. However, it is during the Cold War that we begin to identify corporations systematically converging on the offering of private military services.

In contrast, UK-based PMCs were predominantly small, independent service providers. The requisite membership of the political, business, and military elites in the numerous private gentlemen's clubs in London partly explains the more idiosyncratic links between PMCs and the British establishment. To some extent, these distinctions between the United States and the UK still permeate the corporate constitution of the private military industry of each country.

As experimentation was giving way to an emerging industry, KMS, DSL, KAS, and MPRI were among the companies that surfaced in the 1980s. KMS apparently took on the more aggressive and controversial projects in which Watchguard and the like were not prepared to involve themselves.[25] In Sri Lanka, KMS engaged in fighting against Tamil separatist forces. Peter Tickler comments that KMS pulled some personnel out of Sri Lanka who went on to "Honduras to train and fly missions for the Contras against the Sandinista government."[26] In 1981, former members of the SAS established Defence Systems Ltd. (DSL), which evolved into ArmorGroup International (now part of G4S). DSL became a model for other British PMCs entering the business of providing security services in high-risk areas. In 1986, Stirling set up KAS Enterprises, his last incursion into the business before his death in 1990. In the United States, eight senior military officers created Military Professional Resources, Inc. (MPRI) in 1987. MPRI Inc became a model for the PMCs that went on to offer military and law enforcement instruction. Israeli PMCs, such as Beni Tal, Levdan, and International Security & Defence Systems (ISDS), also started to make their presence felt in what was becoming a quickly expanding market.

Meanwhile, mercenaries have continued their linear journey. Combatants from various nationalities poured into the brutal conflict in Bosnia and Herzegovina during the first half of the 1990s. Between late 1996 and early 1997, some 300 veteran Bosnian Serb soldiers joined the mercenary force recruited by the crumbling regime of Mobutu Sese Seko in Zaïre (now the DRC). After three decades in power, Mobutu was overthrown in May 1997 by the Alliance of Democratic Forces for the Liberation of Congo-Zaïre (Alliance des forces démocratiques pour la libération du Congo-Zaïre or AFDL), a multiethnic Congolese force supported by Rwandans and Ugandans. North and South Yemen (only united in 1990 to become the Republic of Yemen) are breeding grounds for extremists who export their causes abroad or welcome foreign terrorists. American, Israeli, and Eastern European mercenaries have been reported as collaborating with the paramilitary forces maintained by drug-trafficking organizations in South America, and so on.

While the legal and normative status of mercenaries and other adverse private forces will remain unchanged, PMCs work in partnership with governments and assist international and nongovernmental organizations.

Notes

1. Kenneth Fowler, *Medieval Mercenaries*, vol. 1, *The Great Companies* (Oxford: Blackwell, 2001), 6.

2. See Table 3.1 in Peter Wilson, "Warfare in the Old Regime 1648–1789," in *European Warfare 1453–1815*, ed. Jeremy Black (London: Macmillan Press, 1999), 80.

3. John McCormack, *One Million Mercenaries: Swiss Soldiers in the Armies of the World* (London: Leo Cooper, 1993), 72.

4. John Childs, *Warfare in the Seventeenth Century* (London: Cassell & Co., 2001), 105.

5. Colin Jones, "The Military Revolution and the Professionalisation of the French Army," in *The Military Revolution Debate: Readings on the Military Transformation of*

Early Modern Europe, ed. Clifford J. Rogers (Boulder, CO: Westview Press, 1995), 151.

6. Fritz Redlich, *The German Military Enterpriser and His Work Force: A Study in European Economic and Social History*, vol. 1 (Wiesbaden, Germany: Franz Steiner Verlag, 2004), 170.

7. Carlos Ortiz, "Overseas Trade in Early Modernity and the Emergence of Private Military Companies," in *Private Military and Security Companies: Chances, Problems, Pitfalls and Prospects*, ed. Thomas Jäger and Gerhard Kümmel (Wiesbaden, Germany: VS Verlag, 2007), 11–22.

8. Superintendent Government, India, *The Army in India and Its Evolution: Including an Account of the Establishment of the Royal Air Force in India* (Calcutta: Superintendent Government Printing, 1924), 2–3. Topasses was a term used to designate native Asians with a Portuguese background.

9. Raymond Callahan, "The Company's Army, 1757–1798," in *The East India Company: 1600–1858*, vol. 5, *Warfare, Expansion and Resistance*, ed. Patrick Tuck (London: Routledge, 1998), 24.

10. F. S. Gaastra and J. R. Bruijn, "The Dutch East India Company's Shipping, 1602–1795, in a Comparative Perspective," in *Ships, Sailors and Spices*, ed. Jaap R. Bruijn and Femme S. Gaastra, *East India Companies and Their Shipping in the 16th, 17th and 18th Centuries* (Amsterdam: NEHA, 1993), 183.

11. Evan Cotton, *East Indiamen: The East India Company Maritime Service*, ed. Charles Fawcett (London: Batchworth Press, 1949), 29–32.

12. Edgar Stanton Maclay, *A History of American Privateers* (Morristown, NJ: Digital Antiquaria, 2004), 12.

13. Rodney Atwood, *The Hessians: Mercenaries from Hessen-Kassel in the American Revolution* (Cambridge: Cambridge University Press, 1980), 254.

14. Maclay, *A History of American Privateers*, 112.

15. See Table 2 in Congressional Budget Office, *Contractor Support of U.S. Operations in Iraq* (Washington, DC, Congress of the United States, August 2008), 13.

16. Michael Mallet, *Mercenaries and Their Masters: Warfare in Renaissance Italy* (Totowa, NJ: Rowman and Littlefield, 1974), 34.

17. Michael Howard, *War in European History* (Oxford: Oxford University Press, 1977), 81

18. Martin Van Creveld, *The Transformation of War* (New York: Free Press, 1991), 40.

19. Niels Steensgaard, "The Companies as a Specific Institution in the History of European Expansion," in *Companies and Trade: Essays on Overseas Trading Companies during the Ancien Régime*, ed. Leonard Blussé and Femme Gaastra (Leiden, Netherlands: Leiden University Press, 1981), 258.

20. Janice E. Thomson, *Mercenaries, Pirates, and Sovereigns: State-Building and Extraterritorial Violence in Early Modern Europe* (Princeton, NJ: Princeton University Press, 1994), 88.

21. Fred Halliday, *Mercenaries* (Nottingham, UK: Russell Press, 1977), 15–23.

22. Patrick Seal and Maureen McConville, *The Hilton Assignment* (London: Trinity Press, 1973), 19.

23. Steven J. Zamparelli, "Contractors on the Battlefield: What Have We Signed Up For," *Air Force Journal of Logistics* 23, no. 3 (Fall 1999): 12.

24. Deborah D. Avant, *The Market for Force: The Consequences of Privatizing Security* (Cambridge: Cambridge University Press, 2005), 114.

25. James R. Davis, *Fortune's Warriors: Private Armies and the New World Order* (Vancouver, BC: Douglas & McIntire, 2000), 103.

26. Peter Tickler, *The Modern Mercenary: Dog of War, or Soldier of Honour?* (Wellingborough, UK: Patrick Stephens, 1987), 127–28.

CHAPTER 3

Private Military Companies and Adverse Private Forces

A look back at the events that dominated the international headlines at the end of 2008 highlights the various types of private armed forces operating in the world. In Mumbai, the heart of India's prosperity, for 60 hours between November 26 and 29, terrorists brought the city to a state of siege. Some 25 young men rampaged with assault rifles and grenades while staging a series of coordinated attacks. A total of 163 people died and at least 300 were wounded. The same weekend, up to 400 people were killed in clashes between Muslim and Christian gangs in Nigeria; apparently 16 mercenaries from neighboring Niger were also involved.

November 29 marked the 14th day since the Sirius Star was hijacked by Somali pirates off Kenya's coast. The Sirius Star, a supertanker loaded with an estimated two million barrels of oil worth about $100 million, is the largest vessel captured in a piracy attack so far. In Somalia's waters, a day earlier, three security guards employed by the British firm Anti-Piracy Maritime Security Solutions jumped overboard from the tanker MV *Biscaglia* once its seizure became imminent.

A top United Nations (UN) official announced on December 5, 2008, that the government of Nepal had agreed to the release of 2,975 former child soldiers recruited by Maoist rebels some years earlier. Twice as many child soldiers were reported to be active in Sudan's Darfur region by the outgoing representative of the UN Children's Fund (UNICEF) in the country.

On December 8, five employees of the U.S. firm Blackwater Worldwide (now operating under the name Xe) were indicted on charges of unlawfully killing 14 civilians while responding to an ambush in September 2007 in Baghdad.

Around Palermo, in Sicily, over 90 mobsters were arrested in the following week. They were apparently close to establishing a new command structure to reactivate the Cosa Nostra as a major crime organization in Italy and beyond. Under the framework of the Merida Initiative, American and Mexican officials met to discuss progress in the ongoing war on drug-trafficking organizations in Mexico.

A day or two after Christmas Day, dozens of civilians were massacred in a church in Uganda by rebels from the Lord's Resistance Army. UN reports further noted that up to 200 civilians were killed by rebel militias in a week. By the end of December, scores had been killed or maimed in car or suicide bombings in Afghanistan, Iraq, Israel, Pakistan, Russia's North Ossetia province, and Sri Lanka.

Many other events failed to make the headlines or went unreported. Many more people died. News clippings like these instill a sense of urgency into efforts to identify the private armed groups behind the unfathomable surge in violence. However, one point needs to be stressed. On any given day, hundreds of private military companies (PMCs) work on counteracting the advances of the insurgent, terrorist, and organized crime forces undermining global security.

Private Military Companies

Controversies surrounding the activities of a small sample of PMCs are the focal point of news reports. Some media outlets did carry the story of the team of South African security guards helping to safely evacuate about 120 guests from the Taj Mahal Hotel during the Mumbai terror attacks. As they were off duty and armed only with kitchen utensils, the item hardly registered as an exception to the rule. The media focus on controversies surrounding a small sample of PMCs is partly explained by a lack of understanding of what PMCs are and do. Despite disagreements, however, there is some consensus on their identification as commercial enterprises delivering services that used to be considered to be the preserve of the state and to be provided by its security forces. The multi-angle view presented here, which includes discussions of the origins of the study of PMCs and the vocabulary used to describe these firms, will assist the reader in forming a spatially flexible conceptual framework suited to addressing personal interests and key areas of study.

The Genesis of a Scholarly Theme

Early in 1993, reports started to circulate in the world press about a mercenary operation underway in Angola, which was then paralyzed by a protracted conflict between governmental forces and insurgents from the National Union for the Total Independence of Angola (UNITA). Such stories are hardly unheard of in Africa. However, the press dispatches spoke of an operation involving not footloose soldiers in arms, but personnel from a South African security firm. By March 1993, when three employees of the firm were reported wounded and two killed, the activities of Executive Outcomes (EO), the firm in question, arrived irreversibly in the international domain. The involvement of EO in the conflicts in Angola and Sierra Leone in the 1990s generated a great deal of interest within segments of the academic community. With EO frequently used as a case study, the scholarly study of PMCs began.

Under a contract with the Angolan national oil company, Sonangol, EO liberated oil facilities in the coastal town of Soyo that were under UNITA control. The company was thereafter approached by the Angolan government to help reconstitute and train its 16th Brigade.

The strategy EO implemented covered basic and advanced training and tactics. The firm played both supervisory and active roles during combat, with staff spread "sparingly throughout the force, from platoon to command level."[1] By the summer of 1994, the UN reported that the Angolan government had regained control over most of the coastal provinces and the cities of Benguela, Cubal, Lobito, Luanda, Lubango, Namibe, and Sumbe. The eclipsing of UNITA was crucial for the signing of the Lusaka Protocols in November 1994, an important step on the road to peace in Angola.

EO was established in 1989 by Eeben Barlow and ceased operations on December 31, 1998. Barlow was formerly second in command of the reconnaissance wing of the 32nd Battalion of the South African Defence Force (SADF), an elite force, predominantly composed of Angolans and Namibians, that was also known as the Buffalo Battalion.

It was while EO was active that the term "PMCs" was popularized. Because EO personnel on occasion fought rather than simply trained, combat services became irrevocably associated with the firm. EO, in turn, has been characterized by many analysts as the archetypal PMC. Although this analysis is not entirely accurate, it impinges noticeably upon popular perceptions of PMCs.

First, EO offered and provided many services other than those involving a role in combat. Barlow documents in his autobiography, *Executive Outcomes: Against all Odds*, training and consultancy in areas of intelligence and counter-narcotics. In addition, though seldom mentioned in profiles written of the firm, EO was engaged in passive training, conventional security work, and risk assessment.

Second, EO was studied alongside other firms that have nothing to do with combat, including many diversified corporations offering private military services only marginally and away from the sound of battle. Well-known players already discussed in the 1990s include AirScan, Brown & Root (the predecessor of KBR), Defence Systems Ltd. (DSL, the predecessor of Armor-Group), DynCorp International, Group 4 Falck (now part of G4S), MPRI (standing for Military Professional Resources, Inc.) RONCO, and Vinnell Corporation.

The term "PMCs" was and remains an organizing label that is useful in differentiating this type of enterprises from conventional security firms, or from those that do not employ highly specialized security personnel or that are not capable of deploying to dangerous environments. In other words, not every shopping mall guard can aspire to operate proficiently in conflict zones or defuse unexploded ordnance (UXO) effectively. However, the original meaning of the term is sometimes lost in academic translation, so to speak.

A further complexity originates on a different front. Due to the controversies associated with the loose use of the term "PMCs" some firms came to prefer the more innocuous term "private security companies" (PSCs). Together with "security contractors," "PSCs" is now widely used in government circles. On the other hand, some scholars regard PSCs simply as a more elegant name than PMCs. But then again, the term "PSCs" is increasingly taken out of context and applied to conventional security firms.

This is not just a matter of semantics. It is necessary for the reader to become acquainted with the alternative terminology used to refer to PMCs. The term "PMCs," however, I believe captures the essence of this particular type of service provider and facilitates the study of the subject since its origins in the early 1990s, and not just from the Iraq conflict onward.

Typologies of Services

Most analysts use typologies to organize the diverse services that PMCs offer.

The conventional typological approach classifies private military services according to their degree of lethality and apparent proximity to the battlefield (an approach commonly referred to as "the spear" analogy), and groups them into segments corresponding to aspects of state defense and security. The six broad segments frequently identified are combat, training, support, security, intelligence, and reconstruction.

As typologies use generic checklists to help organize data and answer particular research questions, they tend to be developed in different ways in each study. By combat, for instance, one author might imply only direct engagement in hostilities while another also covers support of combat operations both on or away from the battlefield. By training, one author might refer only to military training while another also includes police and law enforcement instruction. By support, one author might mean only deployment logistics while another incorporates also technical and quartermaster supply or assistance. By security, one author might focus only on armed and unarmed protection while another includes risk assessment and security advice as well.

By intelligence, one author might mean surveillance and data collection and analysis for the support of state operations while another also includes commercial intelligence. By reconstruction, one author might only mean mine clearance and UXO disposal while another investigates the building and repair of critical infrastructure in conflict or postconflict zones.

Among typologies cited in the literature, in the 1990s David Shearer classified services into the following categories: (1) military operational support (e.g., as provided by the defunct Sandline International); (2) military advice (e.g., Science Applications International Corporation or SAIC); (3) logistical support (e.g., Pacific Architects and Engineers or PAE); (4) security services (e.g., Control Risks Group); and (5) crime prevention services (e.g., Kroll).[2]

In 2003, Peter W. Singer organized the industry into three types of firms through a framework based on the merging of the spear analogy and the breakdown of the outsourcing business: that is, service providers, consultative firms, and non-core service outsourcing. His typology resulted in three types of firms: (1) military provider firms (e.g., EO); (2) military consulting firms (e.g., MPRI); and (3) military support firms (e.g., KBR). Security and reconstruction firms are not covered by Singer's typology.[3]

In contrast, Deborah D. Avant, in a 2005 study, made contracts rather than services or firms her unit of analysis. She divides contracts into two hierarchical categories based on external (military) support and internal (police) support. The first category covers (1) armed operational support (e.g., EO in Angola); (2) unarmed operational support (e.g., SAIC in the First Gulf War); (3) unarmed military advice and training (e.g., MPRI in Croatia); and (4) logistics support (e.g., Brown & Root in Afghanistan). The second category covers (1) armed site security (e.g., Blackwater in Iraq); (2) unarmed site security (e.g., DSL in the Democratic Republic of the Congo or DRC); (3) police advice and training (e.g., DynCorp in Iraq); (4) crime prevention (e.g., DSL in the DRC); and (5) intelligence (e.g., CACI International in Iraq).[4] Reconstruction contracts are not included in Avant's typology.

As the reader may infer from the examples of typologies provided, the scope of services included in each category varies, as does the unit of analysis (firms, services, contracts).

In terms of the debate about whether to use the term "PMCs" or "PSCs," we further find that either term might be applied to a particular category of services or typologies in its entirety. For example, whereas to Singer "military provider firms" are the only types that can be designated as PMCs, all the contracts collated by Avant fall under the PSCs designation. In addition, in organizing categories, inevitably there are overlaps. That is to say, a particular firm might offer more than one type of services or contracts and thus

Table 3.1 Typological analysis of PMCs

Unit of Analysis	David Shearer (1998) Services	Peter Singer (2003) Firms	Deborah Avant (2005)	
			Military Contracts	Police Contracts
Combat	Military operational support	Military provider firms	– Armed operational support – Unarmed operational support on battlefield	
Training	Military advice	Military advice firms	Unarmed military advice and training	Police advice and training
Support	Logistical support	Military support firms	Logistical support	
Security	– Commercial security – Risk assessment – Crime prevention			– Armed site security – Unarmed site security – Crime prevention
Intelligence	Intelligence gathering*	Military support firms**		Intelligence
Reconstruction	Protection of UN and humanitarian operations*			

The table brings together representative typological analyses of PMCs by three authors.

*In David Shearer's typology, "intelligence gathering" (applicable only to commercial operations) is covered by his "crime prevention" services category, and the "protection of UN and humanitarian operations" by his "logistical support" services category.

**In Peter Singer's typology, intelligence services are covered by "military support firms."

belong to different categories, and vice versa. Table 3.1 summarizes the various typologies.

Understanding what PMCs do is not as complex as the discussion suggests. Upon a closer inspection of the table, the reader can see that the services across the market tend to bear distinctive similarities.

A Working Definition of PMCs

Even though typologies present us with a conceptual view of what PMCs are, it is easy to misinterpret the terminology used because it originates in expert research. Definitions can offer further guidance. However, as there are not many definitions available to construct a comparative analysis, I will offer a working definition.

For the purposes of this book, I define PMCs as legally established international firms offering services that involve the potential to exercise force in a systematic way and by military or paramilitary means, as well as the enhancement, the transfer, the facilitation, the deterrence, or the defusing of this potential, or the knowledge required to implement it, to clients.

To fully grasp the meaning of this definition, some explanations are in order:

- Legally established: Like firms in more conventional spheres, PMCs pay taxes and enter into contractual and binding agreements with governments, international and nongovernmental organizations, and multinational corporations. Some PMCs are also listed on stock exchanges. The debate about whether it is right or wrong to employ PMCs or allow them to operate should not be confused with their status as legally established commercial enterprises.
- International firms: PMCs tend to offer services internationally and enter into deals with both national and foreign clients. The for profit and international nature of their work is what motivates some commentators to label PMCs as mercenary organizations.
- Offering services: PMCs, like defense contractors, operate in the areas of defense and security. However, unlike defense contractors, they are service oriented rather than capital intensive. In other words, they do not manufacture military hardware or equipment, but they can instruct clients in how to handle the implements of warfare and security.
- Potential to exercise force in a systematic way: PMCs regularly employ former military and constabulary personnel, hence the reference to military and paramilitary means. Their work force thus possesses a knowledge of the use of lethal force. This acquired potential to exercise force may materialize when personnel are providing armed protection in dangerous locations. However, often the potential does not materialize and involves only an expertise inherent in service delivery. Either way, alluding to the use of force in a systematic way implies a state of readiness typical of PMCs' personnel but not of ordinary security guards.

The second part of the definition relates to the application or transmission of the knowledge of the use of force. It is constructed with reference to the service segments covered by the typological analysis (combat, training, support, security, intelligence, and reconstruction).

- Enhancement: This occurs when PMCs deliver services that, by directly or indirectly improving the combat capabilities of clients, enhance them.
- Transfer: This is manifest when training services are offered, as they reflect the absence of a particular expertise from the forces or agencies to which it is transferred.
- Facilitation: While not lethal in nature, the provision of operational support and intelligence services facilitates the deployment or exercise of force.
- Deterrence: Security services in the form of armed or unarmed protection act as an active or passive deterrent to the adverse private forces endangering the personnel, infrastructure, or activities of the contracting party.
- Defusing: Reconstruction environments often require services that entail the destruction of otherwise lethal capabilities. UXO and weaponry disposal are good examples of this defusing capability.

The military and security expertise employed to enhance, transfer, facilitate, deter, or defuse the use of force does not originate in states, but in PMCs. Thus, the expertise belongs to private firms profiting from its active or potential use.

Overlapping Fields of Commercial Activity

The working definition proposed is developed from an appreciation of a common denominator between all the seemingly distinctive service segments that PMCs cover: a potential to apply a knowledge of the use of force to the provision of commercial services. However, the definition also introduces a conceptual compact from which it is easier to appreciate the variable corporate structure of PMCs.

It is sometimes possible to categorically identify firms as PMCs. Nevertheless, on many occasions corporations offer private military services while not constituting PMCs in their entirety. Analytically, this suggests a differentiation between what could be called stand-alone and hybrid types of PMCs.[5]

Stand-alone PMCs are those specializing in the provision of private military services, that is to say, services we can classify using the typological analysis. These PMCs may be independent firms or subsidiaries of larger firms. EO and MPRI are examples of stand-alone PMCs. Throughout its existence, EO remained an independent service provider. MPRI was incorporated as such in 1987, but it became a wholly owned subsidiary of L-3 Communications Corporation in 2000. As part of L-3 Communications, a group of over

60 companies, however, MPRI retains its corporate identity and a good degree of operational independence.

At the same time, stand-alone PMCs expand beyond their seemingly discrete competencies. For example, Universal Guardian Inc. is a large and independent firm that also owns UK-based Secure Risks Ltd. For its part, Secure Risks acquired Strategic Security Solutions International Ltd. (SSSI), another British PMC, in July 2004. Here we find one PMC that owns another, which owns another; and the two last mentioned work in partnership. In 2006, the partnership Secure Risks–SSSI was awarded a contract to provide security for personnel at the U.S. Embassy in Kabul, Afghanistan's capital. Similarly, Dyn-Corp International together with McNeil Technologies set up Global Linguist Solutions, which is the key supplier of translators and interpreters for the U.S. Army Intelligence and Security Command. MPRI has expanded beyond its training activity base to include emergency management, strategic communications, maritime and driving simulators, development programs, and full-spectrum logistical advice. Other permutations are found in the industry, including more complex permutations involving hybrid types of PMCs.

Hybrid types of PMCs are segments or integral divisions of corporations offering private military services. However, the overall business of these corporations tends to fall outside the scope of the typological analysis. CACI International, though often labeled as a PMC due to its provision of translators and interrogators in Iraq, is a diversified information technology (IT) services company. Likewise, Lockheed Martin Corporation, an aerospace, electronics, and IT giant, is the largest provider of military aircrew training in the world. Northrop Grumman Corporation, another giant, owns Vinnell Corporation, which in turn is a diversified corporation covering various service segments characteristic of PMCs. Further, practically all the major defense corporations embed hybrid types of PMCs.

Thus, stand-alone PMCs can be, and hybrid types of PMCs are, linked to broader corporate structures. Linkages are commonly established with aerospace, construction, defense, engineering, government services, security, and IT corporations. In addition, some private equity firms, such as the Carlyle Group, totally or partially control the holdings of some PMCs. The Carlyle Group used to own U.S. Investigations Services, Inc. (USIS), a key intelligence contractor that has trained elite units in Iraq. In 2007, USIS was bought by Providence Equity Partners. Hence, we can visualize PMCs as entities at the center of numerous fields of commercial activity. This "atomic" view of PMCs is illustrated in Figure 3.1.

If we were to add a spin to this figure, it would be possible to appreciate an even more dynamic view of PMCs. This is because continuous mergers and acquisitions frequently shift the private military capabilities of firms across corporate identities and commercial sectors.

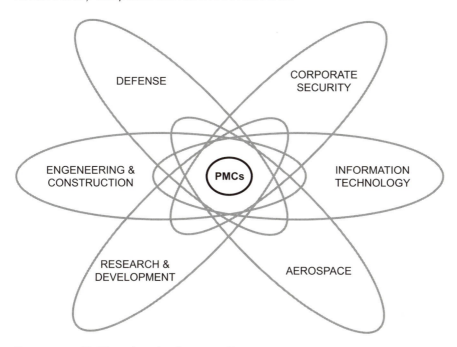

Figure 3.1   PMCs within the Corporate Environment
While some PMCs are units within corporations operating in different commercial
sectors (hybrid types of PMCs), independent PMCs also diversify into those sectors.
This figure is based on an analysis of the variable corporate organization of PMCs and
Figure 2 in Carlos Ortiz, "The Private Military Company: An Entity at the Centre of
Overlapping Spheres of Commercial Activity and Responsibility," in *Private Military
and Security Companies: Chances, Problems, Pitfalls and Prospects,* ed. Thomas Jäger
and Gerhard Kümmel (Wiesbaden, Germany: VS Verlag, 2007), 67.

The reader will not find in the literature or the press references to either
stand-alone or hybrid types of PMCs, just references to PMCs. However, the
analytical distinction gives rise to a more fluid yet accurate view of PMCs.
As this view renders simplistic the characterization of PMCs or private military personnel as just mercenaries, it is another perspective that we need to
examine.

Private Military Personnel

Whether debating companies or personnel, the phrase "private military"
presents us with a clear statement of the way in which state defense and security are partly satisfied nowadays. It superficially justifies the labeling of PMCs
or their employees as mercenaries. There are no easy answers, though. Since

early modern times, governments have employed contractors while gradually moving to monopolize the management of the use of force. Max Weber noted after the First World War that although a myriad of institutions had deemed quite normal the use of physical force in the past, the relationship between the state and violence had become "an especially intimate one."[6] Although the relationship alluded to by Weber is still powerful, the state and private force have ceased to be strange bedfellows. The analysis of patterns of military downsizing since 1989 helps to explain the shifting rationale, as well as the view of PMCs as mercenary forces.

Military Downsizing after the End of the Cold War

Data from key suppliers of private military personnel show the scope and pace of the large-scale downsizing motivated by the end of the Cold War, which was an important factor facilitating the proliferation of PMCs from the early 1990s onward.

In the case of the United States, William J. Perry (secretary of defense 1994–1997) noted in the 1995 Annual Department of Defense report to the president and Congress that by the late 1980s it was clear the forces were going to downsize. The goal was a drop from about 2.2 million active duty personnel in the late 1980s to 1.4 by 1999. In 2000, the active force numbered nearly 1.38 million soldiers, representing 64 percent of the 1989 total. The U.S. Army, Navy, and Air Force all registered reductions of about 35 percent between 1989 and 2000, and the Marine Corps registered a 12 percent reduction.

The British armed forces included a little over 300,000 active personnel in 1989. The Options for Change review of 1990, designed to reassess the military balance after the end of the Cold War, put forward plans for an overall reduction of about 18 percent in British forces by the mid-1990s. By 1999, the active component was 212,000, representing a 31.8 percent drop.

At least in the case of the United States and the UK, there appears to be some correlation between the downsizing and the size of their private military industry. The two countries represent the largest suppliers of private military personnel, followed by South Africa.

The end of apartheid motivated a reorganization of the South African military. In 1994, conscription was abolished and the task of creating the new South African National Defence Force (SANDF) to replace the SADF was initiated. The total strength of the forces was then estimated at approximately 78,500. Elite apartheid-era units were disbanded and the reorganization centered on integrating troops from the Azanian People's Liberation Army (the military unit of the Pan Africanist Congress), Umkhontowe Sizwe (the military unit of the African National Congress), the Zulu Inkatha movement (composed of supporters of the Inkatha Freedom Party), and the tribal homelands districts into SANDF.[7] This consolidation process nearly doubled the forces to a total of 137,900. However, by 1999, SANDF counted only about 70,000 soldiers.

Israel is another important provider of PMCs. Israeli forces did not downsize after the end of the Cold War. With unresolved issues between Israel and its neighbors and contested territorial claims, Israel needs to maintain robust defense and security capabilities. Moreover, Israel remains one of the world's top defense suppliers. The total active strength of the Israeli forces (conscripted and career) stood at about 141,000 between 1989 and 1992, and at about 174,000 throughout the rest of the 1990s.[8] The main supply of recruits for the domestic private military industry comes from the release of soldiers from duty as a result of the normal cycle of service.

Intelligence agencies as well as active forces in the United States, the UK, and South Africa have been scaled down. The CIA, the KGB (the Soviet equivalent), MI6 (the British equivalent), and South African intelligence units from the apartheid era released from duty specialists in possession of rare skills and knowledge.

Given that the private military services industry employs former military and intelligence personnel, the downsizing contributed to the maturation of a market for private military services that had already been identifiable during the Cold War. However, the case of Israel shows that growth can be based on the maintenance of robust defense institutions and the release of soldiers from duty as a result of the normal cycle of service. This is shared by the other countries examined. Neoliberal policies fostering a greater use of the private sector in government areas are important as well. This partly explains the lead the United States and the UK enjoy, but not the case of Russia, which also downsized its forces after 1989.

It would be unrealistic to suggest that this dynamic can be suddenly reversed. Nevertheless, it needs to be asked, has the downsizing leveled off? To some extent, as Table 3.2 shows.

The workings of the private military market provide additional explanations for what appears to be a growth trajectory well after the Cold War downsizing.

The Private Military Labor Market

PMCs, particularly of the stand-alone type, do not tend to maintain permanent workforces. Instead, people are hired for specific operations or to perform particular contracted tasks. Thus, ad hoc teams are assembled and disbanded as contracts require, although team leaders and people in possession of unique skills tend to be retained.

Table 3.2   Patterns of military downsizing 1989–2009

	1989	1999	% of 1989 Number	2009	% of 1989 Number
United States	2,124,900	1,371,500	64.5	1,452,337	68.3
United Kingdom	311,650	212,400	68.2	187,210	60.1
South Africa	103,000	69,950	67.9	62,082	60.3
Israel	141,000	173,500	123.0	176,500	125.2
Soviet Union/ Russia	4,258,000	1,004,100	23.6	1,027,000	24.1

Figures are taken from the International Institute for Strategic Studies' yearly report, *The Military Balance* report.

To facilitate this "just-in-time" hiring practice, databases of past and potential new recruits are commonly maintained. Recruits, for their part, make their details available to more than one firm. Word of mouth and past camaraderie tend to play a role in knowing when and where opportunities open up, and in selecting the best possible employer.

Two sets of factors generally determine employability and pay rates. The first relates to the source of the military, law enforcement, or intelligence expertise, especially in terms of the standing of the force or agency that recruits used to belong to or that has provided training for these recruits. The second is associated with the level of skills, and this focuses on parameters such as the rank reached, the type of force or unit a recruit used to belong to, the specific functions performed, the equipment and weaponry mastered, field experience, security clearance level, accountability record, and so forth. Accordingly, former members of the Special Forces are always in demand and command comparatively high wages. Although the supply of and demand for particular services at any given time can raise or lower recruitment standards and pay rates, the employer's assessment of potential recruits often boils down to nationality issues.

American and British recruits frequently get the best deal for their skills, followed by Australians, Canadians, South Africans, and other Western nationals. At the height of the Iraq conflict (in terms of security contracting, often referred to as the Baghdad or Iraq "bubble"), the news media carried the story of personnel employed to train the new Iraqi police earning up to three times what regular police officers were making in the United States. Meanwhile, the South African press, while agreeing that pay was disproportionate to pay at home, reported that the wages paid to South Africans were about two-thirds of the wages paid to Americans and Britons performing similar functions. We are talking about approximately $50,000 paid monthly to police officers in the United States, while similar work in Iraq attracted $150,000; South Africans received about $80,000–100,000.

In the private military market, there has always been an element of subcontracting, which involves deals between firms as well as the hiring of locals and third-country nationals. During the Iraq conflict a second-tier labor market was consolidated.

Whereas Americans, Britons, and South Africans will not work unless paid the applicable going rates, Chileans, Ecuadorians, Fijians, Filipinos, Colombians, Salvadorans, Namibians, Nepalese, and natives of other African, Asian, Eastern European, and Latin American nations are happy to do the job for less and consider themselves well paid. For example, a representative of a PMC recruiting in Fiji in 2003 reported the following pay scale: private to corporal, $1,300 a month; sergeant to staff sergeant, $1,500; warrant officer I and II, $1800; lieutenant, $1,900; captain, $2,000; major, $2,200; and lieutenant colonel, $2,400.[9] The Salvadoran media reported that their nationals were paid amounts similar to those paid to the Fijians, though under unclear contractual terms. At the same time, due to the abundance of local workers, Iraqis were making even less.

Demand for PMCs often meets with an abundant supply of potential recruits as a result of the internationalization of the private military labor market. Nevertheless, the multiple nationalities and pay differentials between public and private personnel performing similar functions nurture popular perceptions of private military personnel as mercenaries.

Contractors or Mercenaries?

The characterization of PMCs or their employees as mercenaries has developed from two conceptual approaches: legal definitions of mercenaries and the popular understanding of the term.

The international humanitarian law approach to the problem of mercenaries is based on the *1977 Protocol Additional to the Geneva Convention of 12 August 1949*, Protocol I. Protocol I aims to protect the victims of international armed conflicts. Widespread mercenary activity in Africa during the 1960s and 1970s motivated the inclusion of "Article 47—Mercenaries" in Protocol I. Article 47 defines a mercenary as any person who

(a) Is specially recruited locally or abroad in order to fight in an armed conflict;
(b) Does, in fact, take a direct part in the hostilities;
(c) Is motivated to take part in the hostilities essentially by the desire for private gain and, in fact, is promised, by or on behalf of a Party to the conflict, material compensation substantially in excess of that promised or paid to combatants of similar ranks and functions in the armed forces of that Party;

(d) Is neither a national of a Party to the conflict nor a resident of territory controlled by a Party to the conflict;

(e) Is not a member of the armed forces of a Party to the conflict; and

(f) Has not been sent by a State which is not a Party to the conflict on official duty as a member of its armed forces.

The definition is cumulative. This means that to be a mercenary each person needs to meet the six criteria specified by Article 47, which in itself has rendered the definition complex to apply in practice. The legal community agrees about other problems. In particular, to label someone as a mercenary because of a motivation for private gain is contentious and difficult to prove in court.

The other two international instruments dealing with mercenaries are the Organization of African Unity's (now the African Union's or AU's) *Convention for the Elimination of Mercenarism in Africa* (1977) and the UN's *International Convention against the Recruitment, Use, Financing and Training of Mercenaries* (1989). The conventions incorporate definitions derived from those contained in Article 47, thus replicating the problems outlined.

Article 47 and the UN and AU conventions were designed to deal with the problem that the type of mercenaries that were typical of the postcolonial wars of the 1960s and 1970s posed for the stability of developing nations. Therefore, the approach is outdated and fails to reflect the nature of present-day conflicts, which involve a multitude of actors other than state forces and mercenaries. In addition, as PMCs are legally established entities that are contracted by governments or operate with governments' expressed or tacit consent, their activities fall outside the scope of the mercenary definitions in Article 47 and the UN and AU conventions.

The UN created the office of the Special Rapporteur of the Commission on Human Rights on use of mercenaries as a means of impeding the exercise of the right of peoples to self-determination in 1987, and this rapporteur produced yearly reports on the activities of mercenaries until 2005, including PMCs. Nevertheless, this activity yielded little fruit in terms of tuning international instruments to the realities of post-Cold War conflicts. Other than the creation in 2005 of the Working Group on the use of mercenaries as a means of violating human rights and impeding the exercise of the right of peoples to self-determination to succeed the special rapporteur's office, the UN trajectory has stalled.

There is the exception of the 2008 *Montreux Document*, an initiative of the Government of Switzerland (Federal Department of Foreign Affairs) and the International Committee of the Red Cross, which interprets international humanitarian law in a manner applicable to the activities of PMCs.

Diplomats, scholars, and key industry and NGO representatives endorse the *Montreux Document*. However, the incomplete UN and humanitarian law trajectory partly explains why people within the humanitarian community continue to approach PMCs as if they were the mercenaries of past eras.

Indeed, the so-called "footloose soldiers in arms" or "soldiers of fortune" come to mind when thinking about conventional mercenaries. However, the examination of the private military industry offered here strongly suggests that PMCs are organized and behave more like international businesses and less like conventional mercenaries. Secondly, the typological analysis shows that most services offered by PMCs do not require their personnel to be armed. Finally, the globalization environment, in which firms recruit from a truly international pool of candidates, renders the characterization of private military personnel as mercenaries problematic.

The distinction between PMCs and conventional mercenaries is also important because both groups inhabit the fields of conflict. There is also the risk that in spite of vetting procedures, the recruitment practices of PMCs may allow a soldier of fortune in one season to become a PMC employee in the next, and vice versa. Simon Mann, a former British officer, was at some point employed by EO, but he was sentenced in July 2008 in Equatorial Guinea to 34 years in prison for his involvement in a failed coup in the country in 2004. He was pardoned by Equatorial Guinea's president in November 2009 and ordered to leave the country. Some former Soviet soldiers found their way into the private military industry. However, the brutal downsizing that former Soviet forces underwent resulted in some of the unemployed soldiery joining rebel movements in Chechnya and adjacent Russian republics, fighting in the Balkans, becoming members of the Russian and Eastern European mafias, or freelancing in Africa.

Instances of former soldiers going astray do not discredit the notion of PMCs as distinctive commercial enterprises. Rather, it confirms the need to differentiate between PMCs and all the adverse private forces to which the mercenary label can be loosely applied, sometimes including terrorists and rebels.

Terrorists and Rebels

No other security-related topic has produced more textbooks since the beginning of the 21st century than terrorism. The numerous volumes devoted to terrorism during the 1960s and 1970s already described a rich pedigree going as far back as the French Revolution; when the term "terrorism" was coined. It is therefore difficult to do justice to the myriad perspectives on what "terrorism" and "terrorists" represent. These two terms are more slippery than the term "mercenaries." A brief overview of the modern understanding of terrorism is therefore necessary.

Terrorism: Easy Word, Many Problems

One of the most dramatic acts of terrorism of the Cold War era was perpetrated against the Israeli athletes participating in the Munich Olympic Games. In the early hours of September 5, 1972, members of the Palestinian militant group Black September took the athletes and their coaches hostage. The militants wore balaclavas and were armed with submachine guns and hand grenades. During the crisis, among the first to be televised throughout the world, the terrorists demanded the release of 234 convicts, mostly Palestinians, from Israeli jails. By the time the standoff came to a bloody conclusion, 11 Israelis, one police officer, and five terrorists were dead.

Barely two months after the Munich Massacre, as the event is commonly known, Black September operatives hijacked a Lufthansa 727 aircraft and demanded the release of three terrorists who had been held for their role in the attack.

As early as 1972 the UN was preoccupied with the growing threat posed by terrorism, particularly in light of numerous plane hijackings in the preceding decade. Notably, and having echoes in the present, on September 6, 1970, four jets bound to New York from Europe were hijacked by members of the Popular Front for the Liberation of Palestine in the Dawson's Field hijackings. One of the hijacking attempts was foiled, but three days later a fifth airliner fell prey. Consequently, between 1963 and 1971 three international conventions were agreed to on the issue of in-flight safety and violence on board flights.

The Munich Massacre reignited the debate about the need for a broader conceptual approach and for international cooperation to tackle the problem adequately. However, the debate reached a stalemate. Some states were concerned that proposed definitions might undermine genuine "freedom-fighting" movements, which, if they fitted the labels, could be ruthlessly crushed by tyrannical regimes. Other states, in contrast, were worried that the definitions could undermine robust defense and security measures implemented by states to fight terrorism, which could ultimately be regarded as acts of "state terror" by others.

Thus, whereas some states saw the attacks perpetrated by Palestinians as part of a struggle for freedom, some other understood them for what they were: acts of terrorism. Since the 1960s, many more groups and movements have been similarly regarded.

UN General Assembly Resolution 3034 of December 18, 1972, called for a reassessment of antiterrorism measures, for states to submit proposals to deal with the problem, and for the establishment of an ad hoc committee to coordinate the work. This did not result in much change in the established poles of the debate, which to some extent remain.

However, in addition to groups and movements perpetrating acts of terrorism because they seek secession from a state or liberation from something, we now also have anarchists and extremists willing to kill in order to intimidate people into changing consumer behavior or lifestyles. Robert Rudolph, who was behind the bomb attack at the Centennial Olympic Park in Atlanta on July 27, 1996, perpetrated various similar attacks in protest against abortion and same sex relations and saw the Olympic Games as somehow promoting socialism. At the time when this book was being written, the most recent addition to the FBI list of most-wanted terrorists was an American animal rights activist involved in bombings in the San Francisco area. Attacks committed because of animal rights and environmental issues fall under the category of "eco-terrorism," There are also terrorists who oppose capitalism and globalization, are motivated by racial issues, and target particular commercial sectors or countries.

At the international level, groups such as al-Qaeda want to redesign the world according to their own Islamic specifications. In their quest, these fundamentalist terrorists are franchising carnage.

The Counter-Terrorism Committee of the UN Security Council, created after 9/11, promotes 16 instruments dealing with the problem of terrorism. Besides air safety and hostage taking, they cover issues such as terrorist financing and nuclear terrorism; see Appendix III for a summary of all these instruments. No single, universally accepted definition of terrorism guides their formulation. Therefore, while most states recognize the seriousness of the problem and tend to act according to these instruments, each state reflects differently on the nature of terrorism.

Acts and Aspects of Terrorism

Title 22 of the U.S. *Code* defines terrorism as "premeditated, politically motivated violence perpetrated against noncombatant targets by subnational groups or clandestine agents."[10] This definition has been in use since 1983, and the Department of State (DOS) applies it to the annual report on terrorism that it is required to submit to Congress. Important generalizations can be drawn from the definition:

Organized Act of Violence
Terrorism is an act of organized violence. It is premeditated, and carefully planned and executed. To the unfortunate people who fall victim to terrorist attacks, their targeting might appear accidental. Yet, in the mind of

the terrorists, the victims have been chosen for a reason. When attacks are against infrastructure and not specifically against people, terrorists are nevertheless aware that their actions might result in casualties. However, on many occasions the intentions are both to damage property and to inflict death or injury.

This was clearly the case in the April 19, 1995, bombing of the Alfred P. Murrah Federal Building in Oklahoma City, which killed 168 and injured over 800; the June 25, 1996, bombing of the Khobar Towers in Dhahran, Saudi Arabia, which killed 20 and injured over 300; the August 7, 1998, bombings of the U.S. embassies in Dar es Salaam, Tanzania, and Nairobi, Kenya, which killed over 200 and injured thousands; and the 1993 and 2001 attacks on the World Trade Center in New York.

Because of our dependence on technology, the definition contained in the Terrorism Act 2000 (TA2000) in the UK also qualifies as instances of terrorism those actions designed to seriously interfere with or disrupt electronic systems.[11] This aspect of terrorism is also known as cyber-terrorism.

Targeting of Non-Combatants

Even if in practice it is much more complicated than in theory, we all share a basic view of war involving large-scale hostilities between identifiable armed forces. Civilians are meant to be left out of the fighting. In the case of terrorism, whether attacks take place within the context of a conflict situation or not, people who have nothing to do with the machinery of war, state defense and security, or even government, are also targets. Indeed, the organs of the state are common targets.

There have been numerous attacks in Afghanistan and Iraq on soldiers and police, as well as on civilians simply lining up to apply to join the forces. On March 30, 2009, an attack on a police academy in Lahore, Pakistan, resulted in at least eight people killed and over 100 injured. The Organisation for Economic Co-operation and Development (OECD) highlights the fact that "recent terrorist acts accentuate a trend towards targeting large numbers of civilians that began in the 1980s."[12] The *2008 Report on Terrorism* by the National Counterterrorism Center (NCC) recorded that of the nearly 50,000 people killed or injured in terrorist attacks during the year, about 65 percent were civilians.[13]

Besides violence against people and damage to property, TA2000 also prompts us to consider as instances of terrorism broader actions aimed at endangering "a person's life, other than that of the person committing the action"; or those creating "a serious risk to the health or safety of the public." The ultimate concern sketched by this clause deals with the possibility of a chemical, biological, radiological, and nuclear (CBRN) attack. The 1995 sarin gas attack in the Tokyo subway, the 2001 mailing of letters containing anthrax spores in the United States, and the mysterious nonlethal poisoning of schoolgirls in Afghanistan early in 2009 offer noteworthy precedents for such an attack.

Politically Motivated Attacks

Acts of terrorism are politically motivated. In other words, they seek to achieve or advance particular goals or causes through coercive and unlawful means. Hence, the U.S. *Code of Federal Regulations* establishes the intention "to intimidate or coerce a government, the civilian population, or any segment thereof, in furtherance of political or social objectives" as an element of its understanding of terrorism.[14] TA2000 also specifies "religious or ideological" causes. Yet sometimes all of these motives merge as justifications for attacks.

For instance, the terrorist organization al-Qaeda in Iraq operates under the banner of the "Islamic State of Iraq," which communicates a political goal; seeks to establish a state based on Islamic religious law, and expresses disdain for Western values, indicating an ideological inclination.

The 2003 OECD report, *Emerging Systemic Risks in the 21st Century,* notes that anything symbolizing the "Western system" is a prime target of modern terrorism.[15] Nevertheless, there are reasons to suspect that many recent terrorist attacks have been perpetrated out of plain hate, without any discernible political aim sought by their perpetrators. In support of this suggestion, NCC's *2008 Report* recorded the impossibility of determining the perpetrators of over 7,000 terrorist attacks during the year.

Fostering a Climate of Fear

The reader might be able to infer from the characteristics examined that one indication of terrorism is its perpetrators' desire to engender a generalized climate of fear, of terror, within the social groups targeted. We will not commonly find this characteristic itemized in the legal definitions used to criminalize acts of terrorism, as it is subjective and difficult to establish in practice. However, this is what terrorism inflicts on the collective psyche: the fear of finding ourselves at the wrong place and at the wrong time, when violence is suddenly and unexpectedly unleashed.

Fear descended on the inhabitants of Madrid after the March 11, 2004, train bombings that killed 191 and injured about 1,800; and on the inhabitants of London, after the July 7, 2005, bombings targeting London's transport system, which killed 52 and injured about 700. In April 2009, in the Indian province of Jharkhand, Maoist rebels killed over a dozen members of the security forces and blew up a government building. As part of their campaign, they seized a train and held some 300 people hostage. Even though all the passengers were safely released, it would be naive to assume they did not fear for their lives during the ordeal. Terrorism takes into account not only actual attacks but also the threat of carrying out such attacks.

Acts of terrorism are thus unlawful and premeditated actions, fitting the definitions cited as well as the broader picture we have formed, based on these definitions. Terrorists are those individuals perpetrating acts of terrorism. Terrorist groups or organizations are those practicing terrorism; and, as the U.S. *Code* definition indicates, also those groups or organizations that have "significant subgroups" practicing terrorism.

These subgroups can operate through terrorist (or terror) cells, small groups of individuals acting with a certain operational independence but following guidance from a high command upon activation. Yet, in further indication of the organized nature of the crime, terrorism also involves interrelated activities such as financing, planning, the design and engineering of lethal devices, indoctrination, training, and the provision of shelters and sanctuaries. The people involved in these activities are accessories, accomplices, and instrumental to the perpetration of acts of terrorism, and should be therefore considered terrorists.

There are cases in which the perpetrators of acts of terrorism are nationals of the country where the attacks take place. For example, members of al-Shabaab in Somalia, the Real IRA in the UK, the Revolutionary Struggle in Greece, Shining Path in Peru, and lone extremists, broadly, tend to follow this pattern. However, terrorism is increasingly international in character. Hence, the U.S. *Code* regards as instances of "international terrorism" those involving the citizens or the territory of more than one country, and such cases are more the rule than the exception. Al-Qaeda and the terror groups profiled in Appendix II belong here.

What Is al-Qaeda?

Al-Qaeda is an international terrorist organization formed in 1988 in Afghanistan. It evolved out of the Maktab al-Khidamat network established by Abdullah Azzam and Osama bin Laden to recruit volunteers for a jihad against the Soviet invasion of Afghanistan (1979–1989).

"Jihad" is an Islamic term that implies a religious duty under Islam. Islam is a religion based on the teachings of Muhammad, who lived in the seventh century in what is now Saudi Arabia and is regarded by Muslims as a prophet of Allah (God in Arabic). Muslims are the people who practice Islam. A duty of jihad can be that of fighting an enemy. Islamic religious leaders, such as ayatollahs and mullahs, are the ones who issue calls to jihad. The Muslims engaged in jihad are called "mujahedin." "Jihadists" is a term used loosely to refer to the marginal members of the Muslim population who support violent jihad. The desire to impose Sharia (or Islamic religious) law over territories is a common motivation driving jihadists.

Before heading the jihad in Afghanistan and the Maktab network, Abdullah Azzam was one of Osama bin Laden's university teachers in Saudi Arabia. Bin Laden, originally a Saudi Arabian, whose citizenship has now been revoked, adheres to the Sunni denomination of Islam and comes from a very affluent background.

After the Soviets left Afghanistan, analysts agree that there was a split between Azzam and bin Laden about the future of their network, renamed al-Qaeda (Arabic for "the base") by then. While Azzam apparently wanted to use the mujahedin for other endeavors similar to their previous activities, namely, fighting, as in Afghanistan, to expel non-Muslims from largely Muslim countries, bin Laden aimed for a more networked approach. This involved the volunteers returning home and attempting to enforce the strict observance of Islam in their respective countries. The debate ceased after the assassination of Azzam in November 1989, at which point bin Laden assumed control of al-Qaeda.

Al-Qaeda turned anti-American after the First Gulf War. In particular, he resented the large-scale U.S. military presence in Saudi Arabia, perhaps as much as he resented the Soviet presence in Afghanistan in the 1980s. In the period leading up to 9/11, there were many attacks, including the 1998 bombings of the U.S. embassies in Tanzania and Kenya and the 2000 suicide attack on the destroyer USS *Cole* in Yemen.

Bin Laden was based in Sudan between 1991 and 1996. *The 9/11 Commission Report* of the National Commission on Terrorist Attacks upon the United States established that in that area, al-Qaeda's $30 million per year operation covered jihadists, training camps, airfields, vehicles, arms, and the development of training manuals. Bin Laden was expelled from Sudan and went back to Afghanistan, where he was given shelter by the Taliban. The Taliban was overthrown late in 2001 by U.S. forces during the first phase of "Operation Enduring Freedom," but bin Laden evaded capture. It is believed he and his deputy Ayman al-Zawahiri, the former head of the al-Jihad terrorist organization, are hiding in the border region between Afghanistan and Pakistan.

The global campaign against al-Qaeda after 9/11 has crippled its capacity to act as a centralized organization. Nonetheless, the networked nature of al-Qaeda continues to make the organization terrorist enemy number one.

For instance, terrorist organizations such as the Algeria-based al-Qaeda in the Islamic Maghreb (formerly the Salafist Group for Preaching and Combat), the Islamic State of Iraq (formerly the Mujahidin Shura Council), and the Libyan Islamic Fighting Group have declared affiliation to al-Qaeda.

There are also smaller groups named after al-Qaeda in at least Afghanistan, Pakistan, Saudi Arabia, and Yemen. Other groups, such as al-Shabaab in Somalia and Jemaah Islamiya in Indonesia, are suspected to have close links with the organization or its leaders.

Therefore, unlike the case of rebel or insurgent groups that commit acts of terrorism, it is too complex a matter to see al-Qaeda as linked with any specific national struggle. Al-Qaeda increasingly resembles a vast terror nebula, with many different parts diffusely connected to each other and to the core of the organization.

Rebels, Insurgents, and Guerrillas

As the term suggests, "rebels" oppose something. The struggle is violent, as rebellion involves armed fighting. Shared ethnicity and language commonly bind the members of rebel groups together. From an unwillingness to bow to the political or ideological inclinations of governments to a desire to impose the will of the few on the many, the motivations behind rebellion vary. However, claims to the sovereignty or independence of contested regions are common.

While the Zapatistas in the southern Mexican state of Chiapas, the Uighurs in the Xinjiang province of China, the Jundallah group in southwestern Iran, and the Houthi rebels in north Yemen want greater autonomy for their communities, the Liberation Tigers of Tamil Eelam in the northwestern part of Sri Lanka and the Liberation Front of the Enclave of Cabinda in Angola have fought for the outright secession of their provinces since the 1970s. So overlapping terms such as "secessionists" or "separatists," or secessionist or separatist rebels or insurgents, may be used.

In some parts of the world children (boys and girls), as well as adults, are recruited to fight or support rebel fighting. The 1989 UN *Convention on the Rights of the Child* establishes that children are those below the age of 18 and that states should refrain from recruiting for military service those below the age of 15.[16] Thus, according to the 2007 Paris Principles, "child soldiers" are those below the age of 18 who are "associated with an armed force or armed group."[17] Further, the International Labour Organisation's *Minimum Age Convention* of 1973 establishes as "child labor" that which involves children below the age of 15.[18] The International Criminal Court actually regards as a "war crime" the conscription or enlisting of children under the age of 15 into national armed forces or their use in (rebel or insurgent) hostilities.

"Insurgents" and "rebels" are two terms often used without any clear distinction being made between them. Like rebels, "insurgents" are composed of small groups, factions, or militias forcibly opposing governments.

Nonetheless, while rebellions have often a regional character, insurgencies tend to wage violent campaigns across whole countries. Thus, the Taliban insurgency is spread throughout Afghanistan and parts of Pakistan.

A term sometimes used interchangeably with insurgents is "guerrillas." "Guerrilla" refers to a set of paramilitary tactics. In classic warfare, regular armies attempt to annihilate an adversary as soon as possible by using all the means at their disposal. In contrast, fighting between state forces and insurgents using guerrilla tactics is asymmetric, as the insurgents compensate for their relative weakness by conducting small-scale warfare over long periods.

The simplest form of guerrilla tactics is the use of hit-and-run fighting techniques, such as ambushes, assassinations, bombings, and sabotage. To facilitate the task, attacks often occur in rural settings, which offer insurgents ample terrain in which to retreat and hide after attacks. It is said that the strategy allows insurgents to keep political campaigns alive for a long time without risking financial collapse or frontal assaults from security forces.

The insurgents who make extensive use of guerrilla tactics are often simply called "guerrillas." Thus, the word means the paramilitary tactics as well as the people that use them. Guerrillas (or insurgents) in Colombia and Peru have fought state forces using guerrilla tactics since the 1960s.

As the reader might infer, guerrilla tactics are similar to terrorist tactics. In fact, distinguishing between them is a contested field. The U.S. Department of State (DOS) regards some insurgent groups, such as the Revolutionary Armed Forces of Colombia, the Shining Path in Peru, and the Liberation Tigers of Tamil Eelam in Sri Lanka, as terrorist organizations. According to Bard E. O'Neill, the main difference between guerrillas and terrorists is that guerrilla warfare primarily targets state forces rather than unarmed civilians.[19] However, examples come to mind that challenge this assumption.

Indeed, the terms are not mutually exclusive. Moreover, their use is politically charged. Once rebel or insurgent groups become designated as terrorist organizations, negotiations are over, as governments tend not to negotiate with terrorists. When the Sri Lankan forces unleashed a massive assault on the Tamil Tiger–controlled territories in April 2009, which resulted in thousands of civilian casualties, negotiations had been off the table for a while. In addition, in the popular press, terms come into and go out of fashion every now and then.

Therefore, the reader needs to contextualize adverse private forces within the history and evolution of particular conflicts in order to decide whether "rebels," "insurgents," "guerrillas," or "terrorists" would be the best term to apply to them. The ambiguities are patent when we are dealing with the Taliban, which started as one of the many rebel factions emerging after the Soviets left Afghanistan, progressed to an insurgency, employs guerrilla and terrorist tactics, and has links to organized crime.

What Is the Taliban?

We read about the Taliban daily and we get the idea from news reports that it is a clearly defined group, perhaps a conventional terrorist organization. Yet, in spite of the frequent terrorist attacks attributed to it, it is more useful to understand the Taliban as a movement. It draws elements from the tribal composition of Afghan society, the radical interpretations of Islam that many groups in the region embrace, and the consequences of the transition to the post–Cold War state of affairs.

We learned about Cold War rivalries in chapter 2. In Afghanistan, after a military coup in 1978, a power struggle emerged, pitting two rival Communist factions against one another. In 1979, Soviet troops invaded the country and backed the rule of Babrak Karmal, the leader of the Parcham faction of the People's Democratic Party of Afghanistan; the leader of the other faction was killed. An uprising followed and a jihad was called against the "infidel" (non-Muslim) invaders. Following Cold War logic, the United States provided the mujahedin fighting the Soviet troops with funds and weapons. As the Cold War came to a close, the Soviet troops withdrew from Afghanistan in 1989. While this part of the story partly overlaps the origins of al-Qaeda, and the Taliban and al-Qaeda have crossed paths on more than one occasion, the two are very different entities.

After the Soviet left Afghanistan, the country was in a state of civil war, some may say meltdown. For a variety of reasons, warlords and former mujahedin fought one another. There were massive atrocities, and refugees poured into Pakistan and other neighboring countries. Ahmed Rashid documents how a new Afghan generation, the offspring of the mujahedin, many of them born in refugee camps in Pakistan and educated in its madrassas (religious schools), came together under the idea of the Taliban (meaning "Islamic students").[20] Partly to end the fighting, but also to implement the strict religious teachings learned at the madrassas, this group of people endeavored to enforce Sharia law in Afghanistan. With Mullah Mohammed Omar as leader, this group emerged in 1994 in the southern province of Kandahar.

By 1996, the Taliban had taken control of Kabul. The new Taliban government, lacking international recognition but endorsed by a handful of Islamist countries, implemented an aggressive program of oppressive policies. Women were banned from work or education, non-Islamic people lost rights, and religious trials and public executions became the order of the day. In addition to the income generated from allowing and taxing the opium trade, *The 9/11 Commission Report* stated that al-Qaeda paid the Taliban $10–20 million yearly in exchange for being given a haven. Aside from rebellious marginal regions, by the end of the 20th century the Taliban controlled most of the country.

The Taliban government was overthrown in 2001, and some of its leaders fled the country. However, the movement has regained force. Further, it has spread to Pakistan (a state with nuclear weapons), where it has many sympathizers, including members within the security forces and within the system of madrassas. The spread of the Taliban insurgency across Afghanistan and Pakistan has motivated a rethink of the strategy to deal with the escalating conflict in the region and the treatment of both countries as a single theater of war, increasingly called "AfPak."

By April 2009, the Taliban had taken control of the Swat valley, about 75 miles from Islamabad, Pakistan's capital. The government of Pakistan entered into a peace agreement with the fighters, which was later revoked after pressure from the United States. The situation is currently too fluid for us to arrive at reasonable conclusions or even educated guesses about the future of the Taliban, Afghanistan, and the region. However, there is now a Taliban faction linked to former members of the Taliban government and led by a ruling council (the Quetta shura), as well as looser factions operating in the Afghanistan-Pakistan border region and inside Pakistan. Some of the factions inside Pakistan and at the Afghanistan-Pakistan border also appear to work in concert with al-Qaeda.

Organized Crime

Even though the motives behind terrorist attacks may be diffuse and mutate over time, the groups that commit such acts attempt to further political goals. However, when the attainment of private or material gain is the driving force behind acts of unlawful violence, other types of private armed forces come into play. They represent expressions of organized crime. Whereas the term "organized crime" is sometimes used to designate only mafia organizations, in other instances it implies a distinction between petty crime and criminal activities involving higher levels of organization and sophistication. I adopt the latter interpretation in this book and identify pirates, mafia groups, and drug cartels as representing the three main types of organized crime.

Contemporary Piracy and Pirates

Piracy is a water-bound crime. It occurs in oceans, seas, gulfs, harbors, estuaries, and rivers and comprises unlawful attacks against any type of vessel, moving or stationary. Stationary vessels include anchored ships and offshore oil and gas platforms, which are floating vessels. Piracy was endemic during early modern times. The practice was subdued and remained manageable through most of the 20th century. Nonetheless, it seems that piracy as a destabilizing issue has made a comeback, particularly off the coast of Somalia.

Article 101 of the 1982 UN *Convention on the Law of the Sea* (UNCLOS) defines acts of piracy according to the following criteria:

(a) any illegal acts of violence or detention, or any act of depredation, committed for private ends by the crew or the passengers of a private ship or a private aircraft, and directed:
   (i) on the high seas, against another ship or aircraft, or against persons or property on board such ship or aircraft;
   (ii) against a ship, aircraft, persons or property in a place outside the jurisdiction of any State;
(b) any act of voluntary participation in the operation of a ship or of an aircraft with knowledge of facts making it a pirate ship or aircraft;
(c) any act inciting or of intentionally facilitating an act described in subparagraph (a) or (b).

Instances of piracy are those fitting this definition (a, b, and c). Pirates are the persons that perpetrate such attacks (a, b), are accessories to the crime (c), or associated with the people that commit them (c). The attacks are directed toward property, people, or both.

This is not the only definition of piracy available. However, the UNCLOS definition is extensively used by international and professional organizations to establish, first, whether crimes on water or against ships can be catalogued as instances of piracy, and second, to produce statistical reports documenting the evolution of the practice. The definition is also relevant because the international community universally endorses UNCLOS.

Just like other legal terms and definitions we have examined, however, this definition is not perfect. The reader may have noted that UNCLOS emphasizes crimes committed "on the high seas" and "outside the jurisdiction of states" (i, ii). In other words, the approach only covers instances of piracy occurring in international waters (on the "high" or "open" seas), which are the oceanic areas over which no single state has jurisdiction. Crimes committed within the "territorial sea," for example, near the shore, on canals, and in ports, fall outside the definition. As a point of reference, UNCLOS establishes that every state has "the right to establish the breadth of its territorial sea up to a limit not exceeding 12 nautical miles" (13.81 miles or 22.22 kilometers) from the shore.

Acknowledging this problem, the International Maritime Organization (IMO) introduced guidelines in 2001 that define "armed robbery against ships" as

> Any unlawful act of violence or detention or any act of depredation, or threat thereof, other than an act of piracy, directed against a ship or against persons or property on board such a ship, within a State's jurisdiction over such offences.[21]

Thus, for legal and statistical purposes we can distinguish between piracy in international waters and armed robbery against ships in territorial waters. The IMO and other organizations make that distinction. However, to understand the global scope of piracy we can always extrapolate from our knowledge of piracy in international waters when we examine crimes committed in the territorial waters of the United States or any other country.

Pirates are commonly armed. We can gather from the UNCLOS and IMO definitions that instances of piracy (and armed robbery against ships) involve the use of force or the threat of using it. The IMO notes in its 2008 annual piracy report that in many of the attacks recorded, seafarers were violently assaulted by small groups (of five to ten people) armed with guns and knives.[22] The strategy is to attempt to board ships. The intention is often to commit theft, which can range from the theft of a few valuable items in an opportunistic raid to the targeting of the ships' stores or the ships themselves. The kidnapping and ransoming of crews is becoming more common. The IMO documents some 774 seafarers and crewmembers who were taken hostage or kidnapped in 2008; 38 of them remained unaccounted for as of March 19, 2009.[23]

As with other types of crime, piracy may flourish due to law enforcement deficiencies. In conflict-affected countries, such as Somalia, law and order may be minimal or nonexistent. In a weak state, such as Nigeria, the institutions charged with law enforcement may be corrupt or easily corruptible, as well as lacking the ethos and infrastructure needed to tackle crime effectively.

Cultural and geographical factors can also play a part. For instance, if piracy is part of the history of a region and deprived communities living there have extracted rewards from the practice over generations, the chances are greater that piracy will continue. The seas of Southeast Asia and the contiguous Bay of Bengal (the mass of water between India and Myanmar) are examples of this. Adam Young comments that in Southeast Asia there are people who are both maritime oriented and poor and marginalized; hence they provide "a large potential labour pool for piracy."[24]

At the same time, where there is heavy maritime traffic in close proximity to islands and estuaries we are also likely to find regions affected by piracy. This situation offers both bases for attacks and havens to which pirates can retreat in order to divide their spoils or hide their hostages. Such areas include parts of the Caribbean, the Gulf of Guinea, Indonesia, and the Philippines. The reader may wish to use an online satellite imagery service to explore the geography of all these piracy-infested areas.

Some piracy-affected regions, notably Southeast Asia and Northeast Africa, also include countries where terrorists are increasingly active. There are two different attitudes to the potentially explosive combination of piracy and terrorism.

Some analysts believe that the October 12, 2000, suicide attack on the USS *Cole*, an American destroyer, provided a practical example of this explosive combination. The USS *Cole* was anchored in Aden harbor, Yemen, when a small craft hit its port side. Moreover, possible links between Somali pirates and al-Shabaab, the terrorist wing of the ousted Islamic Courts Union, raises further concerns. On the other hand, many analysts see the motivations of pirates and terrorists as too much at odds for the explosive combination of piracy and terrorism to materialize. Whole conference sessions continue to be devoted to the issue. However, I am raising this point for us to consider the actual and possible overlaps between diverse types of adverse private forces and the many scenarios we can construct. Probably we will always be able to find some sort of connection between pirates and local gangs and mafias.

Mafia Groups and Underworld Forces

There are two conventional understandings of the term "mafia." Historically, it is associated with the criminal societies that originated in Sicily, and through emigration, penetrated the U.S. crime scene early in the 20th century. Cosa Nostra (Our Cause) is another term used to refer to these organizations. The word "mafia" is still applied to criminal organizations with some Italian background. However, the term has transcended this specific use and is now used broadly with reference to criminal networks.

Mafias are ingenious, as aspects of their organization resemble firms and conventional business practices. Mafias enforce territoriality, restrictions on membership, rules of operation, and primacy in specific traffics, and they endeavor to achieve the continuation and expansion of their operations.

Mafias control vice and illegal trades such as contraband, counterfeiting, black markets, contract killings, drug-trafficking, money laundering, human trafficking, prostitution, racketeering, usury, weapons smuggling, and so forth. They are also involved in commercial areas involving the employment (and control) of large numbers of workers, for example, in agriculture, construction, ports, and waste disposal (including the international shipping of hazardous wastes in contravention of the Basel Convention).[25]

In addition, mafias extort regular protection payments from honest businesses, large and small. While in some places protection money is part of the cultural fabric, in some others it involves an open battle between underworld forces and those unwilling to yield to their demands. In parts of Italy, for example, protection payments are called *pizzo* and are an old practice, as in Colombia. In Mexico, drug-trafficking organizations and related mafias are currently attempting to introduce the practice at the national level. To varying extents, equivalent practices are found elsewhere in the world, including some neighborhoods in large U.S. cities.

Blurring the lines between the underground and the formal economy, mafias also establish legitimate businesses, albeit often as fronts for illegal activities or money laundering.

Geographical and territoriality issues offer useful parameters for the identification of the various mafia groups operating throughout the world. In Italy, for example, besides the Sicilian mafia, the Camorra organization operates from Naples and the region of Campania, and the 'Ndrangheta from the region of Calabria. During the Balkans conflict in the 1990s, conditions were favorable for Bulgarian mafia groups to consolidate around the creation of a prolific smuggling market leading into the affected countries. The yearly corruption assessment by the Center for the Study of Democracy in Sofia estimated the size of Bulgaria's underground economy at about 14 percent of national income in 2008. Albania has also a prolific mafia profile. Further, the Balkans region remains the main entry route for heroin being transported from Asia to Western Europe.

Beyond the Balkans, the end of the Cold War paved the way for mafia groups to emerge throughout Eastern Europe and the former Soviet republics. Russian mafia groups operate globally and rival the Italians. In Asia, the Japanese Yakuza has a history going back centuries. By the 1970s, Yakuza gangs were active across Southeast Asia and in the United States, particularly in Hawaii. Chinese criminal networks have expanded as China has risen as an economic power. In Latin America, drug-trafficking organizations dominate the mafia scene. In Mexico, the office dedicated to tackle organized crime (SIEDO) estimated in January 2005 that seven drug cartels and numerous associated drug cells dominate the traffic of drugs into the United States.[26] In West Africa, some rebel militias double as criminal gangs, and so on.

In terms of membership, ethnic and cultural factors play key roles. To put it in simple terms, the members of Russian or Italian mafias are overwhelmingly Russians or Italians. They may also be descendants of people of particular nationalities. Symbols, such as initiation rituals (which may include killings), oaths of allegiance, and emblems and logos (sometimes used to indicate the provenance of illicit goods), further reasserts identity traits.

Ethnic and cultural factors guide the geographical areas of traffic, too. Thus, when turf wars erupt between competing mafias, it is often because boundaries established in terms of territories or traffics have been transgressed. Indeed, mafias communicate with each other, and it is through these connections that global operations in illicit trades are organized.

The people commanding mafias vary across the underworld. They range from bosses and heads of clans or families to drug barons, oligarchs, strongmen, and even warlords (rebel or insurgent leaders exercising control over people within discrete conflict domains). Starting from the top, systems of hierarchies all the way down to the level of gang leaders are established.

Similarly, pay scales and systems are set up to distribute the profits derived from trafficking. For example, according to figures provided by the Confesercenti trade association, at ongoing rates the heads of Italian mafia clans (the capos) earn up to €40,000 a month (about $55,000) while operators at the bottom of the pyramid make just about €1,000 (about $1,400).[27]

Ranging from well-established organizations with distinctive historical and cultural backgrounds to looser and sometimes transient criminal networks, this brief examination allows us to see the variable constitution of mafias. Yet we should not discount smaller players as simply petty criminals, because today's large mafia organizations were yesterday's small gangs. Furthermore, mafia organizations can merge or take over the operations of rivals by force. To acknowledge the variable constitution and simplify the analysis, in this book I designate the mafias operating in particular territories as groups involved in "organized crime."

Drug Cartels and Narco Forces

The 1967 report of the Task Force on Organized Crime regarded organized crime activity as "the supplying of illegal goods and services" and singled out gambling, loan sharking, and narcotics especially.[28] It also noted that 24 criminal cartels with a membership of Italian descent formed the core of organized crime in the United States. Four decades later, the Organized Crime Drug Enforcement Task Forces Program, created in 1982, is among the various multiagency initiatives focusing on drug-trafficking. In the interim, organized crime ceased to be chiefly about the Cosa Nostra, drug-trafficking became a problem requiring efforts tailored to tackle it, and drug cartels started to pose a greater challenge to homeland security than ordinary mafias.

In the 1980s there was a shift toward a greater use of cocaine rather than marijuana and heroin. Southern Florida, via the Bahamas, became the gateway for the cocaine supplied by the Cali and Medellin cartels from Colombia. By 1985, fighting between rival gangs for a share of the cocaine trade had turned Miami into the murder capital of the United States. When federal authorities started to gain control over Miami, the fight against drugs shifted to the Andean producer countries (Bolivia, Colombia, and Peru). The Cali and the Medellin cartels were neutralized in the first half of the 1990s. As a means of consolidating the military strategy carried out by the Colombian government with assistance from the United States (including the use of PMCs), Plan Colombia was launched in 1999.

Meanwhile, Mexico emerged as the key transit hub for South American drugs bound for the North American market. The Drug Enforcement Administration (DEA) estimates that the U.S.-Mexico border is now the entry point for about 65 percent of cocaine shipments arriving in the United States.[29]

It took roughly a decade to turn things around in southern Florida, the Bahamas, and Colombia. The Merida Initiative for Mexico, Central America, the Dominican Republic, and Haiti was only launched in 2008. Besides intense fighting between Mexican security forces and drug cartels, as the command structures of the cartels are targeted, there has been an escalation of violence within and between cartels for leadership and turf. Of the seven drug-trafficking organizations identified by Mexican authorities as dominating the illicit trade, in 2009 the most powerful cartels were the Gulf, the Sinaloa, and the Juarez; see Appendix II for profiles of Mexican drug cartels.

"Drug cartels" are organizations trafficking in illegal drugs or substances. According to the U.S. sentencing guidelines (USSG), illegal substances cover heroin, cocaine, cocaine base, PCP (phencyclidine), methamphetamine, LSD (lysergic acid diethylamide), fentanyl, fentanyl analogue, marijuana, hashish, and hashish oil. The description of a "controlled substance offence" by the USSG can be used also as a working definition of drug-trafficking:

> the manufacture, import, export, distribution, or dispensing of a controlled substance (or a counterfeit substance) or the possession of a controlled substance (or a counterfeit substance) with intent to manufacture, import, export, distribute, or dispense.[30]

The Drug Trafficking Act 1994 in the UK also establishes as instances of drug-trafficking the "transporting or storing," or "having possession of or using property" or "using any ship for illicit traffic in controlled drugs."[31] Just as the USSG "application notes" stipulate, we should also understand as part of drug-trafficking the people "aiding and abetting, conspiring, and attempting to commit" the crime.

Even though we commonly refer to drug-trafficking organizations as cartels, the reader should be aware that this name is disputed. Cartels are commercial alliances between producers in the same industry formed to manipulate prices and output with the aim of maximizing profits. For example, OPEC operates as a cartel and its members lower or raise oil output with the intention of affecting international oil prices. However, there is no conclusive evidence suggesting that drug-trafficking organizations can operate with such synergy. Nevertheless, drug-trafficking organizations emulate the workings of business organizations, operate in a transnational fashion, function in cells, and involve paramilitary components.

From production to distribution, the most powerful drug-trafficking organizations are vertically integrated and develop expertise in areas such as agriculture, chemical processing (which requires people with university degrees), R&D (the development of crack cocaine in the late 1970s and the engineering of ever more ingenious methods to avoid detection are examples), and advanced logistics (by air, land, and sea and under tight schedules).

Horizontally, deals are established with mafia groups and other cartels to move drugs from South America or Asia to the lucrative markets in Europe and North America. West Africa is becoming an important transport hub for drugs bound for Europe from South America. The integration of all these processes requires professional management in addition to specialists in laundering hundreds of millions of dollars. Moreover, the undercover nature of the trade makes it necessary to fragment operations into cells. Thus, if one cell falls to law enforcement efforts, the information disclosed does not jeopardize the whole operation.

Huge turnovers also provide the means for cartels to maintain their own paramilitary forces, which may be highly specialized and use advanced military hardware. In Mexico these forces are sometimes called *sicarios*. As an example of such forces, we can take the paramilitary wing of the Gulf Cartel, the Zetas, which originated from 30 or 40 deserters from the Mexican elite forces. From this base, they have expanded by luring other members of the forces to join them and through the recruitment of soldiers of similar backgrounds from Central America.

Media reports over the years have documented the collaboration of American, European, and Israeli mercenaries with the Colombian cartels. Similarly, Eastern European and Russian mafias have incorporated former members of the Soviet-era security forces, which also staff many local security firms and the large security units maintained by oligarchs and state companies. A point emerging here is that while each one of the adverse private forces examined poses a threat to global security, these forces also interact. This introduces destabilizing dynamics that are counteracted by both state forces and PMCs.

Notes

1. Herbert M. Howe, "Private Security Forces and African Stability: The Case of Executive Outcomes," *Journal of Modern African Studies* 36, no. 2 (1998): 312.

2. David Shearer, "Private Armies and Military Intervention," *Adelphi Paper* 316 (1998): 25–26.

3. Peter W. Singer, *Corporate Warriors: The Rise of the Privatized Military Industry* (New York: Cornell University Press, 2003), 91.

4. Deborah D. Avant, *The Market for Force: The Consequences of Privatizing Security* (Cambridge: Cambridge University Press, 2005), 16–17.

5. Carlos Ortiz, "The Private Military Company: An Entity at the Centre of Overlapping Spheres of Commercial Activity and Responsibility," in *Private Military and Security Companies: Chances, Problems, Pitfalls and Prospects*, ed. Thomas Jäger and Gerhard Kümmel (Wiesbaden, Germany: VS Verlag, 2007), 55–68.

6. Max Weber, "Politics as a Vocation," in *From Max Weber: Essays in Sociology*, ed. and trans. H. H. Gerth and C. Mills Wright(London: Routledge, 1997), 77–78.

7. International Institute for Strategic Studies, *The Military Balance 1995–1996* (Oxford: Oxford University Press, 1995), 230–56.

8. See International Institute for Strategic Studies, volumes of *The Military Balance* for 1990 to 1999.

9. "Ratendra's Lifetime Mission," *The Sun* (Fiji), September 14, 2003.

10. United States, *United States Code*, Washington DC, 22USC2656f, http://www.gpoaccess.gov/uscode/.

11. United Kingdom, *Terrorism Act 2000* (London: Stationery Office, 2000), 1.

12. Organisation for Economic Co-operation and Development, *Emerging Risks in the 21st Century: An Agenda for Action* (Paris: OECD Publications Service, 2003), 104.

13. National Counterterrorism Center, *2008 Report on Terrorism* (Washington, DC: National Counterterrorism Center, April 30, 2009), 12.

14. United States, *Code of Federal Regulations*, Washington DC, 28CFR0.85, http://www.gpoaccess.gov/cfr/.

15. Organisation for Economic Co-operation and Development, *Emerging Risks in the 21st Century*, 104.

16. See article 38 in United Nations, *Convention on the Rights of the Child*, in *United Nations Treaty Series* 1577, no. 27531 (September 2, 1990): 3.

17. United Nations Children's Fund (UNICEF), "The Paris Principles: Principles and Guidelines on Children Associated with Armed Forces or Armed Group" (Paris, January 30, 2007), para 2.1.

18. See Article 1 and 2 in International Labour Organisation, *Minimum Age Convention* (Geneva: International Labour Office, June 26, 1973).

19. Bard E. O'Neill, *Insurgency and Terrorism: From Revolution to Apocalypse*, 2nd ed. (Washington. DC: Potomac Books, 2005), 36.

20. Ahmed Rashid, *Taliban: The Story of the Afghan Warlords* (London: Pan Books, 2001), 17–54.

21. International Maritime Organization, *Resolution A.922(22): Code of Practice for the Investigation of the Crimes of Piracy and Armed Robbery against Ships* (London: International Maritime Organization, January 22, 2001), Annex, para. 2.2.

22. International Maritime Organization, *Reports on Acts of Piracy and Armed Robbery against Ships: Acts Reported during April 2009* (London: International Maritime Organization, May 5, 2009), 1.

23. Ibid., 2.

24. Adam J. Young, *Contemporary Maritime Piracy in Southeast Asia: History, Causes and Remedies* (Singapore: ISEAS Publishing, 2007), 57.

25. The Basel Convention is a global environmental agreement that establishes guidelines for the transboundary movements and disposal of hazardous wastes. See United Nations, *Convention on the Control of Transboundary Movement of Hazardous Wastes and Their Disposal*, in *United Nations Treaty Series* 1673, no. 28911 (May 5, 1992): 57.

26. SIEDO (Subprocuraduría de Investigación Especializada contra la Delincuencia Organizada, Mexico), "México y Eastados Unidos Trabajan Coordinamente

Para Combatir El Lavado De Dinero Provenienete Del Narcotráfico," Press Release 025/05 (Mexico City, January 13, 2005).

27. Confesercenti, *Le mani della criminalità sulle imprese. XI Rapporto SOS Impresa—Confesercenti* (Rome: Confesercenti, November 11, 2008), 7.

28. President's Commission on Law Enforcement and Administration of Justice, "Task Force Report: Organized Crime" (Washington, DC, 1967), 1, 6.

29. Donnie R. Marshall, Administrator Drug Enforcement Administration, "Statement before the U.S. House of Representatives Committee on the Judiciary Subcommittee on Crime" (Washington, DC, March 29, 2001). The 65 percent estimate is still quoted by DEA.

30. See 2008 *Federal Sentencing Guidelines Manual*, § 4B1.2(b), available online at http://www.ussc.gov/2008guid/TABCON08.htm.

31. United Kingdom, *Drug Trafficking Act 1994* (London: Stationery Office, 1994), I(1).

CHAPTER 4

Conflict Environments and Private Forces

On December 14, 1995, the Republic of Bosnia and Herzegovina, the Republic of Croatia, and the Federal Republic of Yugoslavia signed the Dayton Peace Accords in Paris. The accords formally ended the Bosnian War, a violent ethnic conflict in central Europe that began in March 1992. The accords invited a multinational military force, the Implementation Force (Bosnia and Herzegovina) or IFOR, under the command of the North Atlantic Treaty Organization (NATO) to implement the peace. IFOR became a stabilization force, SFOR, in January 1996. The Security Council of the United Nations (UN) also sanctioned the establishment of an International Police Task Force (IPTF) under UN command.

Parallel to the contributions of NATO and the UN, on July 9, 1996, President Bill Clinton announced the start of the Train-and-Equip Program (TEP) for the Bosnian Federation. Its aim was to help Bosnia to develop the ability to defend itself.

The start of TEP saw a contingent of some 170 skilled and experienced military personnel dispatched to Bosnia under the command of William M. Boyce, a former commanding general of the First Armored Division in Germany. TEP was an ambitious operation that included assistance in the establishment of a ministry of defense and the development and execution of military training policy. The United States contributed about $100 million worth of defense articles and services, and Saudi Arabia, Kuwait, the United Arab Emirates, Malaysia, and Brunei pledged $140 million to cover the implementation costs of TEP.

Operationally, TEP was an independent endeavor over which NATO and the UN enjoyed neither authority nor command. However, what set TEP apart from other military operations sponsored by the United States was that it was actually implemented by a PMC based in Alexandria, Virginia: MPRI Inc.

MPRI and many other PMCs deployed in the Balkans in the second half of the 1990s largely operated in a reconstruction environment. Before the accords, however, when governmental forces and militias perpetrated monstrous atrocities and mercenaries and jihadists poured in, MPRI assisted the government of the new Republic of Croatia to enhance its defenses. PMCs currently operating in this part of Europe focus primarily on the provision of security services and mine clearance. Military and law enforcement instruction is still provided.

The Balkans provide us with a microcosm of the different types of adverse private forces populating corridors of conflict, as well as the various roles that PMCs assume while assisting governments, international organizations, and private clients to achieve a myriad political, humanitarian, and economic goals. These connections are deeply entangled in global security, and new light can be thrown on them by exploring three themes: humanitarian crises and interventions, trade in dangerous places, and homeland security.

Humanitarian Crises and Interventions

Humanitarian crises and interventions by the international community in the attempt to contain them frequently occur in weak states. With problems ranging from the exodus of refugees and famines to mass killings and the violent indoctrination of child soldiers, these states pose the greatest development and security challenge to the world. Often requiring external support, PMCs become intertwined in the reconstruction agenda engineered by international organizations and donor nations to tackle their many problems. There has been even a debate about whether it is time to privatize peace. However, first we need to identify weak states. Second, the historical discontinuities and trends linked to the transition to the post–Cold War world provide a useful means to analyze the reasons why these states offer fertile ground for the operation of PMCs.

Weak States and Low-intensity Conflict

Commonly affected by endemic conflict, weak states are the most deprived and underdeveloped countries on the planet. To facilitate the analysis, Table 4.1 offers a working list of weak states based on research by the World Bank and the UN. Some omissions and inclusions are open to debate. Nonetheless, this list offers the reader a window into the most disadvantaged countries in the world as catalogued by leading international organizations (IOs). Most of these countries are located in Africa.

Table 4.1 Weak states

A Angola ~	A Gambia *	A Rwanda *
Afghanistan +	A Guinea ~	A Sierra Leone *
A Benin *	A Guinea-Bissau ~	Solomon Islands +
A Burkina Faso *	Haiti +	A Somalia +
A Burundi ~	Kosovo +	A Sudan +
Cambodia +	Lao PDR +	Timor-Leste ~
A Central African Republic ~	A Lesotho *	A Togo ~
A Chad *	A Liberia ~	A Uganda *
A Comoros +	A Malawi *	Vanuatu +
A Congo +	A Mali *	A West Bank and Gaza +
A Cote d'Ivoire ~	A Mozambique *	A Zambia *
A Dem. Rep. of the Congo ~	Myanmar +	A Zimbabwe +
A Eritrea ~	A Niger *	
A Ethiopia *	A Nigeria ~	

(+) LICUS 2006; (*) LHD 2006; (~) Both LICUS and LHD; (A) in Africa
The table includes countries catalogued as "fragile" by the World Bank's Low-Income Countries under Stress (LICUS) initiative, as well as those considered by the UN Development Programme (UNDP) to be affected by "low human development" (LHD).

Conflicts in weak states occur internally (they are intra-state conflicts), tend to originate in ethnic, tribal, or religious quarrels or to be caused by disputes over the control of natural resources, and are of the low-intensity type.

In contrast to conventional wars between states (inter-state wars), in which the aim is to defeat the enemy with the utmost expedition and with massive force, low-intensity conflicts involve intermittent but sustainable levels of fighting over long periods of time. For example, while the Democratic Republic of the Congo (DRC) has experienced periodic uprisings since its independence from Belgium in 1960, Somalia's state of civil war has continued unabated since the early 1990s. Both countries are considered to be LICUS, or low-income countries under stress, broadly defined by the World Bank as states "characterized by weak policies, institutions, and governance."[1]

"Low-intensity conflict" is a term that was first used during the Cold War to refer to warfare involving guerrilla and terrorist tactics. The combined use of both tactics is often subsumed under "irregular warfare." Assassinations, ambushes, bombings, kidnappings, military coups, and the widespread intimidation of the civilian population are regular occurrences in these conflicts.

Basic weaponry, such as semiautomatic rifles, rocket-propelled grenades, and machetes, are the implements of warfare typically used by the insurgents, rebels, militias, and terrorist factions fighting in weak states. Among them, AK-47 rifles and RPG-7 shoulder-held grenade launchers are favored because they are cheap, widely available new or secondhand, and easy to maintain and repair. Once they were part of the state arsenal; now they are the weapons of the poor and the many. Hutus made extensive use of machetes in their massacre of at least 800,000 Tutsis during the 1994 Rwanda genocide, and machetes were also used by militias from the Revolutionary United Front (RUF) in the 1990s in Sierra Leone for indiscriminate mutilations, which included the chopping off of the hands of captured soldiers and male civilians. Rwanda and Sierra Leone are low human development or LHD countries, namely, those ranking lowest in terms of life expectancy, educational attainment, and income in assessments conducted by the UN Development Programme (UNDP).

Low-intensity conflicts easily spill across borders. For example, antagonisms between Tutsis and Hutus continue to create tensions across the border regions between Rwanda and the DRC. Further, deficient or nonexistent law enforcement fosters high levels of criminality and the exploitation of these areas by criminal organizations. Thus, upon becoming a major transshipment hub for cocaine from South America bound for Europe, the West African country of Guinea-Bissau (which is both LICUS and LHD) has been elevated to the status of Africa's first "narco-state."

However, while approaching underdeveloped and conflict-prone countries as weak states helps us to make useful generalizations, we should be careful not to apply the label indiscriminately. For instance, the conflict in Bosnia-Herzegovina was brutal, but the country is not considered a weak state. There are serious separatist and terrorism problems in India. However, the country is catalogued by the UN as a country of "medium human development" (MHD) and by most analysts as an emerging world power. The military campaign against drug-trafficking organizations that is underway in Mexico has made some cities, particularly those along the border with the United States, very violent. However, the country is considered to have "high human development" and is ranked as one of the world's 20 largest economies.

There are certainly high-risk zones in developing countries and emerging markets. Nevertheless, it would be counterproductive to argue that any country in which conflict flares is suddenly becoming a weak state. The movement away from bipolarity (see below) partly explains the weak states' plight, but not the problems affecting nations closer to the other end of the development ladder.

Beyond Bipolarity

During the period of bipolarity the world was organized into two blocs headed by the two superpowers, the United States and the Soviet Union.

The Third World sat in between, with most countries broadly leaning toward either the West or the Soviet side in the Cold War struggle. It was a cold war because the United States and the Soviet Union came close to war, but never actually declared war on each other. However, the Cold War was pretty hot in parts of the Third World. The most contested regions were Africa, the Middle East, and Southeast Asia, where many countries only became independent during the period of bipolarity. Within this group of developing nations, we find those referred to as weak states today.

As the Cold War progressed and many (weak) states became either people's republics or sided with the West, external assistance from the appropriate bloc was provided. This assistance developed into steady patterns of provision of military and financial aid.

The end of bipolarity resulted in a drastic decline in this patronage. In the case of the United States, the number of military personnel deployed overseas went down from 520,000 in 1983 to 344,000 by 1992.[2] This accompanied a reduction of official arms transfers from about $23.6 billion in 1987 to $14.8 by 1992.[3] Facing economic meltdown, the withdrawal of the Soviet Union (Russia since 1991) from the developing world became more accentuated. Arms transfers registered a drop from about $31.2 billion in 1987 to just $2.8 by 1992. Overall, Western influence and military assistance by the United States and its allies was more substantial and organized than that provided by Russia, China, and other former Communist countries.

The demilitarization of world affairs after the end of the Cold War was welcomed by many, who saw it as a "peace dividend." The shift was inevitable, one might have argued. However, weak states went through a harsh introduction into statehood that made their stability contingent on the external military assistance that was now faltering. In some instances, the assistance was discontinued; in others, it simply ceased to be offered unconditionally. In other words, weak states were denied external support unless they reformed and embraced democracy.

This did not occur overnight. The 1990s were the years of transition. Meanwhile, the transformation of world affairs reignited conflicts; far from achieving resolution of these conflicts during the period of bipolarity, the Cold War order merely imposed a straitjacket on them. With the restraints gone, many weak states were engulfed by low-intensity conflict.

Furthermore, the discipline imposed by the superpowers on client states over the use of the weaponry supplied was gone. There were numerous military coups, and guns and ammunition were illegally traded by corrupt officials. In particular, weapons have found their way easily into the wrong hands.

Between 1989 and 1997, the Stockholm Peace Research Institute reported a decline in the number of major armed conflicts, from 36 to 25.[4] This was the apparent peace dividend in the movement away from bipolarity.

However, this was accompanied by an increase in low-intensity conflicts in weak states, which defies accurate measurement. It was hoped that the UN, liberated from the constraints that paralyzed its decision making during the Cold War, would play a greater role in the emerging conflicts.

The Blue Helmets at 50

UN peacekeeping was 50 years old in 1998. During these 50 years, 49 peace missions were established, and over 750,000 international personnel served in them. A total of 36 (73 percent) of the missions were deployed between 1988 and 1998.[5]

At over $3.6 billion, annual peacekeeping costs reached a half a century high in 1993. This reflected growing expenditure due to the missions in Somalia (UNOSOM I and II) and the beginning of the large deployment in former Yugoslavia (UNPROFOR, 1992–1995), which also involved missions in Bosnia and Herzegovina (UNMIBH, 1995–2002), Croatia (UNCRO, 1995–1996; UNTAES, 1996–1998; UNMOP, 1996–2002; and UNPSG, 1998), and Macedonia (UNPREDEP, 1995–9). Costs fell in 1996 and 1997 to about $1.4 and $1.3 billion, respectively.[6]

While the data examined confirm a larger role for the UN in the transition to the post–Cold War world, it also reflects the rise of low-intensity conflicts. The willingness of some weak states to hire PMCs rather than waiting for the Blue Helmets (soldiers under a UN mandate) to achieve results raises questions about the effectiveness of UN peacekeeping. To put it in different terms, it became clear to some governments that they had to find an alternative to the faltering external assistance. The involvement of Executive Outcomes (EO) in Angola (both LICUS and LHD) and Sierra Leone (LHD) adds substance to the claim and puts the UN and the private military alternative into sharp contrast.

Between 1993 and 1997, EO worked alongside the Angolan Armed Forces (Forças Armadas Angolanas or FAA). EO's involvement was controversial. However, it was crucial for the FAA to defeat the UNITA insurgents, recapture the diamond fields they had exploited to generate the funds needed to carry on fighting, and force the UNITA leadership to the negotiating table, which led to the signing of the Lusaka Protocols.

The UN was already deployed in Angola before EO arrived. UNAVEM I (1988–1991) was established to verify the withdrawal of Cuban troops from the territory, and UNAVEM II (1991–1995) to verify the implementation of a previous peace deal agreed between the Angolan government and UNITA (the Bicesse Accords). The contract between EO and the Angolan government was valued at about $60 million.[7] In contrast, the combined cost of UNAVEM I and II was nearly $200 million.[8]

Similarly, in Sierra Leone EO contributed to the neutralization of RUF militias and the signing of a cease-fire. Elizabeth Rubin comments that before EO was deployed, "no one—not the United Nations, not the Organization of African Unity, not the international-conflict-resolution experts who filled up the abandoned tourist hotels in Freetown, Sierra Leone's capital—was able to bring the fighting under control."[9] A small UN observer mission in Sierra Leone (UNOMSIL, 1998–1999) was subsequently established. Meanwhile, as EO departed, a splinter RUF group, the West Side Boys, took to arms.

To assist with the implementation of the Lomé Peace Agreement, which put Sierra Leone on the road to peace, UNAMSIL (1999–2005) was established. Its cost was about $2.8 billion. In contrast, EO's rates were about $31 million per year.[10] In addition, Doug Brooks reminds us that DynCorp International and PAE provided logistical and support services to UNAMSIL peacekeepers and ICI of Oregon provided air charter services to both UN and U.S. Embassy personnel.[11]

Costs ranging in the millions and not billions, and hundreds of private personnel as against thousands of peacekeepers are two of the contrasts it is possible to identify here.

There are no other examples available that parallel what EO achieved in Angola and Sierra Leone. The now-defunct British firm Sandline International attempted to follow in the footsteps of EO. The firm was hired to assist the forces of Papua New Guinea (LICUS until recently) to regain control of the Panguna Copper Mine in the Isle of Bougainville, which was shut down after the Bougainville Revolutionary Army took control of the island. The plan involved subcontracting EO personnel. However, amid an international scandal the operation collapsed. Thereafter, the appetite to hire PMCs for similar endeavors subsided. Nevertheless, EO gave credence to the idea that private "force multipliers" could contribute to making peace.

PMCs as Force Multipliers

"Force multiplier" is a term implying that a comparatively small group of specialists can enhance a larger force (e.g., an army or units within it).

PMCs on occasions act as force multipliers because they possess skills that can significantly enhance the military capabilities of the recipients of services, strategically, tactically, or operationally. While strategy deals with overall plans and objectives, tactics focus on how military units are organized and deployed to attain the objectives. Operationally, various specific tasks can assist either strategies or tactics.

When PMCs are hired to deliver training services, by definition they become force multipliers. First, they provide an expertise that is absent from the forces or agencies to which it is provided. Second, they supply teams that instruct or become embedded within the security forces of the contracting state.

In the case of EO in Angola and Sierra Leone, its role covered strategy, tactics, and operational support up to combat level. However, in most instances the training delivered by PMCs is more specific, provided away from the battlefield, and often organized in form of TEPs.

In TEPs, PMCs and defense contractors forge a security partnership with governments, whereby training is provided to help the recipients of services upgrade their forces. The TEP for Bosnia and Herzegovina developed after the government of the country and MPRI signed a contract. Cubic Corporation has been involved in the U.S.-sponsored TEP for Georgia and has also run simulation programs in Romania, Ukraine, and Lithuania, all of them former Soviet republics. Israeli instructors have also provided military instruction in Georgia. While the UK and other NATO countries engage in similar programs within their areas of influence, Israel, like the United States, has a truly international footprint in the private training field.

PMCs can also work as force multipliers in areas of law enforcement, such as policing, counter-narcotics, and surveillance. For example, DynCorp International has trained the new police force of Liberia (both LICUS and LHD) in addition to training its 4,000-strong army. The firm also spearheaded the creation of the new Iraq police force and is currently focusing on similar tasks in Afghanistan and other countries. The training to support law enforcement operations and technical assistance associated with Plan Colombia and the Merida Initiative (for Mexico and Central America) can be understood as counter-narcotics TEPs. PMCs have played an active role in both programs.

From these examples, it can be seen that PMCs can act as force multipliers not only in weak states but also in emerging markets and advanced democracies. In the United States and the UK, for example, the provision of military instruction is progressively modeled as a security partnership in which contractors participate in the training of the new generation of soldiers. Moreover, the definition of force multiplier incorporated in the army field manual *Contractors on the Battlefield* also addresses "battlefield support functions" and "system contractors necessary to provide technical support."[12]

In using PMCs as force multipliers, the contracting parties attempt to achieve political goals. Often these involve defeating, counteracting, or deterring the adverse private forces attacking the organs of government and undermining "peace and stability," a simple yet powerful expression that the reader will frequently find in official reports and mission statements.

Figure 4.1 shows the model we are constructing here, which involves the goals that the users of PMCs want to achieve when contracting them. Clearly there are overlaps, particularly considering that in attempting to bring peace and stability to entire regions, political goals often encompass

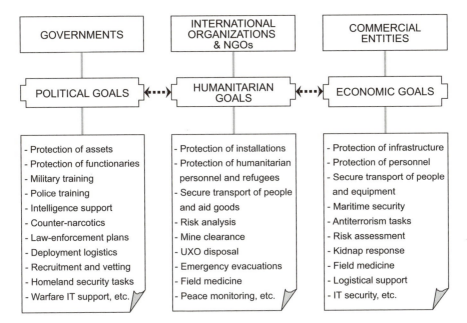

Figure 4.1 PMCs: Goals and Tasks
This figure illustrates the various services PMCs render while assisting governments, IOs and NGOs, and business clients to achieve political, humanitarian, and economic goals. It provides another way to understand PMCs in addition to the conventional typological analysis based on the lethality of services offered.

humanitarian ones, and many more multilateral parties are involved than just the UN.

Multilateral Peacekeeping and Reconstruction

At age 60 in 2008, the challenges the UN faces are daunting. The approved budget for the year to June 2009 was $7.1 billion: about twice the amount spent in 1993, which back then was considered unprecedented.[13] In 2009, there were over 91,000 Blue Helmets involved in 16 ongoing peace-keeping operations. Ten of these operations are in weak states: the Central African Republic (LICUS and LHD), Chad (LHD), Côte d'Ivoire (LICUS and LHD), the DRC (LICUS and LHD), Haiti (LICUS), Kosovo (LICUS), Liberia, Sudan (two missions, one of them in Darfur), and Timor-Leste (LICUS and LHD).

Besides the larger role the UN plays, other IOs and international coalitions of states have become regular features of peacekeeping and reconstruction initiatives. The following examples document the trend as of 2009.

The rapid reaction force of the European Union (EU), called EUROFOR, has been involved in three large operations so far: in Albania (Operation Joint Guardian, 2000–2001), in Macedonia (Operation Concordia, 2003), and in Bosnia and Herzegovina (Operation Althea, 2006–2007).

Although SFOR for Bosnia and Herzegovina was terminated in 2005, NATO maintains a 14,000-strong presence in the region in the form of the Kosovo Force (KFOR). At age 60 in 2009, NATO is also contributing to the training of Iraqi security forces and counterterrorism surveillance in the Mediterranean Sea (Operation Active Endeavour). Yet its most challenging task remains its commitment to help pacify Afghanistan (LICUS), where the UN also maintains a political mission (MONUA).

At the same time, the Organization for Security and Co-operation in Europe (OSCE), which is composed of 56 largely European and Central Asian countries and partly overlaps the membership of NATO, maintains some 20 field operations in Europe and former Soviet republics, including operations in Bosnia and Herzegovina, Kosovo (LICUS), Georgia, and Moldova.

Meanwhile, Russia maintains peacekeeping missions in Georgia and Moldova. Georgia, which aspires to become a member of NATO, had a brief war with Russia in 2008 over disputes involving its pro-Russian separatist province of South Ossetia. The Russian peacekeepers, under the auspices of the Commonwealth of Independent States, are stationed precisely in South Ossetia. The UN has an observer mission in Georgia (UNOMIG) as well.

In Africa, the African Union (AU) is engaged in various peacekeeping tasks throughout the continent. In Somalia, under the AMISOM mission, AU helps the Transitional Government to establish its rule and repel the predatory advances of militias and the terrorist group al-Shabaab. Through a bilateral understanding, Ethiopian forces also assist the Transitional Government. Furthermore, a coalition of nearly 30 nations formed the Contact Group on Piracy off the Coast of Somalia (CGPCS) in January 2009 to tackle the escalating problem of piracy attacks launched from Somalia. The AU, the EU, the International Maritime Organization (IMO), NATO, and the UN are also participating in the initiative. The United States chairs the Commercial Industry Coordination working group of CGPCS.

South Africa under an AU mandate has about 1,000 soldiers deployed in Burundi (LICUS and LHD), where the UN also maintains a peace-building mission. In addition to single states that provide the bulk of forces for a particular mission, coalitions of states are deployed in the field. For example, the RAMSI mission in the Solomon Islands (LICUS) involves 15 nations from the Pacific region working together to return the country to stability. Similarly, Operation Astute has the same aims for Timor-Leste (sometimes called East Timor). Australia and New Zealand are key partners in both missions. The extreme case is Iraq, where at its peak there were some

40 nations involved, though some of them provided only a symbolic handful of troops.

To fill out the picture, we also need to add the numerous nongovernmental organizations (NGOs) and charities also deploying to troubled countries.

I have tried to disentangle as far as possible the overlapping mandates, forces, and goals involved in all these operations and missions. I have also focused on a small sample of countries and IOs; many more humanitarian projects are underway elsewhere. Nevertheless, I am sure the reader will agree that peacekeeping and reconstruction in the 21st century have become incredibly multifaceted. PMCs are also part of this picture and assume a different role in these circumstances.

PMCs as Relief Operators

In August 2003, a massive bomb attack on the UN headquarters in Baghdad injured over 100 people and killed 23, including the UN's special representative in Iraq, Sergio Vieira de Mello. In October 2004, the director of Care International in Iraq was kidnapped and subsequently murdered. At least a dozen people involved in mine clearance in Afghanistan were assassinated in 2008. In January 2009, militants from the terrorist organization Abu Sayyaf Group kidnapped three Red Cross workers in the Philippines. Gone are the days when humanitarians were respected by the belligerent parties in a conflict. As the field becomes more dangerous, humanitarian organizations are increasingly requesting risk advice and private protection from PMCs.

The involvement of private military personnel in humanitarian endeavors is not new, but the recipients of services do not commonly acknowledge it. During the Nigerian Civil War in the late 1960s, NGOs such as Caritas, the World Council of Churches, and the Red Cross employed relief pilots for their operations.[14] In the early 1990s, MPRI, under contract with the U.S. Department of State (DOS) delivered nearly a billion dollars worth of food and medical aid to the states that had newly become independent from the former Soviet Union. Besides logistical support and security services, two areas of growth in which PMCs participate are mine clearance and the disposal of unexploded ordnance (UXO); and police missions.

UXO is composed of items used in low-intensity conflicts that fail to detonate; this includes bombs, grenades, landmines, and other explosive devices. These can explode when they are simply touched or moved. The Landmine Monitor program, an NGO initiative, estimated the casualty toll worldwide at over 5,400 for the year 2007, with about 1,400 people killed.[15] In terms of landmines, between 2003 and 2005 the worst-affected countries were Iraq, Afghanistan, Cambodia (LICUS), and Colombia. About 120 people involved in humanitarian mine clearance were among the casualties.

UXO disposal and mine clearance became partly privatized in the early 1990s, particularly due to the huge demand for these services after the First Gulf War and the conflict in the Balkans. For example, early in 2009 the Conventional Weapons Quick Reaction Force, funded by DOS and operated by DynCorp International, assisted the government of Tanzania in UXO disposal tasks and training. RONCO Consulting Corporation, for its part, is currently engaged in mine clearance in about three dozen countries, including Ethiopia (LHD), Eritrea (LICUS and LHD), Guinea (LICUS and LHD), the Lao People's Democratic Republic (LICUS), and Nigeria (LICUS and LHD).

Together with TEPs, Civilian police missions (CivPols) are another important component of institutionalized plans aimed at fostering peace and stability in troubled countries. CivPols broadly provide the instruction needed to turn around law enforcement deficiencies. Practically all UN peacekeeping missions incorporate forms of CivPols. In countries emerging from conflicts, this can involve the provision of actual policing duties while the basic law enforcement infrastructure is created. For example, the Participating Police Force (PPF) in the Solomon Islands, part of the RAMSI mission, had to focus on restoring law and order before it could provide training.

The first occasion on which the United States participated in a CivPol was in 1994 in Haiti. Other countries to which the United States has provided police officers include Bosnia and Herzegovina (1996–2002), Croatia (1996–2003), Sierra Leone (2003–4), and Timor-Leste (1999–2005). The United States currently participates in CivPols in Afghanistan, Haiti, Iraq,

Afghanistan, UXO disposal team
A UXO disposal team identifying devices in a suburb of Kabul. *Source:* Doug Brooks, IPOA.

Kosovo, Liberia, Sudan (LICUS), and the Palestinian territories in the West Bank (LICUS).

The key contractors assisting the United States in the implementation of CivPol initiatives are Civilian Police International, DynCorp International, MPRI, and PAE-HSC, an alliance between PAE Government Services and Homeland Security Corporation.

However, not all CivPols involve PMCs. The police forces of Australia, New Zealand, and Papua New Guinea have implemented PPF in the Solomon Islands. Moreover, sometimes humanitarians do not regard private protection as necessary, especially when peacekeepers or state forces are there to provide protection. Similarly, military engineers supplied by the security forces of states can handled the disposal of UXO. Yet, given the growing peacekeeping and reconstruction demands the international community faces, PMCs are increasingly filling a myriad operational gaps and participating in the achievement of humanitarian goals, thereby assuming the role of relief operators.

First, PMCs engage in activities that contribute to improving the well-being of the people living in conflict and postconflict zones, or support the IOs and NGOs undertaking such tasks. Private military personnel are providing relief by endangering their life while clearing a minefield, disposing of UXO, or transporting or distributing aid goods in conflict zones. "Relief," in this meaning, relates to welfare and attending the necessities of people in need.

Second, the delivery of services in high-risk environments requires military or security expertise to accomplish the contracted tasks, including the provision of armed protection. Although humanitarians are among the fiercest critics of PMCs, away from the limelight anecdotes abound about their gratitude to private military personnel for saving their lives or those of the people under their care. This reflects another meaning of "relief," which relates to the provision of military assistance to endangered posts or forces.

The role of PMCs as relief operators is hardly just a footnote to the analysis of PMCs working in conflict environments. In light of the many humanitarian catastrophes unfolding in slow motion, as in Sudan's Darfur, some analysts would like to see PMCs used as peacemakers and not just relief operators.

The Time to Privatize Peace?

Executive Outcomes produced plans for the UN to intervene in the Rwanda conflict as the genocide started to unfold early in April 1994. The fee asked was about $100 million for a six-month operation.[16] The plan was rejected. The UN spent nearly half a billion dollars during its Assistance Mission for Rwanda (UNAMIR, October 1993–March 1996). It is futile to speculate whether EO would have succeeded. Nevertheless, since then, conflict analysts and scholars alike have produced similar plans and concept papers involving PMCs.

The analysis commonly involves parameters such as costs, deployment schedules, workforce composition, operational strategies, casualties, and EO as a case study. The reasoning is, why not replicate what EO achieved in Angola and Sierra Leone in other protracted conflicts? This is one side of the debate about the privatization of peace.

To be fair to the UN, it is necessary to bring some other issues to the discussion. The role envisaged for PMCs in many proposals is more one of peacemaking rather than of peacekeeping. The UN pursues the latter and not the former role.

The sovereignty of a state, taken here to mean not interfering in the internal affairs of a state, is a key principle underpinning the work of the UN. Therefore, peace agreements often need to be reached before the UN can deploy its representatives, which it does at the request of the affected governments. Thereafter, besides endorsement by the Security Council, agreement needs to be reached about the mandate of the mission, the projected budget, the size of the peacekeeping force, if any, and the countries that will be supplying the troops. It is a painstaking process, some may say bureaucratic, that mediates the requirements of the affected states while observing international law.

Leaving aside for a moment the improbability of the idea that the international community would accept the notion of using PMCs instead of Blue Helmets, however cheaper and more effective the private alternative can be, the UN cannot bypass the political and administrative entanglements that are involved in the process leading to the deployment of peacekeepers. It is perhaps in this context that we need to understand the often quoted remarks by former UN Secretary General Kofi Annan, that "the world may not be ready to privatize peace."

There is another side to the privatization of peace debate. Its basic premise involves acknowledging that PMCs already participate in peacekeeping and reconstruction initiatives while acting as relief operators. Supporters of PMCs believe it is possible to engineer a stepwise system to broaden this role, as they argue that the private military alternative is cheaper and more effective. PMCs also deploy faster than conventional forces. Thus, a few more lives can be saved when humanitarian catastrophes suddenly strike. Critics, in contrast, see the support of PMCs as incongruous in connection with peace and stability initiatives and argue that too much work has already gone to PMCs.

The reader has probably already decided which side in the debate to support. Even though a compromise on the issue will not be reached anytime soon, the role of PMCs as relief operators is only likely to grow. The reason is simple. As insecurity is on the rise and the peace and stability agenda more ambitious than ever before, state and peacekeeping forces find themselves increasingly overstretched. Unless state forces go back to Cold War levels or conscription is reintroduced, as peacekeeping forces are composed of state soldiers under a UN mandate, it is difficult to see where the relief is going to come from, other than from PMCs. PMCs are also filling security gaps when facilitating trade in weak states and other dangerous places.

Trade in Dangerous Places

A noticeable proportion of our income is spent on hydrocarbon-related products. It is not only the gasoline for our cars or the gas to heat our homes but also a constellation of products incorporating crude oil-based components such as plastics. We all are users and the companies producing the hydrocarbon-related products are proud to be part of one of the key sectors behind our industrial and technological might. Four oil and gas corporations ranked in the top 10 in the 2009 list of the world's largest companies by Forbes (Royal Dutch Shell, Exxon-Mobil, BP, and Chevron), which means hundreds of billions worth of assets and annual turnover.[17] The bulk of the natural riches behind this prosperity comes from the developing world, including weak states. Among the beautiful pictures of people from all over the world adorning the annual reports and Web sites of energy and mining corporations, we are unlikely to find one depicting private military personnel protecting exploration crews or production compounds. However, such a picture would reflect the true situation. Somewhere in the commercial cycle, when and where instability or conflict traits impinge upon the global economy, PMCs are frequently involved.

Underdevelopment and International Trade

Besides being dependent upon military and security advice, stability in weak states is partly dependent upon external financial assistance. Lisa Chauvet and associates estimate the combined cost of the problem of weak states at approximately $267 billion per year.[18] Previously, they estimated the cost of a single LICUS country at $82.4 billion. In other words, these figures reflect what it would cost to help weak states, or a single LICUS country, turn into more typical underdeveloped societies. In 2008, aid originating in countries in the Organisation for Economic Co-operation and Development (OECD) totaled $119.8 billion. The gap between the financial resources needed to assist weak states and the aid budget of OECD countries, which comprise the largest suppliers of aid to the poorest nations, gives us an idea of the scale and complexity of the underdevelopment problem.

Although we tend to see the provision of financial assistance from the richest to the poorest countries as a permanent feature of the international system, it was rare before the Second World War. The prelude to the practice was the Marshall Plan, which was conceived by the United States to help in the reconstruction of Western European nations after the war. The International Monetary Fund (IMF) was part of the framework for economic cooperation then created and remains a key supplier of debt relief and aid.

During the Cold War, the United States and the West were the main providers of financial assistance to the developing world, as the Soviet Union concentrated on only a handful of strategic countries such as Cuba and Vietnam. In the movement away from bipolarity, aid ceased to be offered simply for political reasons. Now the financial assistance is largely conditional on governments demonstrating a willingness to reform and on transparency in the allocation of resources. In particular, donors have grown weary of money supplied failing to reach members of society and becoming involved in in-house transactions flowing from the treasuries of weak states to the private treasuries of their rulers, which can on occasions be impossible to tell apart.

I am not talking here about aid in response to natural disasters, food shortages, famines, or epidemics, which continues to be delivered unconditionally even to serial human rights offenders, but about streams of unrequited funds or lines of credit needed for countries' reconstruction.

Even though financial assistance is important, it is insufficient in itself to trigger economic growth. In particular, there is the risk of creating an aid trap, in which aid can perpetuate rather than alleviate underdevelopment. Therefore, besides the belief in states reforming themselves, there is a shared belief that national economies need to engineer a path to sustainable growth, which involves welcoming foreign trade and investment.

Some weak and underdeveloped states are rich in natural resources but lack the technical expertise and economic capability to exploit them. In exchange for duties, royalties, and taxes, multinational corporations (MNCs) are given rights to exploit these resources.

What follows is that for the governments willing to commit to the state-reform agenda in exchange for financial assistance, MNCs provide foreign investment. For the rulers who want to circumvent these requirements, MNCs provide a solution to the problem of external financial inflows.[19] Either way, the UN Conference on Trade and Development judges that to reduce poverty levels significantly in sub-Saharan Africa, where various oil-rich weak states are located, countries require to sustain levels of growth of around 6 percent for several years.[20] The operation of MNCs in weak states thus becomes, if not the only path toward sustainable growth, an unusually important source of income. Yet economic development is expected to progress against a background of insecurity and instability.

Remote Oil and Gas Fields

We tend to take our oil supply (at current prices) for granted. However, this view is changing rapidly. According to the Energy Information Administration (EIA), in 2006 total world oil supply was about 84.52 million barrels per day (there are 42 gallons of oil per barrel) and demand was 85.20.[21] In 2008, the total world oil supply was about 85.37 million barrels per day and demand was 85.78.[22] The larger oil discoveries occurred during the Cold War. Yet those super-giant oil fields have entered their declining phase. Analysts believe that new discoveries (e.g., in Western Africa, Libya, the new democracies in the Caspian region, and Brazil) and underexploited fields (for example, in Iraq, which holds the world's third largest proven oil reserves) can raise production to perhaps 95 million barrels per day. Above that level, in one or two decades, we enter uncharted territory. Rising demand and bountiful incomes for both industry and governments have moved energy corporations to dig ever deeper and in more dangerous territories.

While the FAA was at war with UNITA in the 1990s, production in existing oil fields and exploration to locate new ones were both underway in Angola. Some important discoveries have been made in Block 17, off the coast of the Zaire province in Angola in which the first EO operation in the country took place. The Girassol field, West Africa's debut deepwater project, was built between 1998 and 2001 at a cost of $2.8 billion.[23] TOTAL (France) holds the controlling stake and operates in partnership with Exxon-Mobil (United States), BP (UK), Statoil (Norway), and Norsk Hydro (Norway). For Angola, the profits from the oil sector represent about 90 percent of exports and 90 percent of government revenue.

The supply and demand picture is tight, which explains in part why production adjustments by the Organization of the Petroleum Exporting Countries (OPEC: Algeria, Angola, Ecuador, Indonesia, Iran, Iraq, Kuwait, Libya, Nigeria, Qatar, Saudi Arabia, the United Arab Emirates, and Venezuela) affect oil prices. However, when rebel attacks or sabotage shut down production at major oil fields, prices also correspondingly adjust.

Oil prices are determined by ongoing patterns of exploration and production as well as future projections. Nigeria's oil output has been in the past cut by up to a fifth or a quarter due to persistent attacks by militants from the Movement for the Emancipation of the Niger Delta (MEND) and linked criminal gangs. As Nigeria is one of the five main suppliers of oil to the United States, this has contributed to spikes in oil prices. In July 2008, the price of crude oil topped $147 a barrel. In addition to rebel attacks, there are many more risks affecting oil producing countries. Table 4.2 shows the different types of political risk affecting a sample of oil-producing countries and the level of development of these countries.

In countries with a background of conflict, kidnappings and the violent intimidation of foreign workers, damage to or sabotage of installations, and the rupture of pipelines to steal oil are common. In Colombia, as in Nigeria, all the major energy corporations operate. Like MEND, the Revolutionary Armed Forces of Colombia (FARC) use poverty and environmentalist rhetoric to justify the damage they regularly inflict on the oil infrastructure. In June 2008, a pipeline transporting oil to the port of Covenas on the Caribbean coast of Colombia was closed after FARC militants launched a dynamite attack. In June 2008, up to 30 MEND militants on speedboats attacked the deepwater Bonga oil field, the largest Royal Dutch Shell offshore facility in Nigerian waters. The attack set a precedent. A great deal of the oil produced in the Gulf of Guinea and West Africa comes from deepwater fields, and until then offshore vessels had been considered immune from the violence onshore.

There are many safe "upstream" (exploration and production) areas in the developing world, though from the Philippines to Bolivia, security and political concerns continue to multiply. In addition to attacks from rebel groups with secessionist or ideological agendas and criminal networks, we need to add the possibility of terrorist acts targeting oil facilities and workers in North Africa, the Arabian Peninsula, Iraq, and Southeast Asia. Al-Qaeda and sympathizing groups are active in these regions, making Western interests (people and infrastructure) targets.

Kazakhstan (holder of the Kashagan oil field, the largest oil find since the 1990s) and Azerbaijan are emerging oil-producing countries in which Western firms are investing. However, not one of the pipelines crisscrossing Central Asia, including the important Kazakhstan-China pipeline, is risk free. In Iraq, besides the pipelines linking the Kurdistan region in the north to the Central Asian network and then to Europe, a great deal of the oil flows to the export terminals in the Persian Gulf, which have suffered heavy damage over the last two Gulf Wars. The oil infrastructure is old and requires massive foreign investment. Through management training and partnerships with the private sector, the USAID-sponsored National Capacity Development program (also called Tatweer) is already modernizing refineries in Iraq. In a country where many view foreign MNCs with suspicion, attacks are likely to continue and perhaps intensify once the U.S. military presence is scaled down.

"Downstream" (refining and distribution of finished products) Saudi Arabian ventures are heavily guarded but always at risk.

Upstream or downstream, once oil and gas corporations have spent billions they cannot simply relocate. State security protects people and investments.

Table 4.2 Selected oil and gas producers and risk

Country	Level of Development	Risk and Security Concerns
Africa		
Algeria*	MHD	Terrorism, kidnaps, crime
Angola*	Weak state	Crime, landmines, rebellion in Cabinda province
Chad	Weak state	Rebellion, political violence, crime
Congo	Weak state	Unrest, political violence, crime
Egypt	MHD	Terrorism, crime, kidnaps, fundamentalist groups
Equatorial Guinea	MHD	Dictatorship, political violence, crime
Gabon	MHD	Unrest, next to a weak state and a dictatorship
Libya*	HHD	Dictatorship, former terrorist haven
Madagascar	MHD	Political violence, rebellion, crime
Malawi	Weak state	Political violence, crime
Nigeria*	Weak state	Rebellion, piracy, kidnaps, political violence
Zambia	Weak state	Militias from DRC, crime, landmines
Asia/Middle East		
Azerbaijan	MHD	Political violence, civil liberties, crime
Cambodia	Weak state	Political violence, civil liberties, landmines
Indonesia*	MHD	Terrorism, crime, piracy
Iran*	MHD	Civil liberties, crime, U.S. sanctions
Kazakhstan	HHD	Civil liberties, extremism in the region
Malaysia	HHD	Terrorism, kidnaps, piracy
Pakistan	MHD	Terrorism, the Taliban, sectarian violence, crime
The Philippines	MHD	Terrorism, crime, kidnaps
Russia	HHD	Political violence, crime, terrorism
Saudi Arabia*	HHD	Terrorism, civil liberties
Syria	MHD	Terrorist haven, U.S. sanctions
Thailand	MHD	Political violence, terrorism, separatism
Latin America		
Bolivia	MHD	Political violence, crime
Brazil	HHD	Crime, kidnaps, rebels in border with Colombia
Colombia	MHD	Terrorism, kidnaps, crime
Venezuela*	HHD	Civil liberties, crime, kidnaps

The table lists selected oil and gas producers together with their level of development (as established by UNDP) and certain risk and security concerns affecting them.

* OPEC countries (Brazil intends to join OPEC in the future)

Weak state: LICUS, LHD, or both

MHD: medium human development

HHD: high human development

However, this can be basic and not strong enough effectively to withstand waves of instability. Therefore, although large energy operations sometimes integrate in-house security units, protection services and risk advice are often contracted out to PMCs.

Contrary to popular stereotypes, private armies are not deployed. Yet the protection offered is necessarily more aggressive than in low-risk environments. Private military assistance often entails small security teams composed of highly skilled former military or law enforcement officers, who direct larger operations employing local security firms or personnel. Major security corporations, such as Andrews International, G4S, and Garda World Security Corporation, operate in this type of market.

Whether local or foreign guards are employed, the connection between private security and the extractive industry remains controversial, in particular because of the unfavorable scenarios that can become involved in the use of mining or oil production in weak or poor states as a route to sustainable development.

The Oil Curse

East of Nigeria is Ghana, chosen by President Barack Obama as a destination during his first official visit to sub-Saharan Africa, in July 2009. Ghana exports cocoa and gold; there have been multiparty elections since 1992; it is catalogued as possessing MHD by UNDP; and according to the World Bank, its economy has grown on average 3.9 percent yearly since 2000. The growth is lower than ideal and the population could be enjoying higher levels of welfare. However, external financial assistance is provided and the country is performing better than most sub-Saharan societies. But here comes the oil.

In 2007, Tullow Oil (UK), an oil firm with interests in over a dozen sub-Saharan countries (about half of them on our list of weak states), made an important discovery off the coast of Ghana: the Jubilee field. Jubilee and other discoveries are likely to change the economic outlook of the country rapidly. Either Ghana will manage its newfound riches responsibly and use the financial boost to jump to the next step of the development ladder, or oil will become a curse.

The oil curse is the other side of the aid trap. Sudden oil riches may lead to autocratic governments, corruption, military coups, and even uprisings. In short, whether it is due to oil or to some other natural resource, unexpected affluence can undermine the democratic structures needed by many states if they are to stop failing their citizens.

In September 2008, the World Bank walked away from helping to finance a multibillion dollar pipeline project connecting landlocked Chad to an export terminal on the coast of Cameroon. Exxon-Mobil, Chevron (United

States), and Petronas (Malaysia) were investors and contractors involved in the project. The reason for discontinuing this novel approach to financial assistance was simply that President Idriss Déby failed to honor his part of the agreement, namely to invest about 70 percent of the oil income in development projects.

While Ghana was the first sub-Saharan African country to gain independence in 1957, Gabon had until June 2009 the longest serving president, Omar Bongo, who had ruled since 1967. About 50 percent of Gabon's income comes from oil. Like other oil economies ruled by autocrats, it reveals enormous wealth inequalities, and civil liberties appear to benefit only those favored by the regime in power. A member of the same league, Teodoro Obiang has been the president of Equatorial Guinea since he seized power in a military coup in 1976, and Muammar al-Gaddafi of Libya has been in power since a coup in 1969. Idriss Déby changed Chad's constitution in 2006 so that he could run for a third term in office. He faced attempted coups in 2006 and 2008 and it is just a matter of time before he is deposed. While autocrats have kept some states together for some time, countries like Nigeria and Chad have gone through many military coups and leaders during their history as independent countries. It is perhaps part of the oil (or natural gas) curse.

No Western nation or oil producer in Africa and other parts of the developing world escapes unscathed from this oil and power game. We have revised the logic that governed international relations during the Cold War. I have also noted that the European powers tried to retain influence over their former colonies after independence. This influence involved securing concessions or preferential treatment for their national companies from rulers willing to acquiesce. In the case of France, for example, this connection was termed "Françafrique" (French Africa). In a 2008 profile of Idriss Déby, the BBC remarked that he came to power (after a coup) in 1990 with the assistance of the French secret service.[24] Omar Bongo had a special relationship with the French establishment until a recent anticorruption investigation of his assets in France. Times are changing, and Western governments cannot easily get away with obscure deals and shadow alliances anymore. Nonetheless, William Reno has a point when he argues that sometimes outsiders prefer "to deal with rulers who claim the mantle of globally recognized sovereignty, rather than trying to organize relations with competing strongmen or abjuring influence altogether."[25]

I have simplified the analysis by omitting the names of many of the energy corporations operating in these countries, as well as scores of smaller independent firms of which Tullow Oil provides a useful example. PMCs are also involved with these smaller firms. Sometimes they only provide security. In certain instances, closer commercial alliances between independent oil firms and PMCs are established. The debate about the exploitation of remote oil and gas fields involves links between commercial goals and the possible use of force to attain them. Understandably, these links attract a great deal of criticism from NGOs and concerned citizens.

Gems and Metals

"Blood" or "conflict" diamonds also figure prominently in discussions about trade in dangerous places. The discussion originates in the fact that proceeds from the illegal trading of rough diamonds have funded parties to conflicts in countries such as Angola, Congo (also known as Congo-Brazzaville), Côte d'Ivoire (Ivory Coast), the DRC, and Liberia. Diamonds are small, highly valuable, easy to smuggle and sell, and function as hard currency. The NGO Global Witness has campaigned intensively on the issue of blood diamonds.

Case studies often explored in the literature on the topic are those of Angola, and of Sierra Leone and Liberia in the 1990s. During the civil war in Sierra Leone, rebels smuggled diamonds into Liberia, which helped keep the warlord-turned-autocrat Charles Taylor in power. Taylor is in custody in Europe and the International Criminal Court at The Hague has filed charges against him for war crimes, including the recruitment of children under the age of 15 as soldiers. In the case of Angola, because UNITA controlled the country's diamond fields, some commentators depicted the conflict as the war of oil versus diamonds. A contrast is also made between examples like these and Botswana, which is the world's largest diamond producer by value but a prosperous, peaceful society in sub-Saharan African.

The Kimberley Process Certification Scheme (KPCS) now compels its subscribers (75 countries by the end of 2008) to certify that the rough diamonds they trade do not originate in conflict regions. However, there are still conflict diamonds in Côte d'Ivoire and Liberia. Moreover, there are countless numbers of informal miners searching for diamonds across Africa, miners who do not go through legitimate channels to sell their findings. The UN estimates that probably half of the diamonds mined in Sierra Leone alone are unlicensed.

Similar cases, involving other gems or metals, have been studied. Tanzanite, for example, is a semiprecious gemstone used in jewelry and found only in Tanzania. Early in the first decade of the 21st century, when the stone became popular and the trade took hold, stories started to circulate about uprisings linked to its production. A major media outlet even argued that there were links between the tanzanite trade and al-Qaeda. Hence, "conflict tanzanite" was born.[26] More recently, there have been reports about rebels in the northeastern part of the DRC profiting from the trade in coltan. Coltan is a mineral from which are extracted niobium and tantalum, which are used in electronic products.

To be frank, if we put our energy into it, we can turn every element in the periodic table into a conflict substance. However, this will not change the fact that we are all users of these gems and metals, whether we are aware of where they come from or not. While overwhelming attention is paid to oil and diamonds, our lifestyle is also dependent on the extensive use of base and precious metals. We just need to realize that our computers, our cellular phones, and all the electronic devices surrounding us incorporate parts made of these metals, as do the means of transportation and the machinery employed to manufacture anything. The script is familiar to us by now. Some of these metals are mined in countries affected by conflict or instability.

Base metals are those used heavily for industrial purposes and include aluminum, copper, lead, nickel, tin, and zinc. Aluminum, for example, is perhaps the most versatile base metal and is heavily used in transport, packaging, and construction. The mining and processing of base metals is messy, and compared to oil and diamonds they attract little value. Nonetheless, at a macroeconomic level their exploitation adds to the mineral riches of a country. As such, they generate income for governments that if poorly managed, enter our analysis of the problems affecting weak states and underdeveloped nations.

The point weighs more heavily when precious metals (e.g., gold, silver, and the platinum group) and minor metals (e.g., cobalt and rhenium) are included in the equation.

Africa has a representative share of the production of most metals. The DRC, in particular, is one of the most promising sites. This weak state is a key producer of copper and the world's main supplier of mined cobalt. Hydrocarbons and gems are also found in the DRC. The issue is establishing when the likely profits that the exploitation of a particular natural resource would generate outweigh the risks involved. In fact, huge industrial requirements of the world at large and the surge in commodity prices have tilted the equation toward production. Meanwhile, the exploitation of mineral resources involves various forms of private security. The production of agricultural commodities also increasingly requires private security.

Agribusiness

Chocolate is made from cocoa, the seed of the cacao tree. Having tasted it first in Mexico, the Spaniards introduced chocolate to Europe during colonial times. Today the main producers of cocoa are in West Africa and the United States is the largest consumer. Côte d'Ivoire, where rebels are still active and there is a UN peacekeeping mission (UNOCI), is the world's largest producer of cocoa (44.6 percent of exports in 2005–6, according to the International Cocoa Organization). Neighboring Ghana (18.2 percent),

Nigeria (6.3 percent) and Cameroon (5.3 percent) come next.[27] With a historical background similar to that of the producers of cocoa, the main producers of vanilla are Madagascar, Indonesia, and China. We could do similar analyses of other agricultural commodities such as coffee (Brazil, Vietnam, and Colombia are the three largest producers), cereals, fruits, nuts, spices, and wood pulp. However, we can gather from these few examples the geographically variable organization of the trade and the instability traits enmeshed within it.

As with hydrocarbons and metals, contracts for agricultural produce are traded in international markets and their price fixed by future projections involving factors such as natural catastrophes and political risk. For example, international price of cocoa was affected when low-intensity conflict took hold of Côte d'Ivoire in 2002; because of Cyclone Nargis, the 2008 rice harvest in Myanmar (also called Burma, LICUS) was discounted; vanilla futures were adjusted in early 2009 as a result of a military coup in Madagascar, and so on.

As food prices rise, the security of plantations, processing facilities, and storing depots is becoming critical. Perhaps we need to turn into amateur agronomists to gain a little insight into the nature of agro-crime. For example, in mature plantations of cocoa and pepper, the trees may be tall and ladders may be required to steal the produce. This can be time consuming and labor intensive. It is easier to steal coffee beans, as coffee plants are of human height. However, if raw cocoa, pepper, or coffee is stolen, the seeds need to be extracted and processed. Vanilla grows on vines, takes a long time to mature, and its pods have a higher value per volume. With quality vanilla selling for $30–40 per kilogram, vanilla warehouses make tempting prey. The same applies to high-quality teas, spices, rice, processed fruits, soybean, natural rubber, and palm oil, which can be stored next to plantations while they are in different processing stages.

Stealing is common to agriculture (and food aid), particularly in small quantities and informally. The point is that agro-crime can be improvised or involve higher degrees of knowledge and sophistication. Therefore, the protection of agribusiness requires flexibility and operators with a basic knowledge of the trade. For instance, they may be required to patrol on horseback or in all-terrain vehicles.

In many parts of the world, farmers still work double shift as night guards and are armed. However, wealthy landowners, cooperative producers, and plantation corporations are increasingly turning to the private sector for security solutions. For example, the surge in the demand for tequila has prompted large distilleries in Mexico to hire private guards to protect plantations of blue agave, the plant from which the spirit is made. The plant is in short supply and the price of high-end vintage tequila is as high as $500 a bottle.

The emergent problem of food security is making the hiring of protection specialists look like a good idea.

Food Security

There is another side to the rising price of agricultural commodities. Governments are increasingly worried about procuring enough food to satisfy the needs of growing populations, whether through public or private means. The alarms went off in 2007–2008, when there was a global food crisis. The combination of changing weather patterns and bad harvests led to shortages of staple crops. There were riots in at least two dozen countries, ministers were fired, and governments found themselves with their backs against the wall. India, Thailand, and Vietnam restricted rice exports (these countries are the leading producers of rice), and in parts of Asia security forces intervened to distribute food rations. In spite of the temporary drop in commodity prices due to the 2009–2010 global recession, which also resulted in lower income for exporting countries, the Food and Agriculture Organization (FAO) projected that the number of undernourished people worldwide would exceed the one billion mark by the end of 2009. The number is likely to increase in the future. The overall consequence has been that almost everyone has had to adjust the household budget to reflect food prices reaching historical highs. It seems humanity has crossed a threshold.

In 2008, Daewo Logistics thought it innovative to lease 1.3 million hectares of fertile farmland in Madagascar to strengthen the food security of South Korea. The aftermath of the now collapsed deal was an uprising, over 100 deaths, and the overthrow of the government of Madagascar in March 2009. Saudi Arabia's Hail Agricultural Development Company is engaged in similar yet smaller projects in Sudan. In what appears to be an emerging trend, the 2009 report *Land Grab or Development Opportunity?* analyzed samples of similar deals in Ethiopia, Madagascar, Mali (LHD), Mozambique (LHD), and Sudan. It is worth highlighting some of the summary findings of the study:

- Most of the deals involve leases rather than purchases of land and are not large scale. The total land allocation in 2004–2009 was estimated at about 2.5 million hectares (about the size of Vermont).
- Private foreign investments with support from governments dominate the deals. The participation of domestic investors was also identified.
- Although food security concerns appear to be a key driver behind the trend, they are also seen as investment opportunities.[28]

As food stocks become as important as oil and gas supplies, we are likely to see an expansion of private security in agribusiness featuring the deployment of agricultural and plantation corporations to high-risk regions.

However, the risk does not stop at the production point, as an important proportion of the commodities bought and sold in Africa or any other continent make their long sea journey to the distant markets where they will ultimately be consumed.

Shipping Routes and Piracy

During early modern times, exotic commodities from Asia and the Americas (the East and West Indies of past times) made their way to Europe. The companies engaged in this trade made extensive use of private force, inland and at sea, while transporting their goods. These commodities have ceased to be exotic, distant trade is the norm, and although the shipping companies concerned do not maintain private navies, an element of private security is indispensable. To understand the problem, we need to be aware of two important shipping routes. The first one involves the Malacca Strait, which has been an important commercial conduit since antiquity.

The Malacca Strait is a narrow stretch of water separating peninsular Malaysia and the city-state of Singapore (the tip of the Malaysian peninsula) from the island of Sumatra, Indonesia. Although at its narrowest point the strait is only about two miles wide, over 50,000 vessels pass through it yearly. It is the quickest route to the Pacific Ocean (and China and Japan) for all the traffic from Europe, Africa, the Arabian Peninsula, and India, and vice versa, hence its importance.

Historically, piracy has been a problem affecting the region, as there are numerous islands and places in which to hide in close proximity to a bottleneck for shipping traffic. For example, in its monthly report for April 2009, the IMO recorded six incidents of armed pirates boarding ships in the South China Sea.[29] Robbery was the main motive, though when the IMO report was written, seven hostages from the *Astaka* tug were still missing. Piracy is even worse in the Gulf of Aden and off the coast of Somalia.

The Gulf of Aden separates the northern part of Somalia from Yemen. Traffic bound for Europe from Asia and the Middle East passes through the Gulf in order to get to the Red Sea (which separates Saudi Arabia from Eritrea, Sudan, and Egypt) and the Suez Canal. The Strait of Bab el-Mandeb connects the Gulf of Aden to the Red Sea. With an island in the middle, it constitutes a narrow stretch of water and a traffic bottleneck. In 2008, the Suez Canal Authority registered 21,415 vessels crossing it, 95 percent of them being commercial shipping (including tankers, cargo ships, and container ships).[30] The problem here is that aside from the fact that Somalia is the closest a weak state can get to statelessness, it has also become a pirate economy.

The International Maritime Bureau's Piracy Reporting Centre noted that between January and May 2009 there were 114 incidents of pirate attacks and

29 successful hijackings launched from Somalia. The figures already exceeded the total for the year 2008 of 111 incidents and 42 hijackings.[31] Among other high-profile incidents in 2008, the cargo ship *Faina* (loaded with military hardware from Ukraine, including tanks and ammunition, and bound for Kenya) was seized on September 25 and the Saudi Arabian supertanker *Sirius Star* (about 330 meters long and loaded with some 2 million barrels of oil) on November 15. Hijackings have also included those of container and cargo ships, fishing vessels, and private yachts. Nearly 800 people went through the ordeal of being taken hostage or kidnapped in 2008.[32]

To complete the catalogue of piracy, for the month of April, 2009, the IMO also recorded pirates in speedboats firing and boarding the *Aleyna Mercan* chemical tanker off the coast of Nigeria; two cases involving the boarding and robbing of tankers in Tanzania's waters; and incidents of robbery in port areas in Colombia, the Philippines, and Malaysia. There were also numerous failed attempts at boarding ships. For a variety of reasons, including insurance issues, public relations concerns, legal uncertainties, and foreign bureaucracies, many incidents of piracy go unreported every year.

Besides risk advice (aimed at companies and crews), PMCs provide guards on board vessels and assistance in the recovery of captured ships and kidnapped seafarers. Escort vessels and maritime patrols are offered in some markets. Off the coast of Somalia, besides the fact that they sometimes use water cannons to repel hijack attempts, guards are increasingly armed.

PMCs as Commerce Facilitators

We have seen that the activities of MNCs in developing nations lead to two schools of thought. First, corporations generate income for governments that can help countries improve their development prospects. They are also a source of employment that would not exist otherwise. Second, because of the enormous profits they make, their role can also be interpreted as one of exploitation and possibly neocolonialism. Depending on the data and arguments one chooses to prioritize, either side in the debate can appear right or wrong. A third approach is to forge a balanced compromise.

In this context, we should not see foreign assistance and investment purely as aid traps or resource curses: there are benefits to be gained from keeping weak states and other affected countries connected to the global economy. However imperfect the situation might be, if there is economic activity going on, the chances of turning societies around when opportunities arise are higher. As the former administrator of UNDP, Kemal Dervis, notes, "you can't solve poverty without working markets."[33] Nevertheless, the catch in the story is that as the world keeps getting more dangerous, private security will increasingly be part of the commercial reality on the ground. When meeting the needs and helping their clients to achieve economic goals, PMCs become commerce facilitators.

The protection of assets and personnel in high-risk zones is perhaps the most common service that PMCs offer. In terms of the number of contracts, not their value, this service segment probably comprises the bulk of the market. Yet other tasks such as surveillance, emergency response, field medicine, secure transport, logistical support, and counter-piracy may be also part of the security cover.

The attainment of economic goals can be intertwined with broader political agendas and even humanitarian aspirations, as in the case of food security. Therefore, in particular circumstances PMCs may act as both commerce facilitators and relief operators. Iraq is an arena in which the activities of PMCs clearly include intertwined economic and political goals. An analysis of PMCs in the homeland security environment expands this model.

Homeland Security

"Homeland security" is a term popularized after 9/11. In a sense, there has always been a field of homeland security in the form of national security. National security has traditionally been seen as involving the preservation of the integrity and stability of states from internal and external aggressors. In the United States, internal aggression has primarily taken the form of organized crime, gang violence, shootings by unstable individuals, and sporadic social unrest and acts of terrorism. As law enforcement has successfully dealt with these internal problems, historically the focus has been on external aggression and national defense. During the Cold War, the biggest threat was that of a nuclear attack from the Soviet Union. However, the picture changed after 9/11. Thus, homeland security has become a way of thinking about serious threats originating from within a state's borders, particularly major terrorist attacks. Progressively, since the Second World War, national defense has incorporated a private sector input, and homeland security has done likewise since 9/11. In all these areas, PMCs play a role.

The Commoditization of Terrorism

There is no easy way to debate 9/11 and its aftermath, as the topic is heavily politicized and polarizing. Yet, in order to assess the threat that international terrorism continues to pose, it seems relevant to recall certain background issues, the response to the 2001 attacks by the administration of George W. Bush, and some of its consequences.

It had already been apparent since the early 1990s that al-Qaeda wanted to hurt America. We read in the chapter 3 about Osama bin Laden's resentment of the stationing of U.S. forces in Saudi Arabia during the 1990–1991 war to liberate Kuwait from Iraqi occupation. In a memorandum dated January 25, 2001, from the outgoing national coordinator for counterterrorism, Richard Clarke, to the incoming national security adviser, Condoleezza Rice, it was stressed that "in retrospect," ties between al-Qaeda and terrorist attacks on American interests abroad since the early 1990s had been discovered.[34] However, it was in 1998 that Osama bin Laden publicly declared war on the United States. It is up to the reader to decide whether 9/11 could have been averted. However, before 9/11 the use of commercial airliners as terrorist weapons seemed inconceivable, especially within U.S. airspace.

The first phase of the response to 9/11 was the October 2001 bombing campaign and subsequent ground assault by the United States and its allies in Afghanistan. The goal was to destroy the command structure of al-Qaeda. The Taliban, which sheltered al-Qaeda, was driven from power, but Osama bin Laden evaded capture. An invasion of Iraq followed in 2003. Back then, the stated goal was to depose Saddam Hussein, end his regime's alleged support of international terrorism, and destroy its arsenal of weapons of mass destruction, which, however, were never found. Thereafter, various justifications for the fluctuating strategies and the goals to be achieved in Afghanistan and Iraq have been offered.

Waging war on the other side of the globe is an incredibly complex endeavor. However, there was a lack of vision about what to do next after Saddam's regime was deposed. Likewise, no exit strategy from Afghanistan ever seems to have been contemplated. There is also the issue of the massive use of contractors (including PMCs) in Iraq and the scandals linked to it. Countless volumes have been written about it, such as Robert Young Pelton's *Licensed to Kill: Hired Guns in the War on Terror*, David Isenberg's *Shadow Force: Private Security Contractors in Iraq*, and Pratap Chatterjee's *Iraq, Inc.: A Profitable Occupation*. The titles tell part of the story. Again, it is up to the reader to decide the rights and wrongs of these wars, as well as of the use of contractors in Iraq.

Whichever position we adopt, the ultimate aim of these wars needs to be understood as, in part, an attempt to defuse the rise of fundamentalist terrorism. However, these military incursions have had precisely the opposite result, as they have contributed to the radicalization of people worldwide, particularly young Muslims.

At the heart of fundamentalism, there is a rift in the relationship between segments of the Muslim world and the liberal democracies. Certain segments of the Muslim world do not welcome the principles of liberal, democratic, and secular governance. The alternative they want to enforce is the strict observance of Islam, or Sharia law. In other words, their actions are inspired by religion, and acts of terrorism have become a standard means they employ to further this cause.

Ironically, while Islamic fundamentalism is at odds with the technological and multicultural interconnectivity that globalization has engendered, people embracing this radical doctrine have taken full advantage of these trends. New media and communications, such as the Internet and cellular telephony, have become cheap and effective vehicles for the propagation of hate by terrorist networks. For instance, blogs and social forums are used for indoctrination, recruitment, and propaganda purposes, including the dissemination of execution videos. Moreover, used as detonators or timers, cellular phones are integral components of improvised explosive devices (IEDs), such as those used in suicide attacks. Instructions on how to build IEDs and other deadly devices are available on the Internet for the new breed of amateur terrorists harboring desires for carnage.

Bruce Hoffman notes that "less discernible and more unpredictable entities drawn from the vast Muslim diaspora in Europe" are of particular concern.[35] Formed by patterns of emigration over the last century and enriched by a generous influx of political refugees since the 1990s, these communities have provided jihadists for the conflicts in the Middle East, as well as members of amateur terror cells and many sympathizers. The ease of international travel has facilitated these patterns of connection and affiliation too. The attacks in Madrid on March 11, 2004, and London on July 7, 2005, were fed from this terrorist pool.

All these trends blend into a powerful mix and characterize post-9/11 terrorism. For the disaffected people willing to cross the line, terrorism can now start as a DIY enterprise. Hence, we can think of this phenomenon as the commoditization of terrorism.

In the 1970s, Brian Jenkins gave us the oft-cited maxim, "terrorists want a lot of people watching and a lot of people listening, and not a lot of people dead."[36] Via online media and the 24-hours-a-day news, it seems that the first part of the maxim is now a given, but current levels of violence contradict the reference to "not a lot of people dead." Above all, deadly terrorist attacks have ceased to be events occurring only in other countries. In this time of rapid transition from old to new paradigms of terrorism, the homeland security market has become part of the security landscape.

The Homeland Security Market

In the wake of 9/11, there was a renewed impetus toward cooperation between states to tackle the problem of international terrorism. As one element of this, UN Security Council Resolution 1373 of September 28, 2001, created the UN Counter-Terrorism Committee. The committee has multiple tasks and addresses issues such as international collaboration in the investigation of terrorism, the criminalization of the financing of terrorist activities, and the strengthening of laws in order to prosecute such crimes fully. As a result, old terrorist conventions have been updated and new ones established (see Appendix III).

This is what we could term the institutional response to the problem of international terrorism after 9/11. It involves a host of new regulations and technologies that states are using to attempt to prevent similar tragedies, with international bodies overseeing compliance. We can see traces of these efforts when we walk into any international airport. Besides the enhanced security checks, we find that our personal details and biometric data are stored in databases and checked against those of people linked to terrorist activities. Similarly, the International Ship and Port Facility Security (ISPS) Code introduced a set of measures aimed at improving the security of ships and port facilities.

The institutional response incorporates systematic input from the private sector. Whereas international bodies have established what needs to be done and governments have taken the steps necessary for compliance, IT, defense, and security corporations have been responsible for the necessary technological developments. Segments within these corporations (hybrid types of PMCs) train airport personnel on how to use the new technologies and sometimes they are contracted by transport authorities to operate them. Garda World does precisely this type of work at Toronto's Pearson International Airport. Likewise, following the introduction of the ISPS Code, many PMCs developed expertise in the area and continue to assist port authorities worldwide with the tightening of maritime security.

Another component of the homeland security market originates in the particular policies each government has adopted to deal with the problem of international terrorism. In the US, the homeland security marked was broadened with the passing of the Uniting and Strengthening America by Providing Appropriate Tools Required to Intercept and Obstruct Terrorism (USA PATRIOT) Act of 2001 and the creation of the Department of Homeland Security (DHS). The DHS has established security partnership with myriad corporations for the design and operation of the new technologies used in the areas of surveillance and intelligence. For example, the Terrorist Identities Datamart Environment (TIDE) is a classified database said to contain the names of about 500,000 terrorists, suspected terrorists, and potential terrorists. Thousands of terminals access daily this gigantic IT enterprise, which was built by Lockheed Martin and under the Railhead program is being upgraded by Boeing, SRI International, and dozens of subcontractors. In the UK, the Monitoring the Internet (MTI) project aims at keeping track of all Internet activity. Lockheed Martin and Detica are apparently the key contractors behind MTI. In the United Arab Emirates, in July 2009, unsuspecting BlackBerry users discovered that the government was using tapping applications developed by California-based SS8 to eavesdrop on their communications.

Outside government spheres, multinational corporations (MNCs) and international organizations (IOs) that see themselves as potential targets of terrorist attacks contract risk advice and security services to PMCs. Moreover, for a while, there has been a supply of and demand for many services now applied in areas of terrorism. U.S. Investigations Services, Inc., which was part of government until 1996, conducts intelligence investigations and background checks on employees for several government agencies as well as commercial clients. In France, a scandal erupted in 2009 when it was found that EDF, the energy corporation, had hired Kargus Consultants to eavesdrop on the activities of Greenpeace across Europe. EDF deals with nuclear energy and Greenpeace is an antinuclear NGO. London-based International Security Solutions handled the whistle-blowing exposure of the expenses abuses committed by many members of the British Parliament. The story dominated the headlines in May 2009. Indeed, it is often when cases like these become known that we realize the extent to which private military and security services permeate any working environment. All these seemingly separate spheres are included in the homeland security market.

International Markets and Organized Crime

In the evolution from national to homeland security, organized crime is proving to be equally a matter of concern and should be also part of the field. In fact, UN Security Council Resolution 1373 noted that "the close connection between international terrorism and transnational organized crime."[37] Terrorists might be politically motivated, but the (illicit) profit motive behind organized crime can become involved in terrorist activities. For example, money laundering, illegal arms trafficking, and the illegal movement of nuclear, chemical, biological, and other potentially deadly materials are specified in Resolution 1373.

Therefore, organized crime needs to be seen as both a means of facilitating terrorism and a threat in its own right, as, in the underground economy, criminal organizations can supply anything while avoiding detection. As long as there are rebels wishing to acquire weapons, terrorists wishing to obtain deadly materials, and ordinary citizens wishing to pay for illicit goods and vice-related services, there will always be mafia groups and criminal gangs willing to supply them. In addition, cyber-crime is inflicting huge damage on the world economy, its cost being estimated at up to $1 trillion yearly by some analysts.

Notwithstanding the many faces of organize crime, because of the threat it poses to peace and stability, drug-trafficking merits special consideration. Worth hundreds of billions of dollars in illicit profits, the drug trade is a transnational enterprise corroding law and order on a global scale. In this connection, the United Nations Office on Drugs and Crime's *World Drug Report 2009* established that Afghanistan remains the leading producer of opium (from which heroin is made), and Colombia (81,000 ha of cultivation), Peru (56,100 ha), and Bolivia (30,500 ha) remain the leading producers of the coca bush (from which cocaine is made).[38] South Africa, Albania, Jamaica, and Paraguay figured as producers of about 25 percent of cannabis herb, and Morocco as the largest supplier of cannabis resin (21 percent of market share). At the same time, the production of amphetamine-type stimulants (covering the Ecstasy group), which are synthesized in clandestine laboratories throughout the world, showed an increase.

This abundant supply meets with equally robust demand, particularly originating in the lucrative European and North American markets. The examples given here provide the reader with an overview of the trafficking webs crisscrossing the world, operated by scores of large drug-trafficking organizations together with countless mafia groups and crime gangs. Insurgent groups, such as the Taliban in Afghanistan and Pakistan, and terrorist organizations, such as FARC in Colombia, fund their violent campaigns through the drug trade and are therefore linked to organized crime.

As in the case of the fight against terrorism, there is an institutional dimension to the actions undertaken by states and IOs to deal with the problem of drug-trafficking. There are also bilateral agreements between countries that require external security assistance and those with large consumption markets. U.S. assistance in support of Plan Colombia since 2000, and the recent Merida Initiative for Mexico, Central America, the Dominican Republic, and Haiti are examples of such agreements. PMCs such as DynCorp International and MPRI have experience in the area and provide counter-narcotics training in Latin America, Africa, and the Middle East. There is extensive classroom instruction as well as live drills, though sometimes private military operatives accompany security forces on the ground.

The involvement of PMCs in counter-narcotics attracts numerous critics, as does the militarization of the field. However, we need to bear in mind that counter-narcotics operations tend to involve a military component because drug-trafficking organizations maintain paramilitary wings. These private forces may include several hundred people and may be well equipped and trained, as they tend to recruit former members of the security forces as well as mercenaries. To defeat them, the use of deadly force is sometimes necessary.

PMCs as Security Enhancers and Defense Operators

Whether the task involves counterterror, counter-narcotics, or counter-crime initiatives, PMCs play an important role in raising levels of security while counteracting the advances of criminal and terror groups. That is to say, in the homeland security environment, PMCs sometimes act as security enhancers. Theirs is an enhancing action because levels of security would be substantially lower in the absence of the private military alternative.

By improving security at home, however, PMCs also affect the configuration of global security. The world is so interconnected that high levels of crime in one country can affect the well-being of whole regions, which increases the enhancing capacity of PMCs.

Indeed, attempts to secure the homeland on occasions involve undertaking actions abroad. The external assistance provided might be essential for the recipients of services to improve their ability to defend themselves from internal aggressors. Thus, Plan Colombia and the Merida Initiative are essential to enable Latin American countries to upgrade their military and police forces and enhance their homeland security. However, when these countries enhance their homeland security, security in the United States is also enhanced.

The use of PMCs in operations abroad is sometimes part of broader defense strategies. There are tasks in which PMCs provide tri-service support (army, navy, and air force): an example is provided by the Logistics Civil Augmentation Program (LOGCAP), which manages the logistical support required for American troops to deploy worldwide. Each military sector also contracts PMCs and other types of contractors to fulfill particular requirements and missions. Among the myriad contracts awarded in 2009 were the following:

- The Navy's Marine Corps Systems Command awarded a $6.8 million modification contract to General Dynamics C4 Systems to increase field service support for the Combat Operations Center for Operation Enduring Freedom in Afghanistan.
- The U.S. Transportation Command awarded Phoenix Air Group a $26 million contract to provide air charter services for the U.S. Africa Command in Germany to locations throughout Europe and Africa.
- The Naval Facilities Engineering Command Europe and Southwest Asia awarded ECC International a $6.6 million modification contract for the design and construction of facilities at Camp Lemonier in Djibouti, Africa. Djibouti is a tiny (roughly the size of New Hampshire) yet strategically located country. It is opposite Yemen on the Strait of Bab el-Mandeb and sandwiched between Somalia, Ethiopia, and Eritrea.

Basic information on the contracts awarded daily by the Department of Defense is available at its Web site. Not all these contracts involve PMCs. However, when PMCs become intertwined with the machinery of defense they become defense operators, as their input becomes essential for government to implement defense strategies.

By identifying the users of PMCs and the tasks contracted by them, the model introduced in this chapter has allowed us to appreciate the widespread though fragmented nature of private military work. We have also dissected some of the key roles PMCs assume while assisting governments, IOs, NGOs, and MNCs to achieve diverse political, humanitarian, and commercial goals, as well as overlaps between these goals and the roles PMCs assume. Even though high-risk environments might attract the involvement of several PMCs, often they are engaged in different tasks, as clients and contracts dictate. This multidimensional dynamic demystifies stereotypical views of PMCs as dark forces working in unison toward the achievement of secret goals. The examination of the logic behind contracting out, contained in chapter 5, strengthens this view.

Notes

1. World Bank Independent Evaluation Group, *Engaging with Fragile States: An IEG Review of World Bank Support to Low-Income Countries under Stress 2006* (Washington, DC: World Bank, 2006), 3.

2. See Department of Defense, *Annual Report to the President and the Congress* (Washington, DC: Department of Defense, February 1995), "Part V: Defense Management," http://www.dod.mil/execsec/adr95/index.html.

3. See Table 32 in International Institute for Strategic Studies, *The Military Balance 1998–1999* (Oxford: Oxford University Press, 1998), 270.

4. See Table 1.1 in Stockholm Peace Research Institute, *SIPRI Yearbook 1998: Armaments, Disarmament and International Security* (Oxford: Oxford University Press, 1998), 20.

5. United Nations, "50 Years of United Nations Peacekeeping Operations, 1948–1998" (New York: October 1998), http://www.un.org/en/peacekeeping/sites/50years/2.htm.

6. United Nations, "United Nations Peacekeeping: Questions and Answers" (New York, September 1998), http:// www.un.org/Depts/dpko/dpko/question/faq.htm.

7. See Appendix B in Eeben Barlow, *Executive Outcomes: Against All Odds* (Alberton, South Africa: Galago Books, 2007), 540.

8. Facts and figures for current and past UN peacekeeping operations can be found at the Web site of the UN Department of Peacekeeping Operations: http://www.un.org/en/peacekeeping/.

9. Elizabeth Rubin, "An Army of One's Own: In Africa, Nations Hire a Corporation to Wage War," *Harper's Magazine* (February 1997): 45.

10. See Appendix B in Barlow, *Executive Outcomes*, 540.

11. Doug Brooks, "From Humble Beginnings in Freetown: The Origins of the IPOA Code of Conduct," *Journal of International Peace Operations* 3, no. 5 (2008): 9.

12. Department of the Army, *Contractors on the Battlefield: Field Manual* (FM 3–100.21) (Washington, DC: Department of the Army, January 2003), paras. 1–29.

13. United Nations General Assembly, "Approved Resources for Peacekeeping Operations for the Period from 1 July 2008 to 30 June 2009," A/C.5/63/23 (New York, May 1, 2009).

14. Guy Arnold, *Mercenaries: The Scourge of the Third World* (London: Macmillan Press, 1999), 22.

15. International Campaign to Ban Landmines, *Landmine Monitor Report: Toward a Mine-Free World. Executive Summary 2008* (Concord, Canada: St. Joseph Communications, 2008), 29.

16. See Appendix B in Barlow, *Executive Outcomes*, 542.

17. Forbes, "The Global 200," (New York, April 8, 2009), http://www.forbes.com/lists/2009/18/global-09_The-Global-2000_Rank.html.

18. Lisa Chauvet, Paul Collier, and Anke Hoeffler, "The Cost of Failing States and the Limits of Sovereignty" (paper prepared for the World Institute for Development Economics Research of the United Nations University, Center for the Study of African Economies, University of Oxford, February 2007), 18.

19. Carlos Ortiz, "Private Military Contracting in Weak States: Permeation or Transgression of the New Public Management of Security?" *Review of African Security* 17, no. 2 (2008): 11.

20. United Nations Conference on Trade and Development, *Capital Flows and Growth in Africa* (New York: United Nations, 2000), 22.

21. Energy Information Administration, "September 2009 International Petroleum Monthly" (Washington, DC, November 10, 2009), http://www.eia.doe.gov/emeu/ipsr/t21.xls.

22. Ibid.

23. See TOTAL, *Girassol: A Stepping Stone for the Industry* (Courbevoie, France: TOTAL, September 19, 2008), 31–36; and "Angola's Deepwater Girassol Field Comes on Stream," Press Release (Courbevoie, France, December 4, 2001).

24. BBC. "Profile: Idriss Deby." *BBC News*, February 2, 2008.

25. William Reno, "African Weak States and Commercial Alliances," 96, no. 383 *African Affairs* (April 1997): 167.

26. See Robert Block and Daniel Pearl, "Much-Smuggled Gem Aids al-Qaida," *Wall Street Journal*, November 16, 2001.

27. See Table 5 in International Cocoa Organization, "Assessment of the Movements of Global Supply and Demand" (Berlin, Germany: April 3, 2008), 33.

28. Lorenzo Cotula, Sonja Vermeulen, Rebeca Leonard, and James Keeley, *Land Grab or Development Opportunity? Agricultural Investment and International Land Deals in Africa* (London/Rome: IIED/FAO/IFAD, 2009), 99–102.

29. See Annex 1 in International Maritime Organization, *Reports on Acts of Piracy and Armed Robbery against Ships: Acts Reported during April 2009* (London: International Maritime Organization, May 5, 2009).

30. Suez Canal Authority, "2008 Report" (Ismailia, Egypt, 2008), http://www.suezcanal.gov.eg/Files/Publications/32.pdf.

31. International Maritime Bureau, Piracy Reporting Centre, "Pirate Attacks off Somalia Already Surpass 2008 Figures" (London, May 12, 2009).

32. International Maritime Organization, *Reports on Acts of Piracy and Armed Robbery against Ships: Annual Report 2008* (London: International Maritime Organization, March 19, 2009), 2.

33. Quoted in Alison Maitland, "Big Business Starts to Scratch the Surface," *Financial Times*, September 13, 2005.

34. Richard A. Clarke, "Memorandum from Richard A. Clarke to Condoleezza Rice, January 25, 2001—Subject: Presidential Policy Initiative/Review—The Al Qida Network" (National Security Archive, George Washington University), http://www.gwu.edu/~nsarchiv/.

35. Bruce Hoffman, *Inside Terrorism* (New York: Columbia University Press, 2006), 288.

36. Brian Michael Jenkins, "International Terrorism: A New Mode of Conflict," in *International Terrorism and World Security*, ed. David Carlton and Carlo Schaerf (London: Croom Helm, 1975), 15.

37. United Nations, "Security Council Resolution S/RES/1373 (2001)" (New York, September 28, 2001).

38. United Nations Office on Drugs and Crime, *World Drug Report 2009* (New York: United Nations, June 2009), 63.

CHAPTER 5

The Privatization of Security: Approaches and Issues

Alongside the military expansion that helped turn the United States into a superpower, after the Second World War (WWII) the Department of Defense (DOD) emerged as the largest public management operation within government.[1] At this time, the defense industry embarked on its trajectory of unabated expansion and a close relationship with government was forged. This was not only the result of the complex geopolitical settings that characterized the Cold War but also the result of the more technological nature of warfare.

This generational shift was given pragmatic meaning in Dwight D. Eisenhower's farewell address to the nation in 1961. He noted that while a large military establishment and arms industry was new to the American experience, only "alert and knowledgeable" citizens could "compel the proper meshing of the huge industrial and military machinery of defense with our peaceful methods and goals."[2]

In *The Military Specialist* (1968), Harold Wool documented patterns of specialization within the forces, the growing convergence of military and civilian skills, and the retention of trained specialists emerging as a "chronic problem for the Armed Services."[3]

By the late 1960s, the escalation of the Vietnam War was in full swing. Though primarily in a support role, contractors in all sectors assisted the expansion. Vinnell, which had already been a DOD contractor during the Korean War, strengthened its ties with government during the Vietnam conflict. PAE had also started collaborating with the DOD in various support roles in the 1950s. SAIC, a key intelligence contractor, opened its Washington, DC, office in 1970. Moreover, many private military operations linked to arms transfers and training requirements were formalized in the Middle East and elsewhere in the Third World.

On the home front, the growing sophistication of jet fighters, avionics, and military vehicles progressed together with the need for members of the forces to be trained privately in their use and maintenance. By the 1980s, specialist firms focusing on distinct military tasks were operating throughout the world in support of U.S. foreign policy goals. In the next decade many of these firms became known as PMCs, including corporations only marginally involved in delivering private military services (hybrid types of PMCs, see chapter 3).

There has been a noticeable expansion of these trends since the 1990s. However, this transformation is continuously packaged in the popular press as a radical post-9/11 development. Maybe we were not "alert," as Eisenhower suggested. Maybe government assumed we were all reading the lengthy defense budgets and reviews in order to become "knowledgeable" of the momentous changes that state defense and security have been undergoing since WWII. Nonetheless, to most people the underlying and unresolved question remains one of how we have "gradually" drifted into a system in which the monopoly of violence is managed with the assistance of PMCs.

Toward a New Security Architecture

In the transition to the post–Cold War world, the diminished political and financial will of Western governments to intervene in conflicts in the periphery of the world has left a security gap for PMCs to fill. The inability of the UN and other international organizations (IOs) to contain these conflicts inevitably compounds the problem. The spillage of intolerance and terrorism into safe societies ignites disputes that require innovative private security solutions. The reinvention of state militaries as leaner and more technological machines fosters a demand for private sector input too. PMCs have clearly been responsive to supply and demand factors. However, it is important to bear in mind that their rise equally marks a profound change in the traditional state monopoly over legitimate violence. The roots of this transformation are partly found in neoliberalism and the emergence of new modes of public management.

Neoliberalism and Privatization

Neoliberalism is intrinsically linked to capitalism and democracy. Ideologically, neoliberal policies have advocated economic and social freedom over authoritarianism and oppression. Operationally, they have encouraged privatization and market competition. Facilitated by heavy privatization throughout the 1980s and into the 1990s, the shift of the global political economy toward neoliberalism was completed upon the demise of Communism, which had dictated the opposite approach.

"Privatization" is a term that lends itself to broad usage and needs to be defined in specific fashion. The state is not privatizing by selling off segments of its military infrastructure to parts of the private sector, which thereafter become PMCs. However, this practice has given birth to some defense corporations. Neither should the reader infer that governments are reconstituting segments of their military or security forces into private firms, which become PMCs, although PMCs do typically employ former military and law enforcement personnel. Instead, we need to focus on the process whereby certain military and security-related tasks, previously state prerogatives, are being shifted onto the market and performed by legally established commercial firms known as PMCs.

These tasks include the protection of government officials and assets in high-risk environments, military and police training, logistics contingent to military mobilization, mine clearance and the disposal of unexploded ordnance (UXO), the design and running of counter-narcotics programs, and intelligence and surveillance support. In short, these are tasks in the areas of combat, training, support, security, intelligence, and reconstruction, the main service areas covered by the private military industry.

We can achieve a useful view of privatization by looking at the process through the theory and practice of public management. Whereas the neoliberal agenda has ideological elements, it has also come to represent a pragmatic response to the need to transform the bureaucratic structure that used to characterize government. This has contributed to the dismantling of the view that sovereign functions should be performed only by the public sector. This has not occurred suddenly or in a vacuum. In order to understand the significance of this transformation, it seems relevant to contextualize it first within the evolution of public management.

The Rise and Decline of the Bureaucratic Model

The managerial approach to government has some longevity, particularly in the United States. Its origins can be traced back to Woodrow Wilson (1856–1924). In his 1887 essay, "The Study of Administration," Wilson noted that it was a field of business lying outside the sphere of politics. Hence, the object of the public sector was to discover "first, what government can properly and successfully do, and, secondly, how it can do these proper things with the utmost possible efficiency and at the least possible cost either of money or of energy."[4] Taylorism, or the scientific management movement, took this approach to the next level.

In 1911, Frederick W. Taylor (1856–1915) published *Principles of Scientific Management*. Taylor was a manager in a Pennsylvania steel company at the turn of the 19th and the 20th centuries. He sought to find the "one best way" to optimize production by looking at the methods and routines employed during production and variables such as the workforce and its members' skills. The conclusion reached by Taylor and others preoccupied with similar problems was that by carefully assessing and managing these variables, it was possible to arrive at more effective and economic methods. This became known as scientific management, an idea that spread from industry to the public sector. Thus, Leonard D. White wrote in 1926, in what is generally regarded as the first comprehensive textbook on the subject, that "public administration is the management of men and materials in the accomplishment of the purposes of the state."[5]

Through most of the 20th century, public management focused on the optimization of the workings of the essential government machinery: the bureaucracy. A key defender of the "technical superiority" of bureaucracies was Max Weber (1864–1920), who was also a proponent of the notion of the state monopoly of violence (or force). In a posthumously published essay, Weber noted that "precision, speed, unambiguity, knowledge of the files, continuity, discretion, unity, strict subordination, reduction of friction and of material and personal costs" were raised to the optimum point through bureaucratic administration.[6] Accordingly, the task of public managers was to make the bureaucracy run smoothly through an organizational method guided by compartmentalization, hierarchical authority, and detailed rules and procedures. By the 1960s, the bureaucratic model had come to be equated with the workings of the public sector.

Dissatisfaction with bureaucracies, the size of government, and the apparent link between the two contributed to the emergence of new approaches to the management and organization of the public sector. In this evolution, synthesized in Figure 5.1, a very influential approach since the late 1980s has been new public management.

The New Managerial Strategy

There is no best way to describe what exactly new public management (NPM) involves. The approach is empirical in its design and comprises a nexus of techniques aimed at reforming government. Out of all these, efficiency considerations, contractual relations, and new managerial practices figure prominently in discussions about NPM.

The attainment of government efficiency is a guiding aspiration of NPM reform, which is largely articulated in economic terms. The idea is to minimize costs while attempting to improve levels of service. Once a particular good, service, or task is identified as the target for total or partial privatization, tender mechanisms put it within reach of the market economy. As Guy Peters observes, "the fundamental intellectual root of the market approach

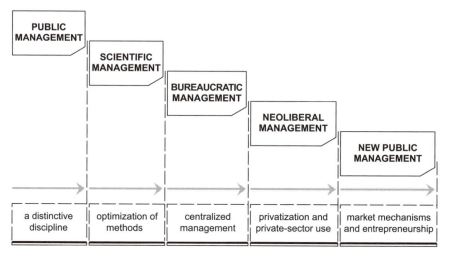

Figure 5.1   Traditions in the Evolution of Public Management
While the information provided here is not exhaustive, it illustrates important and cumulative stages in the evolution of public management traditions.

to changing the public sector is the belief in the efficiency of markets as the mechanism for allocating resources within a society."[7] Therefore, given government-established parameters for the delivery of services, the best mechanism for their satisfaction is often assumed to be that of vetted private firms offering the lowest costs or most attractive financial incentives.

NPM emphasizes the structuring of relations within government and between the public and private sectors through contracts. Contracts arise out of bargaining and negotiations between public managers and contractors and contain parameters such as costs, goals, obligations, and delivery schedules. These contracts put into commercial language the objectives originally set by politicians and delegated to public managers for implementation and follow-through. The implication of this chain of actions is that the contract is placed at "the centre of public governance and not authority as with the traditional approach,"[8] In other words, contracts become a medium for government action. and the public sector turns into a purchaser and supervisor rather than the direct supplier of services.

In deciding on the services to be outsourced, setting up tender mechanisms, and selecting the best firms to be contracted, the managers of government play key roles. While under the bureaucratic model public servants tended to follow inflexible routines and procedures, NPM encourages a hands-on attitude toward public service. In the new managerial state, politicians identify objectives and then instruct public managers to implement them. Managers enjoy a good degree of operational autonomy in the implementation of objectives and are active decision makers and problem solvers. Moreover, numerous methods originally developed for the private sector have been adapted to the running of government. In short, new public managers bring an entrepreneurial spirit to government, which allows, arguably, a shift from political to managerial accountability.[9]

NPM largely emerged with the reform of the welfare state, social services, and local government in mind. From this platform, the strategy has expanded into wider areas of government and reached state defense and security.[10] The embracing of NPM by Western democracies and international institutions, such as the Organization for Economic Co-operation and Development (OECD), has lent NPM the attributes of a global culture or paradigm. Founded in 1961, the OECD brings together countries that embrace democracy and the market economy. These include the leading Western nations and emerging markets such as those of Mexico, South Korea, and Turkey. In the process, novel links have been forged between the state and PMCs, which thereby enter the arena of public goods.

Private Security as a Quasi-Public Good

The theory and practice of public management suggests that there is something inherently distinctive about managing the public, as opposed to the private, sector. A key issue here is the provision of public or collective goods, or those that no one should be excluded from enjoying. We find many public goods in areas of state defense and security, such as defense and law enforcement institutions and the activities that these institutions undertake to ensure our safety.

An economics textbook would tell us that public goods are characterized by nonexcludability and nonrivalry. Nonexcludability means that their consumption cannot be limited to those who have paid for them. Nonrivalry implies that the consumption of public goods by one person does not lessen someone else's opportunities to enjoy the same quantities of the same goods. Tax dodgers, the dispossessed, or people not liable for taxation, all have in principle unrestricted access to these goods.

Theoretically, the private sector is dissuaded from entering the supply of public goods. The fact that governments provide these goods for a seemingly negligible amount, often through taxation, limits the potential profitability of private provision. It is also argued that private companies by themselves are unable to produce the "efficient quantity" of public goods that represents the aggregated and equal requirements of people statewide.

It is possible to imagine this in the case of some complex, expensive, and indivisible public goods, such as the maintenance of criminal and policing systems, a regime of homeland security, national defense, or a nuclear deterrent. In spite of some exceptions, however, distinctions between purely public and purely private goods are imperfect. Hal Rainey observes that many studies confirm the divergence between theory and practice when comparing "public and private delivery of the same services, mostly finding the private form more efficient."[11]

One should reflect on these matters with reference to willing buyers of, for example, basic health care, education, or security services, as their efficient quantity is apparently fully satisfied by the public sector.

Public goods are essential to explain why we have governments and pay taxes, but the definition of public goods does not preclude the private sector from participating in the provision of these goods. Far from that: governments have traditionally relied on private-sector support for the fulfillment of what is judged to be the efficient quantity of public goods. In addition, historically they have been readily available in the market economy for those willing to add to what authorities furnish. The alternative would be a constant enlargement of the public sector and increase in the money needed to tackle the growing needs of populations aspiring to higher standards of living. Some former Communist nations opted for this route and went broke.

Thus, NPM-style reform has simply made it easier for PMCs to become part of the equation in terms of the improvement of the efficient quantity of public goods related to state defense and security, because their participation presupposes a more optimal alternative than exclusive public provision.

The Privatization of Security under NPM

The movement of contractors into the field of the efficient provision of state defense and security has been gradual and accentuated by changing policy imperatives since the late 1980s.

Taking forward the privatization agenda initiated by the administration of Ronald Reagan, the government of Bill Clinton engaged in a modernization program styled according to NPM. Announcing the release of the National Performance Review in 1993, Clinton remarked that the goal was "to make the entire federal government both less expensive and more efficient."[12] The solution Clinton proposed was the creation of "entrepreneurial organizations." In 1995, the final Report of the Commission on the Roles and Missions of the Armed Forces thus advanced the argument for reducing costs through the adoption of "more of the innovative business practices used in the private sector," in particular through the outsourcing of "all commercial type support activities" and the empowerment of DOD managers "to make sound business decissions."[13] By the time of the Balkans conflict, it was estimated that there were as many contractors as military personnel deployed, though only a fraction of them engaged in military and security tasks. Furthermore, the use of contractors has been gradually introduced into military planning. The 2006 Quadrennial Defense Review acknowledges contractors as part of the "Total Force" available to the DOD together with active and reserve military components and civil servants, and considers as policy the incorporation of commercial activities by contractors in operational plans and orders.[14]

Certain allies of the United States have mirrored this transition. In Canada, for example, the 1994 *White Paper on Defence* highlighted the need for the Department of National Defence to adopt a business model incorporating practices such as just-in-time delivery systems, off-the-shelf commercial technology, the contracting-out of support functions, and an enhanced partnership with the private sector.[15] In the UK, the 1998 *Strategic Defence Review* recorded the important role played by the private sector over the previous decade through market testing, contracting-out, and public-private partnerships.[16] In Australia, the 2000 *Defence White Paper* strengthened the commitment outlined in the 1998 Defence and Industry Strategic Policy Statement to incorporate a competitive, efficient, and innovative industry base for the support of the forces.[17]

The policy shift has been accompanied by the development of new methods for the tendering of services, the selection of firms, and the establishment of contractual relations. For instance, the decision to contract out is commonly informed by an exercise in establishing whether private sector use would achieve greater efficiency with regard to public benchmarks set for the delivery of targeted services. When public managers determine that the private sector is better qualified to satisfy preselected services, competition in the market economy ideally fosters optimal selection. A-76 studies, for example, have guided the total or partial privatization of numerous defense and security activities in the United States.

A-76 studies originate in the Office of Management and Budget's Circular No. A-76. This circular establishes guidelines for competition between government and the private sector for the provision of tasks and services. In its simpler modality, the "streamline competition," commercial contracts are fast-tracked once they are proved to be cost effective. For larger projects, the "standard competition" procedure requires the creation of a "most efficient organization" (MEO). Under MEO, teams of technical and functional experts compete with private-sector bids on behalf of government before the most efficient alternative is determined, whether it should be a public, private, or hybrid solution.

Comparator methodology, the practice of estimating what a project would cost if traditional public provision were used and then comparing it with bids from the private sector, is well established and distinguishes NPM-style reform from conventional privatization (the transfer of property rights from the public to the private sector). Instead of A-76 studies, public service comparators (PSCs) and public-private comparators (PPCs) are used in other countries, though the underlying principle is the same.

The New Management of Security

The entrepreneurial nature of the privatization of security under NPM has been enhanced by the development of highly flexible institutions and methods, security partnerships forged between government and PMCs and defense contractors, and civil-military-private military relations.

The New Managerial Infrastructure

Some elements of the managerial infrastructure behind the new management of security are novel, like the FedBizOpps IT interface, and some other elements have been upgraded to fit the emerging strategy, as in the case of the General Services Administration (GSA).

GSA, through its flagship Multiple Award Schedule Program, establishes long-term contracts across government with commercial firms. Orders placed by any governmental agency using the Schedule program are considered to be issued under full and open competition. This is because before orders are placed, the ordering officer has ensured that the selected vendor(s) represent value for money. Moreover, the Schedule program ensures that minority businesses, such as veteran or women-owned firms, are properly represented in the outsourcing process. The Schedule program ensures access to millions of goods and services worth billions of dollars, and their use has grown rapidly.

GSA is an important link in the military supply chain, and the DOD is its largest customer. From translators and IT solutions to law enforcement and security equipment, the Schedule program covers services across the board. GSA supports troops at home as well as while they are on deployment. Well-known private military suppliers such as Blackwater Worldwide (now Xe), CACI International, and MPRI, Inc. have rendered services to government, domestically and abroad, through the Schedule program.

Government contracting through the Schedule program is not an obscure mechanism, as some believe. Vendors are proud to advertise the "Schedules" (a name given to the extensive lists of services on offer under the Schedule program) for which they are qualified suppliers. One could browse the Web sites of defense contractors and PMCs that make the headlines to find frequent references to Schedules, GSA accreditation, or relations with government. Likewise, the Schedules are publicly available at the GSA Web site.

The process is made more expeditious by the Federal Business Opportunities system or FedBizOpps. GSA, through the Federal Supply Service, is in charge of FedBizOpps.gov, which is described as the single point of entry for federal procurement exceeding $25,000. Many of the contracts for the reconstruction of Iraq originated in solicitations posted at FedBizOpps.gov. Other agencies involved in the competitive contracting of private military and security services include the Army Materiel Command, the Defense Contract Management Agency, the Army Contracting Agency, and the U.S. Agency for International Development (USAID). USAID together with the DOD and the Department of State (DOS) are the major government users of contractor support in overseas operations. Outside the United States, Australia and Canada use a tendering approach similar to GSA´s.

It is a two-way process. While the new managerial infrastructure connects government to the private sector in innovative ways, firms in the market economy respond to the ensuing demand and public requirements by specializing, diversifying, or both. Thus, corporations often incorporate government services departments or subsidiaries to manage the supply side of the privatization of security, including the provision of security to foreign governments. For example, the former director of national intelligence, Michael McConnell, who is a member of President Barack Obama's Intelligence Advisory Board, rejoined Booz Allen Hamilton to head precisely its national security business unit. This public-private communication engenders close patterns of collaboration between government and PMCs, patterns of collaboration that, in their most developed form, constitute partnerships.

Security Partnerships

The participation of firms in the management of state tasks is increasingly modeled on the notion of "public-private partnerships" (PPPs), which commonly involve legal relations and transactions.

PPPs integrate selected NPM-style practices into ad hoc programs targeting specific tasks, service sectors, or government-controlled enterprises.[18] For example, a partnership might involve a contract to supply military hardware together with maintenance and ongoing training on how to use it, which might in part take place abroad and under harsh conditions. This type of contract is not uncommon in military mobilizations such as those involving Afghanistan and Iraq. While the training or maintenance might evolve into a jointly owned enterprise between the forces and the contracted vendor(s), clauses may stipulate the requirement to tender or subcontract activities in which vendors do not enjoy a technological lead or which fall outside the original deal.

All the variable parameters and options that make a partnership are specified in the lengthy program details and associated contracts. In areas of defense and security, access to these details and contracts tends to be restricted or classified, which is an indication that the state remains the ultimate arbiter of the uses of force.

It is argued that PPPs allow for a clear specification of objectives, rights, and responsibilities in a legally binding format. In addition, given the long-term and costly commitments PPPs can give rise to, a better allocation of risks between government and contractors is achieved. In the past, government was the designer, the supervisor, and the supplier of services. Through "security partnerships," an expression I use to designate the application of PPP principles to spheres of state defense and security, the field is leveled and government and defense contractors and PMCs work together at each level.

The coveted U.S. Army's Logistics Civil Augmentation Program (LOG-CAP), for instance, is in effect a security partnership. LOGCAP is a program that manages the use of contractors by DOD in full-spectrum logistical support of contingency mobilizations. Through it, thousands of contractors have delivered support to the forces on deployment since the early 1990s. DynCorp International, Fluor Corporation, and KBR are the prime executors of the ongoing LOGCAP IV through competitive biding between them for specific task orders. To facilitate coordination between contractors and buyers in the forces, LOGCAP incorporates a support unit.

The DOS manages the provision of personal protective services and support functions under its jurisdiction through the Worldwide Personal Protective Services (WPPS) contract. WPPS also covers USAID. As of May 2008, it involved 1,090 employees from Blackwater Worldwide (now Xe), 328 from Triple Canopy, and 156 from DynCorp International. Xe no longer participates in WPPS.

In the UK, the production of military knowledge is being reengineered as a security partnership. The Metrix consortium led by Qinetiq is in charge of the multi-billion Defence Training Review Rationalisation Programme, which aims at centralizing the design and delivery of technical training for the British Army, the Royal Navy, and the Royal Air Force. Holdfast Training Services, a consortium of corporations that include Babcock International Group and Carillion, is in charge of a security partnership contract to run the training of British military engineers, or those deployed to war theaters.

In Australia, Defence Force Recruiting is a composite organization in which Manpower Services (Australia) Pty Ltd, a subsidiary of the international recruitment firm Manpower Inc., assists the Australian forces in the recruitment of personnel.

From recruitment and training to military deployment, security partnerships permeate military and security activities throughout the developed world. Because of smaller defense budgets, the Western allies of the United States have perhaps applied PPP principles particularly thoroughly in order

Baghdad Airport, convoy security
Armed guards providing convoy security around Baghdad Airport. *Source:*
Doug Brooks, IPOA.

to reduce spending by sharing financial risks with suppliers in the private sector. In exchange, corporations have gained a fairly permanent foothold in the
management of the monopoly of violence through the partial ownership of
defense and security infrastructure or their operation or support. In the UK,
this method is called the Private Finance Initiative (PFI). Practically the
whole British defense apparatus is operated through an intricate amalgamation of PFIs and security partnerships.

Further, partnerships as patterns of close collaboration are involved in
US foreign relations and development assistance. Hence, Secretary of State
Condoleezza Rice called in 2008 for the establishment of strategic partnerships with well-governed African states. In offering military assistance to
Georgia, the DOS alludes to a charter-guided partnership with the country.
The assistance provided takes the form, in part, of a Train-and-Equip (TEP)
program designed to upgrade Georgia's forces to Western standards in order
to bolster peace and stability in the country. TEPs have been implemented
in other countries and have become a cornerstone of U.S. foreign military
assistance since the end of the Cold War. Thus, Secretary of Defense Robert M. Gates stressed the importance of TEPs for stability operations and to
counter terrorism while announcing his recommendations for the Defense
Budget of 2010.[19] There is a Public-Private Partnership for Justice Reform
in Afghanistan. October 2007 marked the 10th anniversary of the Public-
Private Partnerships to Reinforce Humanitarian Mine Action. Cementing

the trend, under the Obama administration, the DOS has created the office of Special Representative for Global Partnerships.

It should not be forgotten that the reinvention of government might be strongly motivated by a quest for efficiency, but security partnerships bring PMCs to the forefront of state strategies designed to deter the advances of adverse private forces.

The overarching result is a new security architecture in which PMCs and related contractors directly participate in the handling of state defense and security (see Figure 5.2). The implications of the new organization of the monopoly of violence are many, starting with the recasting of traditional civil-military relations.

Civil-Military Relations in the New Millennium

Traditionally, the field of civil-military relations (CMR) is based on the principle that in democracies, control of the military belongs to the civilian authorities. That is to say, democratically elected governments ought

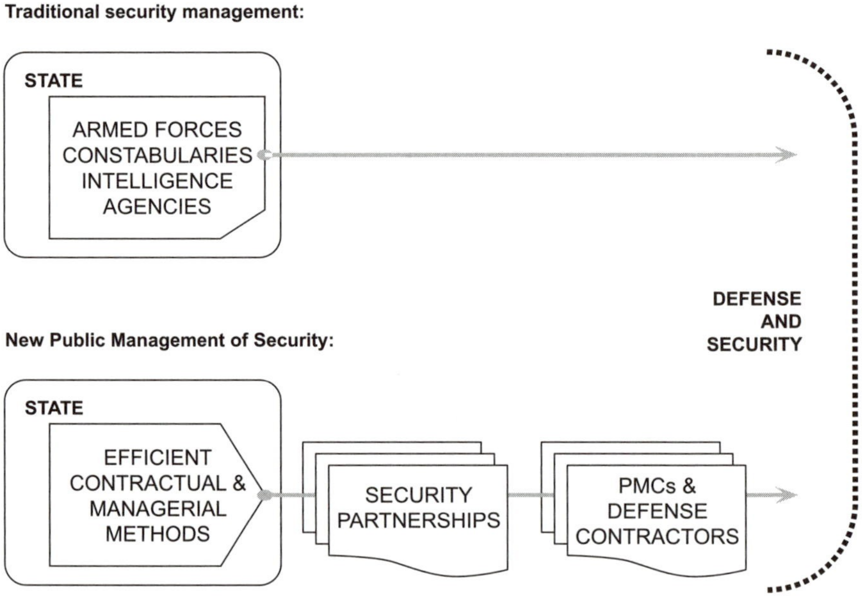

Figure 5.2   Traditional and New Types of Security Provision
In the past, military, constabulary, and intelligence forces and agencies used to provide state defense and security. Through NPM-style reform, contractors increasingly collaborate with the state in the management of its monopoly of violence. The two models coexist and are applied variably from country to country.

to decide the scope and direction that their military takes. Samuel Huntington and Morris Janowitz provided the basis for the study of CMR in the early 1960s.

In *The Soldier and the State*, first published in 1957, Huntington examines the historical roots and development in Western societies of the military as a distinctive professional institution. To Huntington, membership in the military is a "public bureaucratized profession" resting on its own body of knowledge, ethos, hierarchies, and responsibilities.[20] Although in many countries it has proved difficult to achieve or maintain, civilian control of the military in the United States has not been an issue. Instead, the problem has been the artful management of the tensions that emanate from the desire to maintain a robust military institution while ensuring that it remains under civilian and democratic control.

In *The Professional Soldier*, first published in 1960, Janowitz also highlights the professional qualities of the military, but he also elaborated on how fast developments in military technology have shaped the evolution of the field. In the 1971 revised prologue to his book, he adds a comparative analysis of the transferability of skills from the military to the private sector as a means for members of the forces to reintegrate into civilian life and attain employment after service. However, he incidentally touches on a problem of CMR of growing importance, namely that a trend in the opposite direction could already be seen. In noting an apparent convergence of skills between the military and the private sectors, he argues that the practice of having contractors performing logistical and supply roles is fostering a "tendency to assign uniformed personnel to purely military or combat functions."[21] One must stress that this discussion took place in 1971 and not now.

Authorities or the military may err in judgment, strategies, or methods when using lethal force. Hence, from the Vietnam War to the Iraq occupation, the study of CMR has also built on the practical lessons learned from past achievements and misjudgments. However, into the 1990s, conventional CMR continued to emphasize the need to improve synergies between the military and civilian authorities without reflecting on the growing use of contractors.

Recent studies note the deficiencies of traditional CMR when dealing with modern problems, such as humanitarian crises and interventions, in which the United States and its allies find themselves involved, as well as counterterror, counter-narcotics, and counter-crime initiatives. For instance, nowadays segments within the law enforcement community increasingly behave in a paramilitary fashion, and armies are on occasions used for law enforcement and reconstruction matters.

This is obvious in the numerous humanitarian crises in the periphery of the world. However, in the aftermath of Hurricane Katrina we saw the phenomenon unfolding within the United States. This broader understanding of security agencies and their relation to authorities and democratic principles sometimes goes under the term "security sector reform" (SSR); this has become an academic subject that arguably overcomes the limitations of CMR.

Yet SSR, like CMR, fails to acknowledge the bifurcation of the military part of civil-military relations into a public military component and a private military component. In other words, we have former military personnel who incorporate their previously acquired military ethos into their private work and participate in the performance of military tasks.

Professionalism in the private military sector fluctuates, as it is not guided by military codes. Deborah Avant proposes two different types of professionalism: a "cowboy" model that favors the effective use of force and a "starched shirt" model that prioritizes international values.[22] The private military sector, on the other hand, proposes to incorporate professionalism through the observance of corporate codes of conduct. The code of conduct guiding the members of the International Peace Operations Association (IPOA) is a case in point (see Appendix III); the organization is based in Washington, DC, and represents many reputable players.

Further, the civil-military playing field has been leveled and we also find military personnel acting like civilians running businesses. A deputy undersecretary of defense commented that DOD personnel are not just "incorporating best business practices, but also…extending these practices into new, previously unexplored and seemingly unrelated areas."[23] In other words, besides managerial skills, public managers involved in security partnerships need to develop expertise in the command and delivery of military and security functions. At different levels and in different sectors of the forces, this expertise also requires the amalgamation of knowledge in areas such as intelligence, IT systems, logistics, protection, or training, as well as knowledge of specific activities such as drone surveillance, tactical jamming systems, the disposal of man-portable air defense systems, the detection of improvised explosive devices, and any other task in which PMCs may have an input.

Like some other authors, Peter Singer tends to see CMR in the traditional sense and accordingly, PMCs, to him, are an anomalous component.[24] There are no easy answers here. Nevertheless, in light of all the distinctions that are being made, it is starting to make more sense to talk about "civil-military-private military" relations (CMPR) than about CMR or SSR.

Managerial Imperfections

Although NPM has been leading the way since the end of the Cold War, we are just beginning to understand the long-term implications of the new management of security. Even if over the next decade a new approach might eventually bring an end to the normative rise of NPM-style reform, as some analysts suggest, it is likely to evolve out of elements drawn from the current architecture. Therefore, besides considering the challenges of rethinking CMR, it seems relevant to outline other areas of concern and criticism.[25]

Imperfect Tendering

Noneconomic factors can affect the competitive award of contracts for the handling of sensitive defense and security tasks. This is because the disclosure of classified information to bidders is involved. Therefore, sometimes contractors with whom government has already established working relations are favored over other potential bidders. For example, in a Government Accountability Office (GAO) report on contracts awarded for the reconstruction of Iraq for the fiscal year 2003, out of 25 contracts examined, 14 were found to have been awarded on a noncompetitive basis.[26] Contracts need to comply with requirements originating in the Competition in Contracting Act for full and open competition. Otherwise, the contracting officers are required to justify the use of alternative authorized procedures. A $1.2 billion contract awarded to KBR by the Army Corps of Engineers for the rebuilding of Iraq's oil infrastructure was one instance of a contract awarded on a noncompetitive basis. Because of the limited amount of information publicly available about this type of contract, it is difficult to assess the scale of the problem.

As a point of comparison, in the European Union between 2000 and 2004, its 15 older states published on average only 13 percent of all tender opportunities for defense equipment (with Germany providing only 2 percent).[27] Tender opportunities for "sensitive non-military security equipment" were also systematically exempted by governments from publication.

Prioritizing national security over efficiency has traditionally affected defense markets and appears to transfer to broader security areas. For now, however, this practice undermines aspirations to efficiency.

Field Risk and Diminished Efficiency

An important issue to consider in military and security contracts is the environments in which services are rendered, as on many occasions they are conflict or postconflict zones. It can be a complex task to foresee and codify all the eventualities involved in service delivery in climates of instability when formalizing contracts, a novel necessity not integral to traditional security provision. Numerous media reports document the inability to deliver services as promised by various contractors during the most intense periods of fighting in Iraq. The director of defense capabilities and management acknowledged in 2006 that "given the expectation of a relatively benign environment that would require only minimal level of security," private security "costs undoubtedly diverted resources."[28]

Moreover, in spite of the best efforts to protect assets and people, the oil infrastructure was the target of numerous attacks and civilians were kidnapped, maimed, or killed. The special inspector general for Iraq's reconstruction concluded that the lack of security, the absence of protection against looting of infrastructure, and poor prewar maintenance were major contributors to the final cost of KBR's contract to rebuild Iraq's oil infrastructure.[29]

Transnational Transactions

On many occasions, contracting originates at the national level but delivery occurs abroad or evades domestic jurisdiction. The highly developed patterns of cooperation among advanced democracies facilitate the settlement of disputes between them when problems arise out of the import or export of military and security services. However, there are asymmetries of control when the recipients of services are weak states or developing nations. Corrupt practices are of particular concern here.

In a recent high-profile case, for example, the Department of Justice launched an investigating into alleged bribery involved in the multi-billion-dollar al-Yamamah arms deal between the government of Saudi Arabia and BAE Systems. BAE, which evolved out of the privatization in 1985 of British Aerospace, is the largest British defense company and is ranked sixth in the United States. The British Serious Fraud Office abandoned its investigation in 2006 on the grounds of national security.

Limited Oversight

The delivery of services abroad, particularly in harsh environments, can also erode efficiency due to the difficulties inherent in adequately monitoring contracts, which can result in taxpayers' money being misspent or lethal force being misused by PMCs. The defunct Custer Battles, once a rising PMC, was suspended in 2004 from doing business with the U.S. government after allegations of overbilling through a string of sham companies. Blackwater Worldwide unleashed a thunderstorm in Washington, DC, after allegations that security guards employed by the firm unlawfully killed 14 Iraqi bystanders during an ambush on September 16, 2007, at Nisur Square in Baghdad. Moreover, GAO continues to stress the need for better management and monitoring of LOGCAP and recommends that "teams of subject matter experts be created to travel to locations where contractor services are being provided to evaluate the support."[30]

Excessive Lobbying

While there needs to be an element of trust for partnerships to work, excessive lobbying by influential corporations can undermine aspirations to efficiency. Nothing was proved to be illegal about the connections between former Vice President Richard B. Cheney and Halliburton Corporation, the energy giant of which he was CEO between 1995 and 1999. However, Halliburton and its former subsidiary KBR benefited enormously from the Iraq conflict through bountiful contracts.

Onerous Associated Costs

An excessive leaning toward the public sector can equally undermine the spirit of NPM-style reform. In the UK, "quangos" (nongovernmental bodies that in effect advise on or perform government functions) have exploded over the last decade and account for billions of pounds in public funds. Further, privatization under NPM may be so specialized as to motivate the excessive hiring of expensive managers from the highest echelons of business, ultimately risking the creation of onerous bureaucracies rather than streamlining administrative structures.

Away from the West, the privatization of security engenders distinctive problems and opportunities that should not be overlooked.

The Privatization of Security away from the West

The opportunities that PMCs gained from the growing application of NPM principles from the early 1990s onward, when the market in military and security services was enhanced upon the demise of the Soviet system, translated into rapid growth for an industry that established itself during the Cold War. Indeed, the security partnerships between PMCs and governments to which these opportunities gave rise have affected defense and security in Western states. At the same time, however, elements of this architecture have been exported to weak states and the developing world.

Weak States

The reader will most probably have heard either of the terms "failed," "failing," "fragile," "quasi," or "weak" states. These terms began to be widely used in the 1990s to refer to the most deprived countries in the world.

Robert Jackson conceptualized "quasi-states" in a 1990 book with the same title. He argued that although these states are internationally recognized and possess the same rights as any other state, they lack the political will and institutions required to use power constructively and in a manner respectful of the human rights of their inhabitants. This handicap, in his words the lack of "empirical statehood," makes these states incomplete, so to speak; hence to Jackson they are "quasi-states."[31]

The term "quasi" has gone out of fashion and the other terms are used interchangeably. Yet, in our politically correct world, these terms can sometimes be considered controversial. To use an analogy, nowadays a teacher would think twice before describing underperforming pupils as failed, quasi, or weak students. In consequence, more elegant descriptions, such as "countries affected by fragility," are found in official reports. To avoid ambiguities, I have used the term "weak states" in this book.

Weak states are commonly ex-colonial or former Communist countries, characterized by the breaking up of law and order and chronic underdevelopment, and affected, or having recently been affected, by protracted conflicts.

To some extent, the privatization of security in weak states originated in the need for governments to find a substitute for the assistance to which they were accustomed during the Cold War years. The superpowers and their allies used to intervene directly in these governments' political affairs and supplied military and security expertise in exchange for alignment with one side or the other. The end of the Cold War resulted in a drastic decline in military and security patronage, which had included thousands of military advisers and advanced training.

Underdevelopment and Privatization

PMCs have partly filled the security assistance gap in weak states. However, filling the gap has also come to signify the substitution of official assistance by market solutions. This is because Western PMCs tend to engage their clients in a manner that does not contravene the foreign-policy imperatives of their respective governments. Therefore, even though full and open competition between PMCs for the supply of services is a characteristic of the contemporary market, the West retains a strategic edge by exercising a goodly degree of authoritative control over the areas of operation of PMCs.

However, as exemplified throughout the book, assistance offered to weak states nowadays is commonly deployed by or with the support of PMCs. Examples here are the international civilian police missions (or CivPols) implemented by DynCorp International and Pacific Architects & Engineers in places like Afghanistan, East Timor, Kosovo, and Iraq, as well as the TEP programs that many PMCs help to implement.

The privatization of security in weak states was swift. Political and military stability became dependent on private-sector supply. Toward the end of the 20th century, the hiring of PMCs was essential for the daily workings of various public, private, international, and nongovernmental organizations. Anthony Clayton identifies the presence of American, European, Israeli, and South African PMCs as a key feature in the emerging conflict profile of Africa,[32] the continent with the largest concentration of weak states. Governments facing similar problems in Latin America, the Middle East, and Asia have also turned to the market economy for security solutions.

Testimony to the importance attached to these developments was the organization in 1997 of the closed-door symposium "The Privatization of Security Functions in Sub-Saharan Africa" by the Defense Intelligence Agency, a symposium that was attended by government officials together with security experts and representatives of PMCs. The conclusions reached reflected the growing nature of the trend toward the privatization of security. Furthermore, the connection between underdevelopment and conflict had already started to take hold in expert circles.

The Convergence of Security and Development

Traditionally, the fields of homeland and national security relate to the law enforcement, military, and intelligence endeavors undertaken by governments to preserve the integrity of the state from external and internal aggressors. Since the early 1990s, however, these fields have been opened up to new perceptions. Economic, societal, political, and environmental issues are part of new security thinking, as these can also undermine states by fueling or exacerbating conflict.

Moreover, the state has ceased to be the preeminent unit of analysis. In the globalization environment, conflicts easily transcend the countries where they originate and affect distant communities. In addition, non-state actors such as IOs, NGOs, multinational corporations (MNCs), and PMCs play important roles in the international scene. The ongoing conflict in Sudan's Darfur region, for instance, has mobilized all these types of actors, albeit unsuccessfully, to try to work out a solution. Meanwhile, the Janjaweed, a brutal militia thought to be partly funded by the Sudanese government, continues to massacre people for a variety of reasons.

The field of development used to deal primarily with economic issues. In a world where there will always be disparities, the development agenda tended to focus on finding formulas and policies for the poorest nations to find routes to rising and sustainable prosperity. Yet over the last decade, it has become obvious that development and security are two sides of the same coin.

It is not possible to conceive of prosperity without the achievement of at least basic levels of security. Thus, increasingly discussions about security deal with developmental issues and vice versa. Scholars such as Mark Duffield have consistently argued that the virulent nature of conflicts typical of the post–Cold War world impacts both development and security in a way that makes it necessary to link both discourses.[33] Given the role that PMCs play in the new management of the monopoly of violence and development strategies, they figure prominently here.

The use of PMCs for the establishment of secure areas in which economic activity is reactivated (or areas in which IOs and NGOs are able to deploy and operate) has been criticized as a deficient development strategy. Indeed, PMCs represent imperfect, localized, and temporary solutions to development shortcomings. For PMCs, climates of instability are commercial and not development environments. The services they render can be comparatively expensive, too. Nonetheless, the contribution PMCs make to the containment of conflicts makes their characterization as development bandits simplistic.

A scenario emerges in which conflict in economically viable areas of the world turns into business opportunities for PMCs to exploit, opportunities that intersect the neoliberal agenda and the drive toward the attainment of efficient security provision through contracting-out to the private sector.

Toward Efficient Security Provision in Weak States

In weak states, governance is exercised in conditions of political and social turmoil. Insurgent, rebel, and criminal forces constantly challenge state authority and perpetuate instability. Moreover, relations between civilian authorities and the military tend to be tense and in constant flux. On March 2, 2009, for example, the president of Guinea-Bissau was assassinated in what appeared to be a bloody reprisal after the army chief of staff, some hours earlier, had died in a bomb attack. Three months later, a minister and independent contender for the presidency was shot dead by members of the security forces. It is a complex statehood in which, short of expertise in national management, "authorities have to wrestle with the competing demands of economic stabilization and war-related (or peacebuilding) costs."[34] We also need to consider the destabilizing threat posed by terrorist networks, particularly in Africa, the Middle East, and Asia; these networks increasingly target both security forces and segments of the population that refuse to accept extremist or fundamentalist agendas.

In weak states, the privatization of state functions and the delivery of public services by foreign contractors are among the few alternatives authorities can come up with in view of frail public institutions, faltering economies, and corruption. In this context, the highly competitive nature of the international market in private military and security services ensures that a degree of selectivity is available to authorities to make contracts with the best firms. This selectivity, in turn, facilitates a degree of efficiency in the provision of services. Political factors and the personal preferences of rulers might indeed affect contracting procedures, but the potential for optimal selection in light of exploitable market competition exists.[35]

However efficiency and transparency in security contracting can be assured by ensuring that the tendering and selection of firms take place outside the context of the affected weak states. This is particularly the case when tendering and selection take place in advanced democracies and are subject to clear rules.[36] This is often contingent on broader reconstruction and relief initiatives originating from Western donors. Hillary Clinton was prompt to stress several times upon her appointment as secretary of state that together with defense and diplomacy, the other pillar of American foreign policy is development.

The provision of aid by the United States is commonly guided by efficiency parameters. The Millennium Challenge Corporation (MCC), for example, manages development funds intended for responsible countries that encourage economic freedom. In the words of MCC, the task is "to make maximum use of flexible authorities to optimize efficiency in contracting, program implementation, and personnel."[37] MCC is neither a private firm nor a traditional public enterprise, but a corporation established in the spirit of NPM. Guinea, a small African country and candidate for MCC assistance, had its regular stream of aid suspended in January 2008 upon its failure to return to civilian rule after a military coup.

This is a radical departure from the provision of international aid by the United States during the Cold War years, when it was simply contingent on political alignment with the West in order to deter the advance of Communism.

At the multilateral level, the UN Procurement Division (UNPD) vets and buys services that include reconstruction, security, and transport assistance. Some of these services are provided by firms described as PMCs. The Global Compact, a UN initiative that encourages responsible business practices through the adoption of 10 universal principles in the areas of anticorruption, the environment, and human and labor rights, informs the operation of UNPD. At the same time, these requirements are balanced against economic efficiency. This is because the UN, like governments, "seeks the lowest price you can offer."[38]

Exporting efficiency to weak states through transnational transactions is a route to efficient security provision. Overall, however, the incomplete articulation of otherwise identifiable market principles suggests the desirability of a broader convergence toward a recognition of the new security architecture and organization of the monopoly of violence.

Adverse Competition

On a much smaller scale, the problems of weak states also affect the privatization of security in emerging markets, or in those where democratic rule has been achieved and in which sustainable growth and thriving societies are found. Countries such as Brazil, Colombia, India, Indonesia, Mexico, Malaysia, and South Africa belong to this category. There, force has been successfully centralized by the state and the privatization of security develops, if not always efficiently, in an orderly way. Nevertheless, corruption affects political processes, and criminal networks continue to infiltrate the formal economy and terrorize people. I refer to this phenomenon as "adverse competition."

Adverse competition engenders a perplexing dynamic. In emerging markets there are established police and military forces. They are clearly instruments of the state. However, they include both officers with a solid ethos and personnel who are easily corruptible, as well as both highly qualified personnel and people doing the job out of sheer necessity. In Mexico, for example, in 2007 the chief of the state agency charged with combating drug-trafficking was arrested for operating as an informant to the Juarez Cartel. In Colombia, in early 2009 a scandal erupted after allegations surfaced that rogue agents of the Administrative Department of Security, the country's domestic intelligence agency, were engaged in wiretapping activities on behalf of drug-trafficking organizations. In Bangladesh, in February 2009 about 1,000 paramilitary border guards mutinied over pay grievances and massacred about 130 senior military officers. We have a matrix in which we can find any combination of the four types of personnel. In addition, tensions between traditionalists and those that attempt to implement NPM-style reform have been markedly more pronounced than in Western countries.

At the same time, criminal networks and drug-trafficking organizations extract a share of the profits from the formal economy through extortion, ransom demands, and illicit trafficking. The struggle is violent and the organs of the state are under constant attack. In Mexico, for instance, in 2008 over 500 law enforcement and military officers died as a result of the ongoing fight against drug-trafficking organizations.

This climate blends together the best and the worst of government and society. On the one hand, marginal segments of the population succumb to the false security that adverse private forces offer. In the process, they perpetuate the very problems that moved them to bargain their safety. On the other hand, law-abiding citizens contract out any security service they can afford, to supplement inefficient state provision. Robert Mandel stresses that besides governments, "societal groups fearful about their degree of protection" employ private security providers.[39]

In the new conflict between security partnerships and adverse private forces, private security personnel are increasingly becoming a target of criminal and drug forces. In December 2008, for example, the American antikidnapping expert Felix Batista was kidnapped in northern Mexico, he has not been seen since. Hence, in spite of the progress made over the last few decades, there is still a risk that communities in emerging markets could revert to earlier stages of development.

The conflict between security partnerships and adverse private forces is clearly more intense in countries affected by insurgency. In Iraq, the special inspector general for Iraq reconstruction reported in April 2007 that since reconstruction began, 916 death claims for civilian contractors working on U.S.-funded projects had been filed.[40]

While the problems that affect emerging markets call for the overhaul of state institutions, including police and military forces as well as criminal and penal systems, in advanced democracies the controversies surrounding the use of the private sector in the areas of state defense and security can be dealt with by enhanced regulation.

Regulating the Private Military and Security Market

The market for private military and security services is an international one, and universally accepted parameters of regulation remain an aspiration of the international community. Despite the booming nature of the market since the early 1990s, however, there has been little progress in the area. The UN's 1989 *International Convention against the Recruitment, Use, Financing and Training of Mercenaries* has not been amended and continues to reflect conventional mercenaries and not legally established enterprises. A reflection of its contradictions is found in the fact that some of the countries that have signed or ratified the convention (e.g., Angola, the Democratic Republic of the Congo, Georgia, Nigeria, and Saudi Arabia) are noteworthy recipients of private military assistance, and that the major suppliers of PMCs (e.g., the United States, the UK, Israel, and South Africa) do not adhere to it. The management and exercise of force remains a state prerogative. Therefore, it is at this level that the regulatory exercise began and, it should be noted, largely remains. In spite of accountability and oversight issues, the United States enjoys a lead here and it is only to be hoped that other Western nations will at least attempt to emulate its framework.

Licensing Mechanisms: AECA and ITAR

The United States regulates the international supply of defense articles and services through the Arms Exports Control Act (AECA), first implemented in 1968. AECA is contained in chapter 39 of title 22, Foreign Relations and Intercourse, of the *United States Code*.

Section 2778 of AECA confers on the president the authority to control the export and import of defense articles and services, designate what constitute defense articles and services, provide foreign policy guidance to persons from the United States involved in the import or export of these articles and services, and promulgate regulations for these purposes.

AECA implements the control and regulation of the export and import of defense articles and services through the International Traffic in Arms Regulations (ITAR). ITAR is contained in parts 120 to 130 of title 22, Foreign Relations, of the *Code of Federal Regulations*.

The authority of the president to control and regulate the export of defense articles and services was delegated in 1977 to the secretary of state by Executive Order 11958, as amended. At the DOS, this authority is managed by the Directorate of Defense Trade Controls (DDTC) in accordance with AECA and ITAR.

Defense articles and services are designated in the U.S. Munitions List (USML), which comprises part 121 of ITAR. USML covers categories such as aircraft and related articles, vessels of war and special naval equipment, amphibious vehicles, firearms, military explosives and propellants, as well as items such as software and systems, patrol craft, noncombatant auxiliary vessels and support ships, combat logistics support, fully automatic rifles, and submachine guns. There are also classified categories.

Defense services are defined in section 120.9(a) of ITAR and involve, for example, the furnishing of assistance (including training) to foreign persons in the development or maintenance of defense articles, the furnishing to foreign persons of sensitive or classified technical data, and military training of foreign units and forces, including training by correspondence. Section 120.9(b) is "reserved."

ITAR also incorporates the registration and licensing procedures to be followed by U.S. persons willing to export defense articles and services. PMCs and defense contractors offering services internationally are required to be registered with DDTC. The services or articles on offer need to be covered by USML, to be provided under ITAR terms, and to observe the foreign policy restrictions stipulated in AECA.

Thereafter, registered vendors are required to obtain licenses for every contracted activity before the services can be provided. Contractors deployed to Iraq and Afghanistan to work in areas of defense and security have been required to obtain a license to offer and render services. In fact, at the beginning of the campaigns in both countries, the volume of applications created a backlog at DDTC that went largely unreported.

Among other AECA restrictions, if the activity involves the transfer of any "major defense equipment" (section 120.8 of ITAR) valued at over $14 million or any defense article, service, or training valued at over $50 million, special considerations apply. In these instances, the president is required to submit a written and unclassified certification to the House of Representatives and the Committee on Foreign Relations of the Senate. Although Congress has the right to block any such transfer, the president can override the decision if an emergency exists and it can be justified that it is in the national security interest of the United States to deploy any particular article or service.[41]

There are additional restrictions that apply for example, to arms sales destined for sub-Saharan Africa (section 2773 of AECA), foreign military sales to less developed countries (section 2775 of AECA), and transactions with countries deemed to support acts of terrorism (section 2780 of AECA).

AECA, ITAR, and USML are not static documents. They are amended periodically to reflect changing foreign policy goals and international security concerns.

Among recent examples, in May 2007, ITAR was amended to make it policy to grant licenses directed at Somalia only on a case-by-case basis in order to observe UN Security Council Resolution 733 of February 20, 2007.[42] The resolution stressed the need for the external assistance supplied to be solely for the purpose of helping in the development of security sector state institutions. Furthermore, in December 18, 2007, the DOS amended ITAR by adding a list of the countries subject to UN embargoes. On February 7, 2007, Venezuela was added to the list of countries to which exports and sales are prohibited (section 126.1[a] of ITAR) because of its lack of cooperation in antiterrorism initiatives; meanwhile Libya was upgraded to a case-by-case status. The revised status of Libya, a country in which the United States had no embassy for 36 years until the beginning of 2009, was sketched by the newly appointed U.S. ambassador to the country. He indicated that the emerging relationship would initially involve the provision of military training followed by the sale of nonlethal weapons.[43] All such changes are promptly published in the *Federal Register* and are publicly available for inspection.

Other Acts and Jurisdictions

The regulatory exercise is even more complex than the licensing of firms. In addition to periodical updates and amendments of the instruments described, stipulations contained in other acts need to be observed as well.

The Foreign Corrupt Practices Act (FCPA) of 1977

FCPA, significantly revised in 1988, outlines record-keeping rules and antibribery provisions for U.S. listed or domiciled companies. It also applies to foreign firms or persons while they are in the United States. The antibribery provisions prohibit payments to foreign government officials for the purpose of retaining, furthering, or directing business to a particular person. The record-keeping rules enforce the observance of U.S. accounting rules such as the accurate and fair recording of transactions. Many listed corporations that deliver private military services can thus be prosecuted if they engage in corrupt practices abroad. Thus, the investigation of the al-Yamamah arms deal between the government of Saudi Arabia and BAE Systems launched by the Department of Justice aimed precisely to establish whether BAE Systems breached the terms of FCPA.

The Competition in Contracting Act (CICA) of 1984

CICA establishes exceptions to open and full competition when there is an unusual and compelling emergency (such as a military mobilization) making it necessary to limit the number of tendering sources; when there is a need to preserve critical research or facilities; when particular expert services are required for litigation purposes; when government enters into an international agreement with a foreign government or with IOs; when it is in the public interest not to award a contract competitively; when a contracting agency determines that there is only "one responsible source available"; and when the disclosure of sensitive information would compromise national security.[44]

In the case of KBR's $1.2 billion contract for the rebuilding of Iraq's oil infrastructure, GAO concluded that the sole-source contract was properly awarded to the only contractor that the DOD "had determined was in a position to provide the services within the required time frame given classified prewar planning requirements."[45]

The Communications Assistance for Law Enforcement Act (CALEA) of 1994

CALEA, whose application has broadened since it was enacted in 1994, updated the capacity of law enforcement agencies to conduct electronic surveillance. This was in response to the growing use of digital and wireless forms of communication such as electronic messaging and voice-over Internet protocol services (e.g., broadband telephony). Manufacturers of technologies handling these types of communication need to embed the capacity to ensure surveillance capabilities. Contractors producing equipment or software that facilitates the surveillance of digital and wireless communications need to be aware of what it is legal to do, as well as of the periodic policy updates released by the Federal Communications Commission.

The Uniting and Strengthening America by Providing Appropriate Tools Required to Intercept and Obstruct Terrorism (USA PATRIOT) Act of 2001

The USA PATRIOT Act was passed shortly after 9/11. Its stated aim is to deter and punish terrorist acts in the United States and around the world, as well as to enhance law enforcement's investigatory tools. The act increased the surveillance and wiretapping powers of law enforcement and intelligence agencies. Surveillance may involve access to data stored or collected by contractors in their regular operations. In addition, monitoring can be carried out by using contractors. In a case not free of controversy, the act was used in 2004 to prosecute David A. Passaro, a CIA contractor, who was indicted for assaulting an Afghan detainee on a U.S. base in Afghanistan. Key provisions of the act were to lapse on December 31, 2005, though many remain.

The Homeland Security Act of 2002

The act created a new department within the executive branch of government: the Department of Homeland Security (DHS). DHS brings under its umbrella previously independent agencies such as the FBI, the CIA, and NSA. Contractors need to be aware of changing jurisdictions and chains of command, as well as interagency strategies and broader linkages to nonfederal entities. The act also created the Directorate of Science and Technology (DS&T), which is responsible for the research into and development of new technologies and activities to strengthen homeland security. This directorate supervises the amalgamation of civilian research and the use of contractors specializing in intelligence tasks. See, for example, the so-called "Black Helix" project,[46] a DNA database–driven program aimed at tracking terrorists and said to comprise a complex security partnership between DHS agencies, the military, and an undetermined number of contractors.

The National Defense Authorization Act

This act is published yearly and stipulates the defense budget for the coming fiscal year (FY) together with updated rules pertaining to military expenditure and procedures. For example, Section 890 of the FY2008 Authorization Act asked the secretary of defense to prescribe a regulation aimed at ensuring that contractors comply with AECA and ITAR, and to report on the utility of requiring contractors to maintain corporate training plans to disseminate information. Section 861 of the act also called for the DOD, DOS, and USAID to enter into a memorandum of understanding in order to establish clearly the major categories of contracts they have awarded in Iraq and Afghanistan, identify the common databases where this information can be found, and reconcile their rules and procedures governing the movement of contractor personnel in these countries. By July 10, 2008, all three parties had signed the memorandum. Authorization acts commonly introduce bills, thus becoming preambles to new acts.

Besides outlining the defense and security areas in which contractor support is or might be required and under which considerations, acts like these establish alternative prosecution avenues to tackle abuses perpetrated by contractors. There are many more acts and instruments to consider. For example, the Foreign Ownership, Control or Influence (FOCI) procedures ensure that foreign ownership of U.S.-based firms do not endanger national security. In observance of these rules, the 2002 acquisition of Wackenhut Services Incorporated (a provider of armed and unarmed security services) by Group 4 Falck (part of the European security corporation G4S) included the creation of a firewall between the two companies.

The overview so far, summarized in Table 5.1, demonstrates that allegations of the absolute lack of regulation of PMCs are incorrect. However,

Table 5.1   Rules and regulations governing the operations of U.S. PMCs

Commercial Operation	Management of the U.S. Monopoly of Violence	International and Humanitarian Conventions and Codes
Fundamental laws • Commercial Law • Labor Law **Related rules** • Tendering rules issued by contracting agencies • Rules by the Securities and Exchange Commission • Auditing procedures • Arbitration procedures • Contract-award protests • National Industrial Security Program **Codes of conduct** • As established by firms • As established by security and professional associations • As established by international organizations	**Licensing** • AECA • ITAR • FOCI Certification **Deployment** • Rules of engagement • U.S. endorsed conventions on the use of weaponry **Oversight** • UCMJ • MEJA **Complementary acts** • CALEA • CICA • FCPA • Homeland Security • National Defense Authorization • Security and Accountability For Every (SAFE) Port • USA PATRIOT	**International humanitarian law** • Geneva Conventions • Anti-Mercenary Conventions • Convention on Certain Conventional Weapons • Convention on Cluster Munitions **International codes of conduct** • Code of Conduct of the Red Cross • UN Global Compact • Voluntary Principles on Security and Human Rights • Montreux Document on Private Military and Security Companies • International Mine Action Standards **Maritime law** • UN Convention on the Law of the Sea • International Convention for the Safety of Life at Sea (SOLAS) • International Ship and Port Facility Security (ISPS) Code

While not exhaustive, this table includes rules and regulations that PMCs falling under U.S. jurisdiction need to observe, or of whose existence they need to be aware. The United States does not endorse all the international conventions listed. However, PMCs need to know whether the foreign countries in which services are rendered subscribe to them.

much more needs to be done, particularly in the areas of accountability and oversight.

Accountability and Oversight: UCMJ and MEJA

Licensing mechanisms do not govern the use of force, only which firms are entitled legally to sell private military and security services, which specific services, and the countries where they can be deployed. However, an area of critical concern is the accountability and oversight of PMCs on the ground, where deadly force might be exercised. There are currently two alternative avenues through which this can be addressed: the updated Uniform Code of Military Justice (UCMJ) and the enhanced Military Extraterritorial Jurisdiction Act (MEJA).

UCMJ, which became effective in 1951, is the fundamental code of military law in the United States. It applies to all branches of the forces and is administered by military authorities through a court martial system. Whether one is a member of the Army, the Navy, or the Air Force, or a reservist called for duty, UCMJ governs one's actions while on the ground and under the chain of command.

UCMJ imposes a distinction between civilians and members of the forces. The former are subject exclusively to criminal law and not to military codes. Herein lies the problem with regard to applying UCMJ to contractors. In the eyes of the law, contractors have been seen as civilians, even if accompanying or supporting the military or providing armed protection services in conflict zones. This has recently changed, however.

The 2007 National Defense Authorization Act called for the amendment of UCMJ to apply not only to wars but also to "contingency operations" such as those in Iraq and Afghanistan. The amendment in effect brings "persons serving with or accompanying an armed force in the field," for which read here private military personnel, under court martial jurisdiction.[47]

In assessing the relevance of the amendment, it must be remembered that in spite of the numerous military engagements in which the United States has been involved, there has not been a formal declaration of war since 1941.

MEJA is the other route to the prosecution of unlawful activity committed by employees of PMCs and contractors in general. In 2000, MEJA established federal jurisdiction for federal offenses committed outside the United States by civilian persons employed by or accompanying the forces. An amendment in 2004, the year in which the Abu Ghraib prison scandal exploded, expanded the reach of MEJA to cover personnel employed by any other federal agency or provisional authority whose work relates to supporting the DOD abroad. However, here we are not talking about minor offenses but about those that would warrant imprisonment of more than one year if they had been committed within the United States. Unlike the situation under

UCMJ, prosecution devolves upon the United States and the federal court system. MEJA thus allows contractors to circumvent court martial jurisdiction and military tribunals.

By late 2008, there were some 50 ongoing cases involving contractors being handled through MEJA. However, the first high-profile indictment likely to create a legal precedent involves five Blackwater Worldwide security guards charged with voluntary manslaughter, the attempt to commit manslaughter, and weapons violations for their alleged role in the shooting at Nisur Square.

In February 2007, Barack Obama, then a senator, introduced the Transparency and Accountability in Security Contracting Act. This Obama Bill (S.674) broadens the scope of MEJA by attempting to ensure that it applies to all U.S. contractors participating in contingency operations. It also stresses the need for the FBI to create theater investigative units. At the time when this book was being written, the bill was in its early stages and had not yet become law.

It remains to be established whether UCMJ or MEJA provides the better means to bring to justice contractors that act unlawfully. It is likely that the systematic prosecution of offenses will involve a mixture of the two acts. Section 861 of the FY2008 Authorization Act requires the aforementioned memorandum of understanding between the DOD, DOS, and USAID to include database information on offenses by contractor personnel both under UCMJ and under MEJA. Positive outcomes of the scandals involving contractors and PMCs in Iraq are that regulation reform has been accelerated and that the scandals have forced the involved parties to address regulatory gaps seriously.

An International Impetus for Regulation?

I have outlined the regulation trajectory of the United States, but the market for private military services is truly international. Western countries generally operate some sort of licensing system to regulate their domestic defense markets. In a manner similar to the working logic of ITAR, for example, Israel allows the export of articles and services in a manner that does not contravene its foreign policy imperatives, and Australia has a Defence and Strategic Goods List with some resemblance to USML. However, most allies of the United States have not amended their frameworks to address the private military industry, which is service oriented and not capital intensive like the defense sector. Armed protection services, for instance, commonly fall outside the jurisdiction of most licensing mechanisms. The cases of South Africa and the UK are often cited in the literature and illustrate the point.

In the case of South Africa, no legislation existed to regulate its booming private military industry until the Regulation of Foreign Military Assistance

Act came into force in 1998. The act aims to controls the offering of foreign military assistance both by South African citizens and by foreign nationals based in the country. The act differentiates between foreign military assistance and mercenary activity. It regulates the offering of the former and effectively bans the latter, which is defined as the "direct participation as a combatant in armed conflict for private gain."[48]

Like the U.S. framework, the act establishes a two-step licensing procedure. First, any person seeking to offer military assistance needs authorization from the National Conventional Arms Control Committee. Second, if authorization is granted, subsequent scrutiny and approval of every agreement reached with potential clients is necessary. However, South Africa has not introduced a thorough codification of the services likely to be exported, along the lines of USML, which limits the operational flexibility of the act. In addition to the limited applicability of the act due to its wide-brush codification, the enforcement sheet is practically blank.

If in the United States enforcement and oversight have proven to be a highly complex task, South Africa lacks the infrastructure to bring its regulatory efforts to fruition. It appears that the only licenses for the thousands of South Africans who have operated in Iraq have been their plane tickets. Moreover, there is no official record of how many South African citizens have been to Iraq.

An upcoming set of regulations, the *Prohibition of Mercenary Activity and Prohibition and Regulation of Certain Activities in an Area of Armed Conflict Bill*, is even more ambiguous. This bill, not yet law at the time when this book was being written, goes as far as criminalizing the provision of humanitarian assistance unless authorized by government. Once more, a detailed list of the services susceptible to regulation is not contained in the proposed instrument.

In the UK, in 2002, a green paper, *Private Military Companies: Options for Regulation*, was released. In the statement announcing its release, PMCs were not conceived as freelance mercenary soldiers but as business enterprises. In terms of options for regulation, the green paper proposes a ban, self-regulation, or the establishment of a licensing system for PMCs. The ban could cover certain activities deemed by some to be objectionable, particularly "direct participation in combat."[49] The option of self-regulation considers the possibility of PMCs becoming members of or forming a trade association, which would then be charged with formulating a code of conduct for international work. The licensing system proposed follows the same methodology as the American system.

Surprisingly, and after seven years, the British Foreign and Commonwealth Office (FCO) announced in April 2009 that a code of conduct was the preferred option for regulation. In other words, the second largest private military supplier in the world is bypassing the scrutiny attached to licensing mechanisms. The reason given by the FCO was that the "UK based industry has a favourable reputation and operates to high standards" and therefore alternative regulation is "not proportionate to the scale of the problem in the UK."[50]

Thus, there is an imperfect licensing system in South Africa, and there is a code of conduct (on the drawing board at the time when this book was being written) in the UK to be implemented by a private trade association. Oversight through something similar to UCMJ or MEJA does not currently exist in either of these countries and it is unlikely it will emerge any time soon.

In the Obama Bill, it is noted that nationals of many other countries, including Australia, Chile, Colombia, Croatia, Fiji, India, Nepal, New Zealand, Nicaragua, Russia, Serbia, and Sri Lanka, have been deployed to Iraq in a private capacity. It would be presumptuous for the government of any of these countries (and the governments of the UK and South Africa) to assume that their own citizens have not committed or will not commit abuses of force and that therefore there is no need for regulation. Using colloquial terms, there is no inoculation that would prevent unscrupulous cowboy cases from emerging in an international and multi-billion-dollar industry employing thousands of people.

Governmental apathy at home also ignores vociferous calls for universal standards of regulation. Table 5.2 highlights the percentage of contractor personnel recorded by the DOD in Iraq and Afghanistan as being non-U.S. citizens.

Table 5.2   DOD contractors—December 2008

	IRAQ	AFGHANISTAN	Other USCENTCOM
U.S. Citizens	39,262	5,960	7,749
	(26.5%)	(8.3%)	(19.6%)
Host Country Nationals	37,913	60,563	4,878
	(25.6%)	(84.4%)	(12.3%)
Third-Country Nationals	70,875	5,232	26,989
	(47.9%)	(7.3%)	(68.1%)
Total	148,050	71,755	39,616

USCENTCOM countries: Afghanistan, Bahrain, Egypt, Iran, Iraq, Jordan, Kazakhstan, Kuwait, Kyrgyzstan, Lebanon, Oman, Pakistan, Qatar, Saudi Arabia, Syria, Tajikistan, Turkmenistan, UAE, Uzbekistan, and Yemen

Figures as reported by the assistant deputy under secretary of defense for program support for December 31, 2008. Up-to-date figures are available on the office's Web site. PMC employees account for probably no more than 10 percent of the reported figures.

NPM-style reform has given rise to a novel security architecture in which private firms assist in the management of state defense and security. It permeates countries to varying degrees. This asymmetric dynamic compels governments to more effectively inform their citizens about the extent to which state defense and security have been privatized and to enact appropriate regulations.

Notes

1. David H. Rosenbloom and Robert S. Kravchuck, *Public Administration: Understanding Management, Politics, and Law in the Public Sector,* 5th ed. (New York: McGraw-Hill, 2002), 50.

2. White House, "Farewell Radio and Television Address to the American People by President Dwight D. Eisenhower" (Washington, DC, January 17, 1961).

3. Harold Wool, *The Military Specialist: Skilled Manpower for the Armed Forces* (Baltimore: Johns Hopkins University Press, 1968), 117.

4. Woodrow Wilson, "The Study of Administration," in *Classics of Public Administration,* ed. Jay M. Shafritz, Albert C. Hyde, and Sandra J. Parkes, 5th ed. (Belmont, CA: Wadsworth, 2004), 22.

5. Leonard D. White, "Introduction to the Study of Public Administration," in *Classics of Public Administration,* ed. Jay M. Shafritz, Albert C. Hyde, and Sandra J. Parkes, 5th ed. (Belmont, CA: Wadsworth, 2004), 57.

6. Max Weber, "Bureaucracy," in *From Max Weber: Essays in Sociology,* ed. and trans. H. H. Gerth and C. Wright Mills (London: Routledge, 1997), 214.

7. Guy Peters, *The Future of Governing: Four Emerging Models* (Lawrence: University Press of Kansas, 1996), 22–23.

8. Jan-Erik Lane, *New Public Management* (London: Routledge, 2000), 212.

9. Bruce Baker, "Uneasy Partners: Democratisation and New Public Management," in *Contesting Public Sector Reforms: Critical Perspectives, International Debates,* ed. Pauline Dibben, Ian Roper, and Geoffrey Wood (Basingstoke, UK: Palgrave Macmillan, 2004), 46.

10. The discussion about the NPM-style reform of state defense and security in this chapter is based on an argument about the problems inherent in the "NPM of security" in Carlos Ortiz, "The New Public Management of Security: The Contracting and Managerial State and the Private Military Industry," *Public Money and Management* 30, no. 1 (2010), 35–41.

11. Hal. G. Rainey, *Understanding and Managing Public Organizations,* 4th ed. (San Francisco: Jossey-Bass, 2009), 87.

12. White House, "Remarks by President Clinton Announcing the Initiative to Streamline Government" (Washington, DC, March 3, 1993).

13. Department of Defense, *Directions for Defense: Report of the Commission on Roles and Missions of the Armed Forces* (Washington, DC: Department of Defense, May 24, 1995), 3-1–3-6.

14. Department of Defense, *2006 Quadrennial Defense Review Report* (Washington, DC: Department of Defense, February 6, 2006), 75–82.

15. Department of National Defence (Canada), *1994 Defence White Paper* (Ottawa, ON: Ministry of Supply and Services, 1994), para 59.

16. Ministry of Defence (UK), *The Strategic Defence Review—1998* (London: Stationery Office, 1998), 170.

17. See Department of Defence (Australia), *Defence 2000: Our Future Defence Force* (Canberra: Defence Publishing Service, 2000), 99; and "Defence and Industry: Strategic Policy Statement" (Canberra, June 2, 1998).

18. Elke Krahmann, "Private Military Services in the UK and Germany: Between Partnership and Regulation," *European Security* 14, no. 2 (2005): 279.

19. Department of Defense, "Defense Budget Recommendation Statement: As Prepared for Delivery by Secretary of Defense Robert M. Gates" (Arlington, VA, April 6, 2009).

20. Samuel P. Huntington, *The Soldier and the State: The Theory and Politics of Civil-Military Relations* (Cambridge: Belknap Press, 2002), 1–18.

21. Morris Janowitz, "Prologue," *The Professional Soldier: A Social and Political Portrait* (New York: Free Press, 1971), xxiii.

22. Deborah D. Avant, *The Market for Force: The Consequences of Privatizing Security* (Cambridge: Cambridge University Press, 2005), 226.

23. Quoted in T. Lukach, "Installations Transforming to Support Joint Warfighting Needs," *American Forces Press Service*, April 12, 2005.

24. Peter W. Singer, *Corporate Warriors: The Rise of the Privatized Military Industry* (New York: Cornell University Press, 2003), 197–200.

25. I discuss managerial imperfections inherent in the NPM of security with more detail in Ortiz, "The New Public Management of Security," 35–41.

26. Government Accountability Office, *Rebuilding Iraq: Fiscal Year 2003 Contract Award Procedures and Management Challenges* (Washington, DC: Government Accountability Office, 2004).

27. European Commission, "Annex to the Proposal for a Directive of the European Parliament and of the Council on the Coordination of Procedures for the Award of Certain Public Works Contracts, Public Supply Contracts and Public Service Contracts in the Fields of Defence and Security" (Brussels, Belgium, December 5, 2007), 13–14.

28. William M. Solis, *Testimony before the Subcommittee on National Security, Emerging Threats, and International Relations* (Washington, DC: Government Accountability Office, June 13, 2006), 7.

29. Special Inspector General for Iraq Reconstruction, *Cost, Outcome, and Oversight of Iraq Oil Reconstruction Contract with Kellogg Brown & Root Services, Inc* (Arlington, VA: Office of the Special Inspector General for Iraq Reconstruction, January 13, 2009).

30. Government Accountability Office, *High-Level DOD Coordination Is Needed to Further Improve the Management of the Army's LOGCAP Contract* (Washington, DC: Government Accountability Office, 2005), 12.

31. Robert H. Jackson, *Quasi-States: Sovereignty, International Relations, and the Third World* (Cambridge: Cambridge University Press, 1990), 21.

32. Anthony Clayton, *Frontiersmen: Warfare in Africa since 1950* (London: UCL Press, 1999) 155–56.

33. Mark Duffield, *Global Governance and the New Wars: The Merging of Development and Security* (London: Zed Books, 2002).

34. Gilles Carbonnier, "The Carrot and the Stick: Reconsidering the Conditions Imposed on Aid," *Forum* 2 (2000): 15.

35. I first discussed the export of NPM-style practices in areas of state security in Carlos Ortiz, "Private Military Contracting in Weak States: Permeation or Transgression of the New Public Management of Security?" *Review of African Security* 17, no. 2 (June 2008): 8.

36. Ibid., 9.

37. Millennium Challenge Corporation, "Factsheet on the Millennium Challenge Corporation: Reducing Poverty Through Growth" (Arlington, VA, February 2, 2004).

38. United Nations Development Programme, "UNDP: Frequently Asked Questions," http://www.un.org/depts/ptd/ (accessed September 1, 2007).

39. Robert Mandel, *Armies without States: The Privatization of Security* (Boulder, CO: Lynne Rienner, 2002), 156.

40. Special Inspector General for Iraq Reconstruction, *Quarterly Report to the United States Congress* (Arlington, VA: Office of the Special Inspector General for Iraq Reconstruction, April 30, 2007), 11.

41. United States, *United States Code*, Washington, DC, 22 USC 2753, http://www.gpoaccess.gov/uscode/.

42. *Federal Register*, 72(98), May 22, 2007, 28602, http://www.gpoaccess.gov/fr/.

43. Quoted in Haba Seleh, "Thaw Spurs Prospect of Arms Sales to Libya," *Financial Times*, March 11, 2009.

44. *United States Code*, 41 USC 253.

45. Government Accountability Office, *Rebuilding Iraq: Fiscal Year 2003*, 4.

46. Defense Science Board Task Force on Defense Biometrics, *Report of the Defense Science Board Task Force on Defense Biometrics* (Washington, DC: Office of the Under Secretary of Defense for Acquisition, Technology, and Logistics, March 2007), 37.

47. See *United States Code*, 10 USC 802; and Marc Lindemann, "Civilian Contractors under Military Law," *Parameters* 37, no. 3 (Autumn 2007): 83–94.

48. Republic of South Africa, *Regulation of Foreign Military Assistance Act* (Cape Town: Government Gazette, May 20, 1998).

49. Foreign and Commonwealth Office (UK), *Private Military Companies: Options for Regulation* (London: Stationery Office, February 2002), para 71.

50. Foreign and Commonwealth Office (UK), *Consultation on Promoting High Standards of Conduct by Private Military and Security Companies (PMSCs) Internationally* (London: Stationery Office, April 2009), 12.

CHAPTER 6

Conclusions

At the height of the Iraq conflict, when controversies and scandals involv-ing contractors dominated the headlines, I was on my way to a conference in Europe. On my journey, I came across some of the most representative is-sues in and arguments about the debate about the privatization of security and PMCs.

I first met a civil servant. He found it refreshing to discuss the practicali-ties of the contracting process rather than the controversies or virtues sur-rounding the use of contractors in conflict zones.

Later, at an airport lounge, I met a soldier heading back to the United States after a stint in Iraq. While he was critical of the extensive use of con-tractors in Iraq, he wanted to retire early and continue his "military" career working as a "civilian" in the private military industry.

On a train, it seemed that I had jumped on a coach filled with a young crowd heading to a rock concert. They were actually activists on their way to a "stop the war" demonstration in London. I listened to views about the "privatization of war" and the activists' shared belief that PMCs were the result of the Iraq conflict and the policies of George W. Bush.

Then it was on to the academic gathering. The themes covered were broadly the same, although they were discussed with an emphasis on some of the theoretical insights the reader has found in this book.

An unexpected reappraisal came from a doctor I met on my way back home. She was returning home after participating in a vaccination cam-paign in a sub-Saharan African country. She explained that private person-nel (a mixture of local and foreign guards) protected the medical compound where she had been based. As we said goodbye, she just said, "I wish it was different, but I felt safe, and we managed to do our work."

Inspired by similar exchanges, this book has offered the reader a technical understanding of PMCs and the adverse private forces they are hired to protect various parties from or to counteract. However, we need to reflect further on the book's themes in order to map the road ahead. The frequent allusion to PMCs as a new phenomenon since the early 1990s makes it convenient first to touch on the historical understanding of the private uses of force.

Private Military History, between Evolution and Randomness

The year 1989 was momentous indeed. While the world converged on France to celebrate the bicentenary of the French Revolution, Eastern Europe liberated itself from Communism. The piercing of the Berlin Wall, which had separated Western and Eastern communities for decades, was symbolic of the start of a new era. Away from Europe, Soviet forces withdrew from Afghanistan and popular protests across China rattled the old order. Many Communist leaders used lethal force against their people in a last attempt to resurrect what they were used to. They largely failed. The world had taken an irreversible turn.

Michael Howard commented that 1989 was likely to be seen by future generations as the turning point that ended a century of warfare in Europe.[1] Optimism predominated, initially. Francis Fukuyama summarized the mood in his influential essay "The End of History?" in which he argued that the "universalisation of Western democracy" was "the final form of human government."[2]

The point here is that we can see history as evolution; that is to say, as one event logically leading to another while humanity progresses as if by natural design. Conversely, historical change can be understood as something precipitated by fortuitous events.

In *The Black Swan*, Nassim Nicholas Taleb discusses the randomness of history, the way in which unexpected events like 9/11 demolish assumptions we have previously accepted as the established order of things. In Taleb's words, history is merely "*any succession of events* seen with the effect of *posterity*."[3] We now live in the post-9/11 world, but before it, our perceptions of reality were quite different. Similarly, 2008 brought established notions about the world economy and our financial well-being crashing to the ground.

The year 1989 encapsulates the notion of historical randomness. Soviet troops withdrew from Afghanistan, but the mujahedin who fought them for a decade wanted to continue their crusade elsewhere. Their leader Abdullah Azzam was killed in 1989, which gave control of the nascent al-Qaeda terrorist organization to Osama bin Laden. There was a violent ethnic conflict in the Balkans. The end of the Cold War turned into a destabilizing development in Africa as well, with rebellion and insurgency emerging or intensifying in many countries.

Together with the rise of instability in weak states and criminal activity in the developing world, 1989 also marks the beginning of the proliferation of PMCs. Executive Outcomes, the now defunct South African PMC that captured most of the attention of scholars and the press in the 1990s, was established in 1989, as was AirScan, a leader in the airborne surveillance field.

Many of us see history through one of the two lenses, as evolution or randomness. Yet we need to bear in mind that the manner in which we see it can influence our understanding of the private uses of force, as well as their implications for global security.

Let us go back to our historical exploration of the early modern period and recall the trajectory leading to the state's assumption of a monopoly over the legitimate uses of force.

First, I classified key patterns of military organization with a private element into mercenary companies, the forces commanded by military entrepreneurs, the armies of rulers, militias, the armies and navies of the overseas trading companies, pirates, and privateers. Retrospectively, it is possible to establish these distinctions. To someone living in those times, however, it was probably not that clear, as distinctions between the public and private uses of force were in constant flux.

Second, I superimposed evolutionary overtones on the exploration of key events contributing to the state's monopolizing of force. Most academics do, as it facilitates the overview of three centuries of history. However, history seldom travels in a straight line. The process was highly accidental and involved unforeseen events with profound consequences. In fact, the Boston Tea Party (which led to the American War of Independence) and the storming of the Bastille in France (which signaled the onset of the French Revolution) are only two among many historical events with significant implications for the rise of the nation-state and its national army. It would be simplistic to imply that this rise was inevitable. Nonetheless, either as a result of evolution or as a result of a series of random historical events, the idea of a state monopoly of violence had developed by the late 19th century.

If we approach the monopoly of violence as the result of centuries of evolution leading to a universal norm, then we would probably regard PMCs as an affront to the system. In furtherance of this view, some analysts have established parallels between PMCs and the mercenary companies of the past, arguing that the parallels might signify a possible return to the anarchy that characterized the period of these companies. Martin Van Creveld is often quoted in these accounts. In *The Transformation of War*, he argued that the defense of society against the depredations of low-intensity conflicts might be privatized and "the organizations that comprise that business will, like the *condottieri* of old, take over the state."[4]

There is an alternative approach. The use of contractors by governments is a historical constant. During the American Civil War (1861–1865), "requirements for specialized personnel in support-type roles were filled largely by civilian employees or contractors."[5] For major military mobilizations, such as wars between states, it is difficult to assess this civilian role, as everything is subordinated to the war effort. Therefore, it is a nearly impossible task to establish how many contractors in what capacities assisted the allied forces during the Second World War, but we can assume the number was quite high. There was conscription during the Vietnam War, which meant that consideration of the scale and scope of contractor support was hardly the main concern. Iraq is a different matter. It is complex to disentangle fully the use of contractors in Iraq as a result of the trends examined in this book from those entering the conflict as a result of poor planning and mismanagement.

Nevertheless, by acknowledging the use of contractors as a constant, while at the same time recognizing the state as the ultimate arbiter of the use of force, we can establish that these seemingly contradictory requirements have resulted from gradual policy changes over at least the last few decades. Thus, James Larry Taulbee reminds us that what marks the post–Cold War era as significantly different from the previous period is not the fact that defense contractors and PMCs exist but their sheer numbers, "the scope of services offered and the visibility of their operations."[6]

If the reader sees history as progression, then this is a recent evolutionary trait starting to take shape sometime in the second half of the 20th century. However, maybe we need to explore the past century in more detail in order to find the key factors that persuaded governments to start making more use of firms in the management of the state monopoly of violence. I have mentioned some possible factors in this book.

The Changing Corporate Environment and Labor Market

The new security architecture involves numerous tasks in the areas of combat, training, support, security, intelligence, and reconstruction. These are the main areas so far covered by PMCs. The field might expand in the future to incorporate new service segments. While training has been offered since the Cold War, combat was involved mainly in the 1990s, and reconstruction has gained importance since the beginning of the 21st century.

Conventionally, we would think of PMCs as easily identifiable firms offering services in one of these service segments. Media reports convey this impression. Many PMCs, particularly small firms, specialize in a particular service segment. However, large corporations whose business lies largely out-side the private military sector also offer private military services.

For example, an information technology (IT) corporation might become involved in the development of a highly classified intelligence system or database for the Department of Defense (DOD), though most of its business deals with commercial or aerospace electronics. Similarly, a construction and engineering corporation might derive a great deal of its profits from the building of oil refineries or production compounds, yet also help the DOD to deploy forces abroad and run barracks. For analytical purposes, I have referred to such suppliers of private military services as hybrid forms of PMCs, com-prising units within large and diversified corporations.

It should be noted that continuous mergers and acquisitions shift the pri-vate military capabilities of firms across sectors and corporate identities.

For example, the civilian interrogation work provided by CACI Interna-tional in Iraq was chiefly the result of its acquisition in May 2003 of Premier Technology Group Inc., the original holder of the contract with the U.S. Army. Armor Holdings sold ArmorGroup International to a group of private investors backed by the private equity firm Granville Baird Capital Partners in November 2003. In 2005, ArmorGroup was floated on the London Stock Exchange. In March 2008, ArmorGroup was acquired by G4S, the largest security provider in the world, which also merged with Group 4 Falck in July 2004. Wackenhut Services Incorporated (WSI) took over RONCO Consult-ing Corporation in April 2008. As Group 4 Falck acquired WSI in March 2002, though this was done through a proxy agreement with the U.S. au-thorities that establishes a firewall between the two companies, RONCO falls under the umbrella of G4S. In 2005, L-3 Communications merged with Titan Corporation. In June 2009. Andrews International agreed to acquire the guarding operations of Garda World Security Corporation in the United States and Mexico, and so on.

Therefore, an identifiable PMC today can become a hybrid type tomor-row, and vice versa. Alternatively, it could disappear from the spotlight in the next round of corporate consolidations.[7] For instance, in February 2009, Blackwater Worldwide (formerly Blackwater USA) was reorganized and changed its name to Xe. In the process, the firm formerly known as Blackwa-ter lost its previous prominence. Further, corporate identities are sometimes created to manage commercial alliances or specific contracts. They can also be registered in offshore centers, which can make it difficult to identify the firms behind particular contracts.

Determining whether a firm, as a whole or in parts, can be approached as a PMC may not be a straightforward task. Armed with the working defini-tion provided in chapter 3, and the analysis of typologies of services, and the "atomic" view of PMCs, the reader will need to use personal judgment.

Given the dynamic corporate environment, members of the services have become widely aware of the prospect of applying for early retirement to continue a military, law enforcement, or intelligence career as well-paid civilians working for PMCs. This development has intensified the competition between the public and private sectors for the retention of personnel. In 1995, Secretary of Defense William J. Perry noted in his annual DOD report to the president and Congress that it was a matter of concern that pay in the military had not kept pace with the private sector.[8] However, we have seen in this book that the issue has been under discussion since the late 1960s.

As the length of military service shortens, authorities need more funding for the training of new recruits. In turn, rising recruiting and training costs might persuade governments to contract out more functions to PMCs rather than face the prospect of justifying larger defense and security budgets. It is a two-edged sword and possibly a looping cycle in need of further investigation.

This is no longer a problem affecting only tier-one suppliers of private military personnel, such as the United States, the UK, Israel, and South Africa. Tier-two developing nations and probably UN peacekeeping forces, which largely come from the developing world, are affected as well. As of December 31, 2008, the top 10 suppliers of Blue Helmets were Pakistan, Bangladesh, India, Nigeria, Nepal, Rwanda, Ghana, Jordan, Italy, and Uruguay.[9]

The huge demand for security services in Iraq at the height of the conflict injected momentum into this dynamic. The private security boom in Iraq is largely gone now. Iraqis satisfy more and more of their own (public and private) security requirements. Yet rumor has it among soldiers from various Asian, African, and Latin American countries that their skills attract higher pay in the international market.

Private security is neither new nor strange to the developing world. Local security firms and workers have been subcontracted by tier-one PMCs for a while. However, they are no longer reluctant to deploy to countries they do not know about or whose language they do not speak. Many of the Latin American former soldiers who worked in Iraq went back home to establish their own firms, some of them advertising their services internationally. Time will tell whether this newfound entrepreneurship remains in the longer term a force for good. If not, these firms may compound the conflict problems in Latin America.

Living in Insecure Times and in a Smaller World

The Stockholm Peace Research Institute established that between 1990 and 2005 only four of the 57 active conflicts occurred between states.[10] The rest were intra-state conflicts, commonly fought between security forces and all sorts of adverse private forces. By the time the Coalition Provisional Authority assumed control of Iraq (this control lasted from April 2003 to June 2004) with the assistance of an impressive array of contractors, the consultancy firm Control Risks was reporting a 23 percent increase in the number of countries moving from low to medium political risk.[11] These emerging markets are home to expanding societies and substantial investments, and their security requirements continue to multiply. If in corners of the Western world the police and intelligence agencies on occasion find themselves unable to contain internal violence, this is becoming closer to the rule in developing nations. Amid the displacement of populations due to civil strife and capricious natural disasters, organized crime and terrorist networks increase the incidence of conflict.

This book has illustrated the link between conflict and the hiring of PMCs in an attempt to help reengineer a regime of security lost to the predatory advances of adverse private forces. PMCs are not a substitute for regular armies or police, but they have become an enhancing, and some may argue indispensable, complement to them. To delineate the scope and limitations of the variable roles that PMCs assume, I classified conflict environments into humanitarian crises and interventions, trade in dangerous places, and homeland security. However, it is worth highlighting certain recent developments that are likely to affect global security as we move further into the 21st century.

In terms of humanitarian crises and interventions, I noted that the demands imposed on peacekeeping forces continue to multiply. Peacekeeping is no longer undertaken exclusively by the UN and its Blue Helmets, as many other international organizations (IOs), nongovernmental organizations (NGOs), and coalitions of states participate in peace and reconstruction initiatives. For example, at the time when this book was being written, France had a force of a few hundred soldiers in the Central African Republic (Operation Boali). This force was focusing on the training and reorganization of the Central African Republic's forces and supporting FOMUC (Force multinationale en Centrafrique). FOMUC, for its part, was being sponsored by the Economic and Monetary Community of Central Africa and replaced MINURCA (1998–2000), a UN-led mission. As part of Operation EUFOR Tchad/RCA, the European Union (EU) had also a force of some 3,000 soldiers in the northeast part of the Central African Republic and in neighboring Chad until March 2009, when the UN peacekeeping mission MINURCAT was established.

Many more examples provided in the book confirm the overlapping mandates and multilateral forces characterizing peace and reconstruction initiatives. The soldiers in these forces come from national armies. Hence, the problem of competition between the public and private sectors for the retention of personnel, amplified by growing peacekeeping and reconstruction demands, resonates here.

There are also health and development issues affecting weak states, which bring in other types of IOs and donors, including foundations led by very wealthy individuals. For instance, with HIV/AIDS infection rates exceeding 15 percent of the population in Botswana, Lesotho, Mozambique, Namibia, South Africa, Swaziland, Zambia, and Zimbabwe, this disease is considered a serious destabilizing factor in sub-Saharan Africa. It is not uncommon for PMCs to provide risk advice and security services for aid missions, or to facilitate the rapid deployment of humanitarian personnel and aid when natural disasters strike.

In addition, the quest to secure energy resources may turn natural riches into sources of new conflicts. For example, the autonomous Kurdish region in northern Iraq is oil rich, but it is in disagreement with the central government in Baghdad over production and revenue issues. At the other end of the country, where Iraq's export terminals are located, there are territorial disputes between Kuwait, Iraq, and Iran. The uninhabited Spratly Islands in the South China Sea were until recently the site of a (merely) symbolic territorial dispute between Brunei, China, Malaysia, the Philippines, Taiwan, and Vietnam. Now, the possibility of important oil finds in the area complicate negotiations. Politically and environmentally, the exploration of the Arctic for oil and gas would be disastrous. Canada, Denmark, Norway, Russia, and the United States are the potential and seemingly overlapping claimants to these resources.

The China factor, or its insatiable appetite for raw materials to manufacture our goods, has injected momentum into the race to secure the supply of natural resources. In the period leading to the 2009–2010 global recession, while the West nurtured a credit bubble, China amassed reserves estimated at $2.27 trillion in September 2009,[12] which it has used to tap into Africa's natural riches. For instance, in April 2008, the Democratic Republic of the Congo entered into a $9.25 billion agreement with China for the long-term supply of cobalt and copper in exchange for infrastructural development and mining investment. The coming generation of hybrid cars and the implements of new green technologies will incorporate all the metals that China has been securing and stockpiling.

Again, large investments require a security cover, which in the case of China comes from guarantees offered by the recipients of the funding as well as Chinese personnel. Some news outlets have reported the use of Chinese convicts in Africa. Like Gazprom, the Russian energy giant that maintains its own security units, China might find its own answer to PMCs. With Brazil, Russia, and India also competing for resources (together with China they are called the BRIC group: the four largest emerging economies). Trade in dangerous places is expanding beyond the scope of our analysis.

The homeland security environment will continue to face the risk of sudden assaults originating in international terrorist organizations and organized crime. Historically, assassinations and kidnappings have been familiar terrorist methods. In the 1960s and 1970s, the hijacking of commercial airliners became a new problem. The introduction of plastic explosives, which are difficult to detect but lethal, raised the bar and motivated the 1991 counterterror *Convention on the Marking of Plastic Explosives for the Purpose of Detection*. Since the beginning of the 21st century, bombings have become widespread. In Bangladesh alone, on August 17, 2005, there were over 400 small-bomb explosions in about 50 cities. The advent of cheap but reliable means of mass communications has facilitated the perpetration of similar coordinated or synchronized attacks.

The National Counterterrorism Center records that most terrorism-related fatalities in 2008 occurred as a result of armed attacks (including the use of mortars, rocket-propelled grenades, and missiles); bombings (including the use of improvised explosive devices and vehicles to carry them); and suicide attacks (including suicide bombers wearing explosive vests or vehicle-borne improvised explosive devices).[13] There were also numerous arsons, assassinations, assaults, hijackings, incidents of vandalism, and hoaxes, as well as an increase in kidnapping. Acts of nuclear terrorism, perhaps involving the detonation of a "radiological dispersal device" (RDD) or "dirty bomb," fortunately remain so far a hypothetical scenario.

We have become numb to reports about suicide bombings. Alas, this only shows how common and widespread the practice has become. The activities of drug-trafficking organizations engender a generalized climate of fear within society, they increasingly verge on acts of terrorism. We cannot think otherwise of assassinations, executions, and constant attacks on the organs of government, the news media, and ordinary citizens. If nuclear terrorism is a latent threat, "narco-terrorism" is a growing reality in corners of Latin America.

On a different level, through many parts of the world, particularly the West, programs have emerged that empower citizens to take on law enforcement roles. These programs vary from country to country, but often they involve community police officers dealing with minor offenses, members of voluntary organizations trained to respond in case of natural or terrorist disasters, and varied forms of crime awareness reporting. While for the most part these programs are designed to add to state efforts and encourage citizens to be alert, they in effect form part of the broader reconfiguration of the monopoly of violence.

As well as ordinary citizens becoming part-time police officers, the forceful response by the state to organized crime, often assisted by PMCs, only strengthens the view that defense and security is nowadays an enterprise shared by the public and private sectors.

A New Security Paradigm or Rushed Privatization?

When announcing the introduction of America's Economic Bill of Rights in July 1987, former president Ronald Reagan (1981–1989) proposed a judicious pruning "from the Government that which goes beyond the proper realm of the state."[14] Finding "additional ways for contracting outside of government to perform those tasks that belong in the private economy" was part of the strategy. Over two decades later, upon his inauguration, President Barack Obama noted that the question asked today "is not whether our government is too big or too small, but whether it works."[15]

We have heard similar pronouncements from every president in turn. These ideas touch state defense and security, which comprise the single biggest part of government. However, one question I have been asked (and ask myself often) is how these ideas filter down to the different offices and parts of government in which everyday decisions about outsourcing and contracting out are taken.

In an attempt to provide simple answers, I constructed a model based on the theory and practice of public management. This model involves an interlocking chain of developments and draws elements from the visions of successive administrations, their defense and security strategies, and the practical need to find better ways to manage government. The model makes extensive use of the private sector through numerous techniques ranging from outright privatization to public-private partnerships. It is worth recalling some of the key parameters guiding the logic behind the approach:

- *Efficiency:* Government wants to minimize costs and maximize outcome.
- *Competition:* If competition exists between alternative service providers, which can be firms, different parts of government, or both, efficiency can be attained.
- *Contracts:* By using contracts, government can hold the providers of services accountable.
- *Flexibility:* By granting public servants greater flexibility in the decision-making process, better and more creative solutions can be achieved.
- *Performance:* To establish whether results are being delivered as expected or promised, performance needs to be documented and quantified.
- *Experimentation:* The feedback loop that performance measurement introduces facilitates making decisions about the introduction of new practices.

These parameters guide the use of the private sector in the areas of defense and security. Private input includes the contracting of specific training, support, security, intelligence, or reconstruction tasks to PMCs. Patterns of close collaboration between government and PMCs are forged as a result of this process. I have termed these "security partnerships."

Security partnerships permeate the management of the state monopoly of violence across the board. Some noteworthy examples include the following:

- *Training:* Lockheed Martin is the largest provider of aircrew training in the United States and MPRI is a key contractor in areas of law enforcement and military instruction.
- *Deployment:* The LOGCAP contract provides full-spectrum logistical support for the deployment of troops worldwide. In addition, DynCorp International provides support to the Navy Expeditionary Medical Support Command.
- *Security:* The WPPS contract organizes the private protection needs of DOS and USAID.
- *Intelligence:* The Terrorist Identities Datamart Environment is a counterterror database that has involved Lockheed Martin, Boeing, SRI International, and many subcontractors. SAIC is a key intelligence contractor and collaborates with government on numerous related tasks
- *Reconstruction:* The Conventional Weapons Quick Reaction Force is currently operated under contract with DynCorp International, which also collaborates with PAE-HSC and MPRI in the implementation of civilian police missions globally.

The ensuing movement of defense and security knowledge from the state to the private sector will continue. Hence, I have argued in this book that perhaps it makes sense to start thinking about civil-military-private military relations along with security partnerships. However, the management of the monopoly of violence through security partnerships so far suffers from many imperfections, particularly in the areas of regulation and accountability. Although the growing number of prosecutions of contractors demonstrates that these issues are now taken seriously in the United States, questions have been raised about the large-scale use of contractors after the global financial downturn.

The larger defense and security contracts depend on steady financial flows. As credit contracted in 2009–2010, it became difficult to attract investors for ongoing and new projects. At the same time, though the defense industry is particularly resilient, long-term investment decisions have proved difficult to make without a clear idea of when, where, and for how long government plans to make cuts. Meanwhile, in the United States, as in almost any other country, reining in public spending will be critical in the second decade of the 21st century:

- *Defense equipment:* In April 2009, Defense Secretary Robert Gates outlined plans to scale back defense spending. The strategy is likely to be the consolidation of ongoing commitments rather than embarking on ambitious new plans.

- *Security partnerships:* They are essential for the management of the monopoly of violence and cannot be discontinued. However, the monitoring of performance and costs and issues of accountability will increasingly take center stage.
- *Future plans:* The reorganization of defense priorities in light of constrained budgets and the need to preserve jobs is underway. This partly involves mediating between the different requirements of the U.S. Army, Navy, and Air Force. In particular, there will be a greater emphasis on counterinsurgency and reconstruction technologies and support.

Many defense and security projects will be downgraded or their implementation schedules extended, which is not rare. However, security partnerships unfold in reference to strategies conceived for execution over periods ranging anywhere from a few years to one or two decades. They are vital to the achievement of long-term defense and security goals and cannot be simply discontinued. Indeed, intense negotiations between government and firms to guarantee the future of agreed contracts (and jobs attached to them) are likely to result in a tighter and more mature public-private interface. Therefore, there are reasons to suspect that security partnerships and PMCs will metastasize into cornerstones of state defense and security in the 21st century. The new phenomenon will become the status quo.

Notes

1. Michael Howard, "The Springtime of Nations," *Foreign Affairs* 69, no. 1 (1990): 32.

2. Francis Fukuyama, "The End of History?" *The National Interest* 16 (Summer 1989): 3–4.

3. Nassim Nicholas Taleb, *The Black Swan: The Impact of the Highly Improbable* (London: Penguin Books, 2007), 101.

4. Martin Van Creveld, *The Transformation of War* (New York: Free Press, 1991), 207.

5. Harold Wool, *The Military Specialist: Skilled Manpower for the Armed Forces* (Baltimore: Johns Hopkins University Press, 1968), 10.

6. James Larry Taulbee, "The Privatization of Security: Modern Conflict, Globalization and Weak States," *Civil Wars* 5, no. 2 (2002): 2–3.

7. Carlos Ortiz, "The Private Military Company: An Entity at the Centre of Overlapping Spheres of Commercial Activity and Responsibility," in *Private Military and Security Companies. Chances, Problems, Pitfalls and Prospects,* ed. Thomas Jäger and Gerhard Kümmel (Wiesbaden, Germany: VS Verlag, 2007), 66–67.

8. Quoted in Department of Defense, *Annual Report to the President and the Congress* (Washington, DC: Department of Defense, February 1995), "Part V: Defense Management," http://www.dod.mil/execsec/adr95/index.html.

9. United Nations, *Year in Review 2008: United Nations Peace Operations* (New York: United Nations, 2009), 52.

10. Stockholm Peace Research Institute, *SIPRI Yearbook 2006: Armaments, Disarmament and International Security* (Oxford: Oxford University Press, 2006), 108.

11. Control Risks Group, "RiskMap 2004: International Political and Security Risks: What Can We Expect in 2004," Press Release (November 11, 2003).

12. National Counterterrorism Center, *2008 Report on Terrorism* (Washington, DC: National Counterterrorism Center, April 30, 2009).

13. People's Bank of China, "Gold and Foreign Exchange Reserves," Beijing, China, September 2009.

14. Quoted in White House, "Remarks Announcing America's Economic Bill of Rights" (Washington, DC, July 3, 1987).

15. Quoted in White House, "Inaugural Address By President Barack Hussein Obama" (Washington, DC, January 21, 2009).

World Map

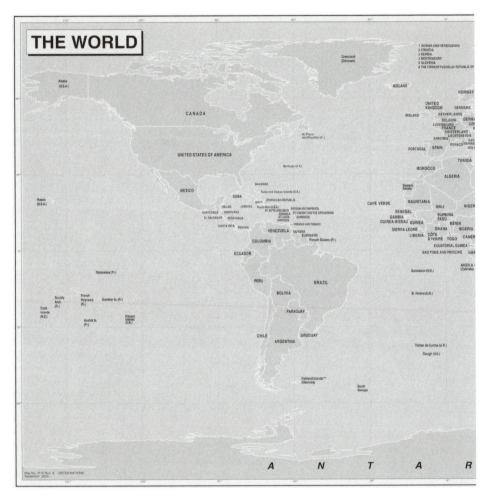

UN Cartographic Section.

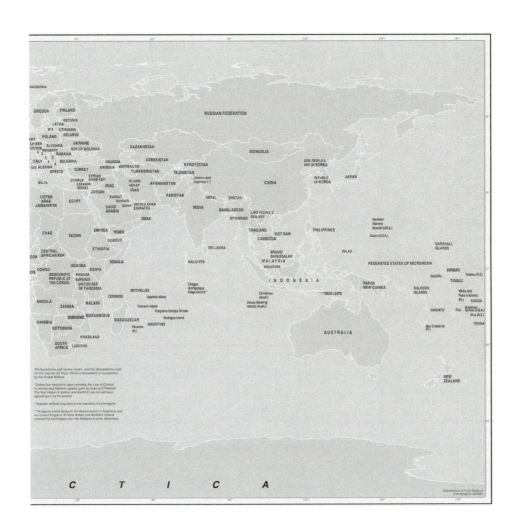

MACEDONIA

SWEDEN   FINLAND

ESTONIA
LATVIA
R.F.   LITHUANIA
POLAND   BELARUS

RUSSIAN FEDERATION

CH REP.   SLOVAKIA   UKRAINE
USTRIA   HUNGARY   REP. OF MOLDOVA   KAZAKHSTAN
ROMANIA

ITALY   BULGARIA   GEORGIA   UZBEKISTAN   KYRGYZSTAN   MONGOLIA
see ALBANIA   GREECE   TURKEY   ARMENIA   AZERBAIJAN   TURKMENISTAN   TAJIKISTAN

MALTA   CYPRUS   SYRIAN   ARAB REP.   ISLAMIC   Jammu and   DEM. PEOPLE'S
LEBANON   REP. OF   Kashmir (*)   REP OF KOREA
ISRAEL   IRAQ   IRAN   AFGHANISTAN   CHINA   REPUBLIC   JAPAN
JORDAN   PAKISTAN   OF KOREA

LIBYAN   KUWAIT
ARAB   BAHRAIN   NEPAL   BHUTAN
JAMAHIRIYA   EGYPT   QATAR   UNITED ARAB
SAUDI   EMIRATES   INDIA   BANGLADESH
ARABIA   LAO PEOPLE'S
OMAN   MYANMAR   DEM. REP.

CHAD   SUDAN   ERITREA   YEMEN   THAILAND   VIET NAM   PHILIPPINES   Northern
DJIBOUTI   CAMBODIA   Mariana
Islands (U.S.A.)
CENTRAL   ETHIOPIA   SRI LANKA   Guam (U.S.A.)   MARSHALL
AFRICAN REP.   BRUNEI   ISLANDS
OON   SOMALIA   MALDIVES   DARUSSALAM   PALAU
UGANDA   KENYA   MALAYSIA   FEDERATED STATES OF MICRONESIA
SINGAPORE
NGO   DEMOCRATIC   RWANDA   KIRIBATI
REPUBLIC OF   BURUNDI   NAURU   Tokelau (N.Z.)
THE CONGO   UNITED REP.   I N D O N E S I A   TUVALU
OF TANZANIA   SEYCHELLES   Chagos   PAPUA   Wallis and
Archipelago   NEW GUINEA   SOLOMON   Futuna Islands
ANGOLA   COMOROS   Agaléch Island   Diego Garcia**   ISLANDS   (Fr.)   SAMOA
Christmas   TIMOR LESTE
ZAMBIA   MALAWI   Island (Austr.)
Tromelin Island   Cocos (Keeling)   VANUATU   FIJI   American
ZIMBABWE   MOZAMBIQUE   Islands (Austr.)   Samoa (U.S.A.)
Cargados Carajos Shoals   Niue (N.Z.)
NAMIBIA   MADAGASCAR   MAURITIUS   Rodrigues Island   New Caledonia   TONGA
BOTSWANA   Réunion   AUSTRALIA   (Fr.)
(Fr.)   SWAZILAND
SOUTH   LESOTHO
AFRICA

The boundaries and names shown and the designations used
on this map do not imply official endorsement or acceptance
by the United Nations.

*Dotted line represents approximately the Line of Control
in Jammu and Kashmir agreed upon by India and Pakistan.
The final status of Jammu and Kashmir has not yet been
agreed upon by the parties.

**Appears without prejudice to the question of sovereignty

***A dispute exists between the Governments of Argentina and
the United Kingdom of Great Britain and Northern Ireland
concerning sovereignty over the Falkland Islands (Malvinas).

NEW
ZEALAND

C   T   I   C   A

Department of Field Support
Cartographic Section

Actors

Selected PMCs Operating in Iraq in 2003–2004

In an April 2, 2004, letter, Representative Ike Skelton requested from Secretary of Defense Donald H. Rumsfeld a "breakdown of information regarding private military and security personnel in Iraq."[1] Skelton wrote in his capacity as ranking minority member of the House Armed Services Committee, which he subsequently chaired, and in response to the Fallujah incident in Iraq, which resulted in the killing of four employees from the firm formerly known as Blackwater USA.

Rumsfeld replied on May 4, 2004. His communication contained an attachment entitled "Discussion Paper. Private Security Companies Operating in Iraq."[2] The paper argued that these companies "provide only defensive services" and were either contracted directly by the Coalition Provisional Authority (CPA, April 2003–June 2004) or subcontracted by companies doing work for CPA. The attachment contained a list of 60 such companies. Some of these companies are old players, some others emerged during the Iraq conflict, and a few of them are no longer active. I use the exact names provided in the list contained in the attachment:

1. AD Consultancy
2. AKE Limited
3. Al Hamza
4. Armor Group
5. Babylon
6. Bechtel
7. BH Defense
8. BHD
9. Blackheart International LLC
10. Blackwater

11. BritAm Defense
12. Castleforce Consultancy
13. Control Risks Group
14. CTU ASIA
15. Custer Battles
16. D.S. Vance
17. Diligence Middle East
18. DTS Security
19. Dyncorp Intl
20. EODT
21. Erinys
22. Excalibre
23. GE International Inc.
24. Genric
25. Global
26. Group 4 Falck A/S
27. Hart Group
28. Henderson Risk Ltd
29. Hill & Associates
30. ICP Group Ltd
31. IRC
32. ISI
33. KBR
34. Kroll Associates
35. Meteoric Tactical Solutions
36. Meyer & Associates
37. MVM
38. NAF Security
39. Nearest Security
40. Olive
41. Omega Risk Solutions
42. Optimal Solutions Services
43. Orion Management
44. Overseas Security & Strategic Information, Inc/Safenet—Iraq
45. Parsons
46. RamOPS Risk Management Group
47. Reed
48. RONCO
49. Rubicon
50. SAS/SASI
51. Sentinel
52. SGS
53. Smith Brandon Int
54. SOC-SMG
55. Summer International Security
56. Tarik

57. Triple Canopy
58. Unity Resources
59. USA Environmental
60. Wade-Boyd and Associates LLC

International Peace Operations Association (IPOA)

Founded in 2001 and based in Washington, DC, IPOA is an organization that represents the interests of firms participating in peacekeeping and reconstruction initiatives. Most of these firms fit the working definition of PMCs put forward in chapter 3.

IPOA sees itself as a nongovernmental, nonprofit, nonpartisan association of companies providing ethical services to international peacekeeping, peace enforcement, humanitarian rescue, stabilization, and disaster relief efforts.

The origins and aspirations of IPOA cannot be dissociated from those of its founder and president, Doug Brooks. Mr. Brooks was a scholar before founding IPOA and has traveled the world extensively to research and campaign for a broader use of the private sector in peacekeeping and reconstruction.

In this light, although IPOA is often approached as simply a trade association, its work also unfolds along the lines of a typical NGO. The organization is a key source of information for scholars researching the privatization of security, produces independent research, publishes a quarterly journal, and promotes the regulation of PMCs.

As of May 2009, IPOA had 60 full members:

1. AECOM
2. Agility
3. AMECO
4. American Glass Products
5. Arkel International
6. ArmorGroup
7. ASPIC
8. Aviazapchast
9. Burton Rands Associates
10. CMSS
11. Crowell & Moring LLP
12. CTG Global
13. Cyrus Strategies LLP
14. Danimex
15. DLA Piper LLP
16. Dreshak North America
17. DynCorp International
18. Ecolog International
19. EOD Technology, Inc.
20. Evergreen International Airlines

21. Exploration Logistics Group
22. FSI Worldwide
23. GardaWorld
24. Ge2b Seguridad Internacional
25. Global Fleet Sales
26. Global Operations Resources Group, Inc.
27. GlobeComm Systems, Inc.
28. Gold Coast Helicopters
29. HART
30. Holland & Hart LLP
31. Insitu, Inc.
32. International Armored Group
33. J-3 Global Services
34. Medical Support Solutions
35. Mission Essential Personnel
36. MPRI
37. New Century
38. Olive Group
39. OSSI-Safenet
40. Overseas Lease Group
41. Pax Mondial
42. Paxton International
43. RA International
44. Reed, Inc.
45. Rutherfoord
46. Securiforce International
47. Securiguard, Inc.
48. Security Support Solutions (3S)
49. Shook, Hardy & Bacon LLP
50. SkyLink USA
51. SOS International, Inc.
52. Swift Freight International
53. Tangiers International
54. Threat Management Group
55. TOIFOR GmbH
56. Triple Canopy
57. Tundra Strategic Security Solutions
58. Unity Resources Group
59. URS Corporation, EG&G Division
60. Whitney, Bradley & Brown, Inc.

International Terrorist Organizations

As established in Section 2656f of Chapter 38, Department of State, of Title 22, Foreign Relations and Intercourse, of the *United States Code,* the Department of State (DOS) is required to submit to Congress by April 30 of each year an annual report on terrorism. This appendix incorporates terrorist groups designated by DOS as of July 7, 2009. The descriptions provided are compiled from information contained in the *Country Reports on Terrorism 2007* and *2008*,[3] as well as recent noteworthy activity reported by the news media. Two groups profiled here but not detailed in the *Country Reports on Terrorism 2007* and *2008* are Kata'ib Hizballah and the Revolutionary Struggle.

Abu Nidal Organization (ANO)

Other names: Arab Revolutionary Brigades, Arab Revolutionary Council, Black September, Fatah Revolutionary Council, the Revolutionary Organization of Socialist Muslims.

Background: ANO was founded by Sabri al-Banna (also known as Abu Nidal) after splitting from the Palestine Liberation Organization in 1974. Killing or injuring some 900 people, its most notorious attacks occurred in the 1980s. Abu Nidal died in Baghdad in August 2002.

Recent activity: ANO is considered largely inactive.

Abu Sayyaf Group (ASG)

Other name: al Harakat al Islamiyya.

Background: ASG is an Islamic group operating in the southern Philippines that seeks to create a separate Islamic state for the Muslim minority in the country. The group split from the Moro National Liberation Front (MNLF) in 1991. MNLF and the Moro Islamic Liberation Front are the two largest separatist groups operating in the Autonomous Regions in Muslim Mindanao in the southern Philippines, but ASG is the most radical one. In February 2004, ASG planted a bomb on a passenger ferry in Manila Bay, killing 132 people. Radullan Sahiron is apparently the current leader of ASG.

Recent activity: On January 15, 2009, ASG gunmen kidnapped three Red Cross workers in the Philippines: Eugenio Vagni (Italian national), Andreas Notter (Swiss national), and Mary Jean Lacaba (Philippines national). ASG threatened to behead Vagni and Notter unless government forces withdrew from certain southern villages. The three hostages were subsequently released; Vagni nearly six months later, on July 12.

Al-Aqsa Martyrs Brigade (AMB)

Other name: al-Aqsa Martyrs Battalion.

Background: AMB emerged in 2000 as a militant offshoot of the Palestinian Fatah political party. The group attacks Israeli military targets and settlers with the intention of persuading Israel to leave the West Bank and Gaza. The ultimate goal is the establishment of a Palestinian state. AMB, composed of loose cells, has no central leadership.

Recent activity: In 2008, the majority of the attacks suspected to have been carried out by AMB consisted of rockets shot from Gaza into Israel.

Al-Jihad (AJ)

Other names: Egyptian Islamic Jihad, Egyptian al-Jihad, New Jihad, Jihad Group.

Background: AJ, active since the 1970s, aims to overthrow the Egyptian government and to establish an Islamic state. The group was responsible for the 1981 assassination of Egyptian President Anwar Sadat. AJ's former head, Ayman al-Zawahiri, is the deputy to Osama bin Laden, the leader of al-Qaeda. In 2001 AJ merged with al-Qaeda and has not claimed responsibility for independent attacks since then.

Recent activity: The Egyptian faction of AJ was dormant in 2007–2008. However, Ayman al-Zawahiri, as al-Qaeda's deputy leader, continues to issue regular threats.

Al-Qaeda (AQ)

Other names: al-Qa'ida, al Qaeda, International Front for Fighting Jews and Crusaders, Islamic Army, Islamic Army for the Liberation of Holy Sites, Islamic Salvation Foundation, the Base, Group for the Preservation of the Holy Sites, Islamic Army for the Liberation of the Holy Places, World Islamic Front for Jihad against Jews and Crusaders, Usama bin Ladin Network, Usama bin Ladin Organization. Due to AQ's strong links with AJ, also al-Jihad, the Jihad Group, Egyptian al-Jihad, Egyptian Islamic Jihad, New Jihad.

Background: AQ was established by Osama bin Laden in 1988 with jihadists who fought the Soviet forces in Afghanistan during the 1980s. AQ's aims include uniting Muslims to fight the United States and its allies, overthrowing regimes it deems "non-Islamic," and expelling Westerners and non-Muslims from Muslim countries. AQ has reconstituted some of its pre-9/11 operational capabilities through affiliation with other terrorist organizations and the use of sympathizers. The leadership of al-Qaeda is believed to be sheltering in the border region between Afghanistan and the Federally Administered Tribal Areas of Pakistan. AQ remains terrorist enemy number one.

Recent activity: Ayman al-Zawahiri, bin Laden's deputy, claimed responsibility on behalf of AQ for the terrorist attacks in London on July 7, 2005, which resulted in 52 civilians killed and over 700 injured.

Al-Qaeda in Iraq (AQI)

Other names: al-Qa'ida in Iraq, al-Qa'ida Group of Jihad in Iraq, al-Qa'ida Group of Jihad in the Land of the Two Rivers, al-Qa'ida in Mesopotamia, al-Qa'ida in the Land of the Two Rivers, al-Qa'ida of Jihad in Iraq, Al-Qa'ida of Jihad Organization in the Land of The Two Rivers, Al-Qa'ida of the Jihad in the Land of the Two Rivers, Al-Tawhid, Jam'at al-Tawhid Wa'al-Jihad, Tanzeem Qa'idat al Jihad/Bilad al Raafidaini, Tanzim Qa'idat al-Jihad fi Bilad al-Rafidayn, the Monotheism and Jihad Group, the Organization Base of Jihad/Country of the Two Rivers, the Organization Base of Jihad/Mesopotamia, the Organization of al-Jihad's Base in Iraq, the Organization of al-Jihad's Base in the Land of the Two Rivers, the Organization of al-Jihad's Base of Operations in Iraq, the Organization of al-Jihad's Base of Operations in the Land of the Two Rivers, the Organization of Jihad's Base in the Country of the Two Rivers, al-Zarqawi Network.

Background: In January 2006, AQI created the Mujahidin Shura Council (MSC) as an umbrella organization meant to bring together the various Sunni terrorist groups operating in Iraq. AQI originally claimed its attacks under the MSC banner. As Abu Ayyub al-Masri succeeded Mus'ab al-Zarqawi (killed in June 2006) as leader of the group in mid-October 2006, the group declared Iraq as the "Islamic State of Iraq" (ISI). Since then, new AQI attacks have been claimed under ISI. Besides frequent attacks on Coalition and Iraqi forces, suicide and car bomb attacks on crowded and symbolic targets continue unabated.

Recent activity: The ferocity and regularity of AQI attacks decreased in 2007–2008. In 2009, April proved particularly violent: on April 6, seven car bombs exploded across Baghdad, killing at least 37 and injuring scores; on April 23, two suicide attacks in Baghdad and near Baquba resulted in at least 80 killed and 100 wounded; and on April 24, in a double suicide attack at a Shia shrine in Baghdad over 80 were killed and 125 injured. The number of attacks will probably rise as the bulk of the U.S. forces start to leave.

Al-Qaeda in the Islamic Maghreb (AQIM)

Other names: al-Qa'ida in the Islamic Maghreb, Tanzim al-Qa'ida fi Bilad al-Maghrib al-Islamiya, Le Groupe Salafiste pour la Prédication et le Combat, Salafist Group for Call and Combat, Salafist Group for Preaching and Combat.

Background: AQIM originated out of the merger of the Salafist Group for Preaching and Combat, formed in Algeria in 1998, with al-Qaeda in September 2006. The group seeks the overthrow of the Algerian government and its replacement with an Islamic regime. On April 11, 2007, AQIM for the first time carried out suicide attacks and vowed to continue the strategy. Outside Algeria, in December 2007 the group carried out an attack in neighboring Mauritania and declared France its "public enemy number one."

Recent activity: In December 2008, the UN special envoy to Niger, Robert Fowler, and his assistant, Louis Guay, were kidnapped. The two were released in April 2009. Meanwhile, AQIM told Algerian newspapers that it was holding six Western hostages seized in adjacent Niger in December 2008. There are growing concerns that the group might intend to spread its activities throughout northwestern Africa.

Al-Shabaab (AS)

Other names: The Harakat Shabaab al-Mujahidin, al-Shabab, Shabaab, the Youth, Mujahidin al-Shabaab Movement, Mujahideen Youth Movement, Mujahidin Youth Movement.

Background: AS is the militant wing of the abolished Union of Islamic Courts (USC) in Somalia. USC, which aimed to establish Sharia law in the country, rose in 2006 as a rival to the Transitional Federal Government endorsed by the UN and the African Union. Ethiopian and Transitional Government forces dissolved USC rule. AS emerged as a militant force pursuing USC's original goal. The group, composed of radicalized young men in their 20s and 30s, has links with al-Qaeda. It is believed that some AS leaders have previously trained or fought with al-Qaeda in Afghanistan.

Recent activity: On April 13, 2009, mortars were fired toward the plane carrying U.S. Congressman Donald Payne during a visit to Mogadishu, Somalia's capital. On April 19, 2009, two workers of the NGO Médecins Sans Frontières were kidnapped. The National Counterterrorism Center established that in 2008 AS was the second deadliest international terrorist group.

Ansar al-Islam (AI)

Other names: Ansar al-Sunna, Ansar Al-Sunnah Army, Devotees of Islam, Followers of Islam in Kurdistan, Helpers of Islam, Jaish Ansar Al-Sunnah, Jund Al-Islam, Kurdish Taliban, Kurdistan Supporters of Islam, Partisans of Islam, Soldiers of God, Soldiers of Islam, Supporters of Islam in Kurdistan.

Background: AI was formed around 2001 in Iraq and aims to expel the Coalition Forces from the country and to establish a state based on Sharia law. AI has ties to the central leadership of al-Qaeda and has become the second most prominent terrorist group in Iraq.

Recent activity: AI continues to issue threats and up to 2007 conducted numerous high-profile attacks against a wide range of Coalition targets.

Armed Islamic Group (GIA)

Other names: Jama'ah al-Islamiyah al-Musallah, Groupement Islamique Armée.

Background: GIA, which began its violent activity in 1992, aims to overthrow the Algerian regime and to establish a state based on Sharia law.

Recent activity: GIA's last significant attacks occurred in August 2001.

Asbat al-Ansar (AA; Band of Partisans)

Other names: League of Partisans, Band of Helpers, League of the Followers, Partisan's League, Usbat al-Ansar, Usbat ul-Ansar, Osbat al-Ansar, Isbat al-Ansar, Esbat al-Ansar.

Background: AA, which emerged in the early 1990s, is a Lebanon-based extremist group composed primarily of Palestinians with links to al-Qaeda.

Recent activity: AA operatives have been involved in fighting or in supporting jihadists fighting in Iraq since at least 2005.

Aum Shinrikyo (Aum)

Other names: A.I.C. Comprehensive Research Institute, A.I.C. Sogo Kenkyusho, Aleph, Aum Supreme Truth.

Background: Aum was established by Shoko Asahara as a religious cult in Japan in 1987. Its recognition as a religious organization was revoked by the Japanese authorities after the group's deadly sarin gas attack on Tokyo's subway in March 1995. The cult now goes under the name Aleph.

Recent activity: In July 2001, Russian authorities arrested a group of Russian Aum followers who had apparently planned to set off bombs near the Imperial Palace in Tokyo. In July 2009, a refusal to open a retrial for Shoko Asahara was upheld by a high court. He was sentenced to death in 2004.

Basque Fatherland and Liberty (ETA)

Other names: Askatasuna, Batasuna, Ekin, Euskal Herritarrok, Euzkadi Ta Askatasuna, Herri Batasuna, Jarrai-Haika-Segi, K.A.S., XAKI.

Background: ETA was founded in 1959 as a Marxist-oriented group seeking to establish an independent territory encompassing the Spanish Basque provinces of Vizcaya, Guipuzcoa, and Alava, the autonomous region of Navarra, and the southwestern French territories of Labourd, Basse-Navarre, and Soule. ETA began its lethal attacks in the late 1960s. These attacks primarily consist of bombings and assassinations. ETA operatives also intimidate and seek to extort money from the business community.

Recent activity: On March 26, 2009, a bomb exploded outside the home of a businessman in Spain's northern Basque country. In April 2009, ETA issued a warning that the incoming regional government was a priority target. On June 19, 2009, Eduardo Pulles Garcia, a senior police officer, died after his car exploded near Bilbao.

Communist Party of the Philippines/New People's Army (CPP/NPA)

Background: CPP/NPA is a Maoist group formed in March 1969 with the aim of overthrowing the government of the Philippines. The group's primary targets are members of the security forces, government officials, local infrastructure, and businesses that refuse to pay extortion money.

Recent activity: Telecommunications infrastructure belonging to the firm Globe Telecom has been targeted since September 2008 by suspected CPP/NPA rebels. A series of bomb blasts in Mindanao in early July 2009 killed about a dozen and injured scores. No group claimed responsibility for the attacks, but it is believed that they were committed by CPP/NPA militants. Governmental sources reported over 400,000 people displaced in Mindanao as a result of the ongoing violence.

Continuity Irish Republican Army (CIRA)

Other names: Continuity Army Council, Continuity IRA, Republican Sinn Fein.

Background: CIRA was formed in Northern Ireland (part of the UK) in 1994 as the clandestine armed wing of Republican Sinn Fein, which in 1986 split from Sinn Fein (the largest nationalist party in Northern Ireland). CIRA cooperates with the larger Real IRA. CIRA's terrorist activity has decreased since 2005, though the group has become increasingly active on the criminal front.

Recent activity: On March 9, 2009, a policeman was gunned down in Northern Ireland. The Independent Monitoring Commission, established by the British and Irish governments in 2004 to help promote the peace in Northern Ireland, said in its 21st report in May 2009 that "dissident activity since early summer 2008 has been consistently more serious than at any time since we started reporting in April 2004."[4]

Gama'a al-Islamiyya (IG)

Other names: Al-Gama'at, Egyptian al-Gama'at al-Islamiyya, Islamic Gama'at, Islamic Group. Gama'a is sometimes spelled in media reports as Jamaa or Jamaat.

Background: IG, based in Egypt, has been active since the late 1970s. However, it is now a loosely organized network. IG's spiritual leader, Sheikh Omar Abd al-Rahman, was sentenced to life in prison in January 1996 for his involvement in the 1993 World Trade Center bombing. In 1997, IG shot and killed 62 people, 58 of them tourists, in Luxor. Subsequently, IG's membership was the object of a large-scale crackdown.

Recent activity: IG has apparently renounced mass violence and there has not been a major incident involving members of the group since the 1997 Luxor attack.

HAMAS (Islamic Resistance Movement)

Other names: Harakat al-Muqawama al-Islamiya, Izz al-Din al Qassam Battalions, Izz al-Din al Qassam Brigades, Students of Ayyash, Student of the Engineer, Yahya Ayyash Units, Izz al-Din al-Qassim Brigades, Izz al-Din al-Qassim Forces, Izz al-Din al-Qassim Battalions, Izz al-Din al Qassam Forces.

Background: HAMAS was formed during the Palestinian uprising of 1987 and controls the Gaza Strip. With strong links to Syria, HAMAS includes military and political wings. Its military wing has conducted numerous armed attacks on Israeli civilian targets. After winning Palestinian Legislative Council elections in January 2006, HAMAS formed an expanded and overt militia called the Executive Force. In an interview with the *Financial Times* in May 2009, Sheikh Naim Qassem, the deputy leader of Hizballah, admitted offering full support to HAMAS.[5]

Recent activity: HAMAS attacks and Israeli retaliations are a regular feature of international press dispatches. Between late December 2008 and January 2009, HAMAS factions fought a 23-day war with Israel.

Harakat ul-Jihad-i-Islami/Bangladesh (HUJI-B)

Other names: Islami Dawat-e-Kafela, Harakat ul-Jihad e Islami Bangladesh, Harkatul Jihad al Islam, Harkatul Jihad, Harakat ul Jihad al Islami, Harkat ul Jihad al Islami, Harkat-ul-Jehad-al-Islami, Harakat ul Jihad Islami Bangladesh.

Background: HUJI-B, designated as an international terrorist organization by DOS in February 2008, is based in Bangladesh. The group is a hard-line Islamist organization targeting government figures and security forces. Its methods include bombings and grenade attacks.

Recent activity: On April 16, 2009, Mufti Abdul Hannan and 13 other militants were charged with murder over a bombing in 2001 that killed 10 and injured many more. Hannan was the leader of HUJI-B.

Harakat ul-Mujahadeen (HUM)

Other names: Al-Faran, Al-Hadid, Al-Hadith, Harakat ul-Ansar, Harakat ul-Mujahideen, Harakat ul-Mujahadin, Jamiat ul-Ansar.

Background: HUM is an Islamic militant group based in Pakistan. It operates primarily in the disputed Kashmir region, where it has conducted numerous operations against Indian troops and civilian targets. However, activity involving HUM members spreads across the Middle East, Asia, and Europe. There are apparent links between HUM and the Pakistani secret service.

Recent activity: In 2005 the Pakistani press reported that Badr Munir had become the new head of HUM. Based on a secret report submitted by regional police to Pakistan-administered Kashmir authorities, the BBC reported in June 2009 that HUM together with Jaish-e-Mohammad and Lashkar-e-Taiba are expanding their activities in Kashmir.[6]

Hizballah (Party of God)

Other names: Islamic Jihad, Islamic Jihad Organization, Revolutionary Justice Organization, Organization of the Oppressed on Earth, Islamic Jihad for the Liberation of Palestine, Organization of Right against Wrong, Ansar alla, and Followers of the Prophet Muhammed. The group is also commonly spelled Hizbollah

Background: Hizballah was formed in 1982 in response to the Israeli invasion of Lebanon. The group has strong links to Iran and Syria and is guided ideologically by Iranian Supreme Leader Ali Khamenei. Hizballah remains the most technically capable terrorist group in the world, and, before 9/11, was responsible for more American deaths than any other single terrorist organization. The Lebanese government and the majority of the Arab world recognize Hizballah as a legitimate group and political party.

Recent activity: Between November 2008 and April 2009 some 50 people linked to Hizballah were arrested in Egypt on suspicion of planning attacks on government targets and Israeli tourists. In April 2009, Hizballah also admitted smuggling weapons from Egypt onto the Gaza Strip. Ahead of the June 2009 parliamentary election in Lebanon, Hizballah held talks with IMF and European Union (EU) officials.

Islamic Jihad Union (IJU)

Other names: Al-Djihad al-Islami, Dzhamaat Modzhakhedov, Islamic Jihad Group of Uzbekistan, Jama'at al-Jihad, Jamiat al-Jihad al-Islami, Jamiyat, the Jamaat Mojahadin, the Kazakh Jama'at, the Libyan Society.

Background: IJU opposes secular rule in Uzbekistan and seeks to replace it with a government based on Islamic law. IJU split from the Islamic Movement of Uzbekistan. In July 2004, the group carried out coordinated suicide bombing attacks against the U.S. and Israeli embassies and the Uzbek prosecutor general.

Recent activity: In September 2007, Germany reported having foiled an IJU plan to carry out large bomb attacks against U.S. installations. In 2008, IJU claimed responsibility for attacks on the Coalition Forces in Afghanistan. In June 2009, two men, a German of Afghani background and a Turkish national, were charged in Germany for supporting IJU.

Islamic Movement of Uzbekistan (IMU)

Background: IMU aims to overthrow the secular regime in Uzbekistan and replace it with a government based on Islamic law. The group, which has links to al-Qaeda, includes militants from Uzbekistan as well as other Central Asian countries.

Recent activity: Media reports in April 2009 noted the apparent presence of IMU operatives in the Federally Administered Tribal Areas of Pakistan. In June 2009, the press reported the arrest of nearly 18 people on terror charges; five of them were apparently trained abroad and others were involved in fighting against the Coalition Forces in Afghanistan.

Jaish-e-Mohammed (JEM; Army of Muhammad)

Other names: Army of Mohammed, Jaish-i-Mohammed, Khudamul Islam, Khuddam-ul-Islam, Kuddam e Islami, Mohammed's Army, Tehrik ul-Furqaan.

Background: JEM was formed in 2000 and is based in Pakistan. The group aims to unite the disputed Kashmir region with Pakistan, but has also declared war against the United States. The Indian government blames JEM for the December 2001 attack on the Indian Parliament.

Recent activity: In April 2009, the Indian government reported its belief that JEM was now working in cooperation with other terrorist organizations active in Kashmir. According to the BBC, JEM and HUM are planning to open madrassas (religious schools) in Kashmir.[7]

Jemaah Islamiya (JI)

Other name: Jemaah Islamiyah

Background: JI is a group based in Southeast Asia that seeks the establishment of Islamic rule across Indonesia, Malaysia, Southern Thailand,

Singapore, Brunei, and the Southern Philippines. JI was behind the 2002 and 2005 bombings in Bali, Indonesia, in which over 240 people were killed.

Recent activity: There have been various arrests of JI members since the 2005 Bali bombing. The arrested people have been accused of plotting violence against diverse targets, including Christian priests and tourist destinations. On July 17, 2009, bombs exploded at the Ritz-Carlton and Marriott hotels in Jakarta, Indonesia's capital, killing at least nine people and injuring over 50. Preliminary reports suggested that JI militants might have been behind the attack.

Kahane Chai (KC)

Other names: American Friends of the United Yeshiva, American Friends of Yeshivat Rav Meir, Committee for the Safety of the Roads, Dikuy Bogdim, Forefront of the Idea, Friends of the Jewish Idea Yeshiva, Jewish Legion, Judea Police, Judean Congress, Kach, Kahane, Kahane Lives, Kahane Tzadak, Kahane.org, Kahanetzadak.com, Kfar Tapuah Fund, Koach, Meir's Youth, New Kach Movement, Newkach.org, No'ar Meir, Repression of Traitors, State of Judea, Sword of David, Committee against Racism and Discrimination, Hatikva Jewish Identity Center, International Kahane Movement, Jewish Idea Yeshiva, Judean Legion, Judean Voice, Qomemiyut Movement, Rabbi Meir David Kahane Memorial Fund, Voice of Judea, Way of the Torah, Yeshiva of the Jewish Idea, Yeshivat Harav Meir.

Background: KC is a splinter group of Kach, a hard-line political group seeking to restore the biblical state of Israel. Kach was founded by the radical Israeli-American rabbi Meir Kahane, who was assassinated in New York in 1990. Upon Kahane's death, his son Binyamin Ze'ev Kahane established Kahane Chai ("Kahane lives" in Hebrew). Israel designated both groups as terrorist organizations in 1994. Binyamin was killed in Israel in 2000.

Recent activity: On April 7, 2005, the press reported the arrest of two Kach people suspected of planting fake bombs in Jerusalem. Kach and KC have unsuccessfully attempted to overturn their terrorist designation by the Israeli government and DOS.

Kata'ib Hizballah (KH)

Other names: Hizballah Brigades, Hizballah Brigades in Iraq, Hizballah Brigades–Iraq, Hizballah Brigades–Iraq of the Islamic Resistance in Iraq, Islamic Resistance in Iraq, Kata'ib Hezbollah, Kata'ib Hizballah fi al-Iraq, Katibat Abu Fathel Al A'abas, Katibat, Zayd Ebin Ali, Katibut Karbalah, Khata'ib Hezbollah, Khata'ib Hizballah, Khattab Hezballah.

Background: Based in Iraq, KH is believed to have been established by Iran's Qods Force, an arm of the Islamic Revolutionary Guard Corps, and has received weapons training (e.g., IEDs, arms attacks, sniper attacks, mortar attacks, and rocket attacks) and support from Hizballah. In 2007 and 2008, KH launched various attacks on the Coalition Forces. Between February and September 2008, videos showing some of those attacks were broadcast in Lebanon.

Recent activity: On July 2, 2009, the U.S. Department of the Treasury targeted Kata'ib Hizballah for threatening the peace and stability of Iraq, thereby freezing any identifiable asset under U.S. jurisdiction.

Kongra-Gel/Kurdistan Workers' Party (KGK/PKK)

Other names: Freedom and Democracy Congress of Kurdistan (KADEK), Halu Mesru Savunma Kuvveti, Kurdistan Freedom and Democracy Congress, Kurdistan People's Congress, Partiya Karkeran Kurdistan, People's Congress of Kurdistan, the People's Defense Force.

Background: KGK/PKK was formed in 1978 as a Marxist separatist organization aspiring to establish an independent Kurdish state in southeastern Turkey. However, in recent years the group has spoken more often simply of the establishment of an autonomous region. KGK/PKK-initiated attacks rose from just five in 2000 to more than 70 in 2007.

Recent activity: At the end of 2008, Turkey hit PKK targets inside Iraq. In March 2009, the Iraqi president issued a warning to PKK members using northern Iraq as a base for their attacks to lay down their arms or leave the country. Meanwhile, a Turkish military spokesperson noted the killing of up to 375 PKK members between October and December 2008.

Lashkar-e Tayyiba (LT; Army of the Righteous)

Other names: Al Mansooreen, Al Mansoorian, Army of the Pure, Army of the Pure and Righteous, Lashkar e-Toiba, Lashkar-i-Taiba, Paasban-e-Ahle-Hadis, Paasban-e-Kashmir, Paasban-i-Ahle-Hadith, Pasban-e-Ahle-Hadith, Pasban-e-Kashmir.

Background: LT was formed in the late 1980s or early 1990s as the militant wing of the Markaz Dawa ul-Irshad (MDI), a Pakistan-based extremist organization that opposed the Soviet occupation of Afghanistan during the 1980s. LT now operates chiefly from Kashmir and preaches hate toward the United States, India, and Israel.

Recent activity: The sole terrorist captured alive during the Mumbai terror siege of 2008 disclosed that LT was responsible for the operation, which resulted in 163 people killed.

Lashkar i Jhangvi (LJ; Army of Punjab)

Background: LJ is based in Pakistan and is an offshoot of the Sunni Deobandi sectarian group Sipah-i-Sahaba Pakistan. The group targets Shia religious and community leaders. LJ has links with the Taliban. In May 2006, two LJ militants suspected of involvement in the March bombing outside the U.S. Consulate in Karachi were arrested.

Recent activity: LJ militants were suspected of being involved in the attack on a police academy in Lahore on March 30, 2009, which resulted in eight cadets killed and about 100 injured. In April 2009, five men were arrested in relation to apparent planned attacks on government offices and security forces in Karachi.

Liberation Tigers of Tamil Eelam (LTTE)

Other names: Ellalan Force, Tamil Tigers.

Background: LTTE is a secessionist group formed in 1976 with the aim of establishing an independent Tamil state in the northern and eastern provinces of Sri Lanka. The group has blended a battlefield insurgent strategy with a terrorist program targeting dissident Tamils, security forces, and government officials.

Recent activity: Early in 2009, Sri Lanka's security forces launched a large operation with the intention of terminating the secession once and for all. By April 2009, LTTE combatants were cornered in an 87 sq km pocket in the northeast part of the country along with some 250,000 civilians. Amid claims by NGOs on the ground about thousands of civilians killed as a result of the fighting, on May 18, 2009, Sri Lanka declared that it was "free from terror" after Velupillai Prabhakaran, LTTE's leader, was killed by the security forces. Selvarasa Pathmanathan was reported in July 2009 to be the new leader of the organization.

Libyan Islamic Fighting Group (LIFG)

Background: Libyans who oppose the regime of Muammar al-Gaddafi (the leader of the country since a military coup in 1969) and fought Soviet forces in Afghanistan during the 1980s formed LIFG in the early 1990s. The group have attempted to assassinate al-Gaddafi on four occasions, the last time in 1998. Because of tightened security, LIFG has been largely inactive since the late 1990s and many members have fled to various Asian, Arabian Gulf, African, and European countries, particularly the UK. On November 3, 2007, senior al-Qaeda leaders announced that LIFG had officially joined them.

Recent activity: On April 8, 2009, a major antiterror raid was launched in the north of England. The 12 men arrested were apparently planning to detonate bombs over the Easter Holiday in targets including a shopping mall and a nightclub. One of the arrested men was living in a property belonging to Mohammed Benhammedi, an LIFG financer wanted by Interpol.

Moroccan Islamic Combatant Group (GICM)

Other name: Groupe Islamique Combattant Marocain

Background: GICM, formed in the 1990s, was a clandestine transnational terrorist group centered in the Moroccan diaspora communities of Western Europe. The group has disintegrated. Many of the leaders in Morocco and Europe have been killed, have been imprisoned, or are awaiting trial. It is believed that the few remaining members no longer operate on behalf of any single terrorist organization.

Recent activity: Members of GICM were among those responsible for the train bombings in Madrid on March 11, 2004, which resulted in 191 people killed and about 1,800 wounded.

Mujahedin-e Khalq Organization (MEK)

Other names: Mujahadin-e Khalq, Muslim Iranian Students' Society, National Council of Resistance, Organization of the People's Holy Warriors of Iran, National Liberation Army of Iran, People's Mujahadin Organization of Iran, National Council of Resistance of Iran, Sazeman-e Mujahadin-e Khalq-e Iran.

Background: MEK emerged in Iran in the 1960s and was one of the more violent political movements opposing the rule of Mohammad Reza Pahlavi, whose monarchy was overthrow by the Iranian Revolution on February 11, 1979. In addition to its terrorist credentials, MEK has also displayed cult-like characteristics. Maryam Rajavi, MEK's leader, claims to emulate the Prophet Muhammad and is viewed by members of the group as the "Iranian President in exile." Since 2003, about 3,400 MEK members have been at Camp Ashraf in Iraq, under the protection of the Coalition Forces; though the group maintains its main headquarters in Paris and has members across Europe. The armed wing of MEK is known as the National Liberation Army of Iran.

Recent activity: The legal status of the MEK residents at Camp Ashraf remains unusual and ambiguous.

National Liberation Army (ELN)

Other name: Ejército de Liberacion Nacional.

Background: ELN, formed in 1964, is a Colombian group inspired by Marxist ideology. ELN has minimal conventional military capabilities and engages in kidnappings, hijackings, bombings, drug-trafficking, and extortion. The group targets foreign employees of large corporations and over the years has inflicted huge damage on oil and energy infrastructure. Exploratory peace talks between the Colombian government and ELN began in Cuba in 2005, but they remain inconclusive.

Recent activity: ELN continues its campaign of low-level intimidation and crime. On March 30, 2009, the Colombian Army reported the capture of 25 ELN rebels.

Palestine Liberation Front—Abu Abbas Faction (PLF)

Other name: PLF-Abu Abbas.

Background: PLF split from the General Command of the Popular Front for the Liberation of Palestine. Subsequently, this group divided into three factions: pro-Syrian, pro-Libyan, and pro–Palestine Liberation Organization. The pro–Palestine Liberation Organization faction was based in Baghdad prior to Operation Iraqi Freedom. Abu Abbas, PLF's leader, died of natural causes while in U.S. custody in Iraq. The current leadership and membership of the relatively small PLF appear to be based in Lebanon and the Palestinian territories.

Recent activity: The PLF took part in the 2006 Palestinian parliamentarian elections, but failed to win a seat.

Palestinian Islamic Jihad—Shaqaqi Faction (PIJ)

Other names: PIJ-Shaqaqi Faction, PIJ-Shallah Faction, Islamic Jihad of Palestine, Islamic Jihad in Palestine, Abu Ghunaym Squad of the Hizballah Bayt Al-Maqdis, Al-Quds Squads, Al-Quds Brigades, Saraya Al-Quds, Al-Awdah Brigades.

Background: PIJ was formed in the 1970s by militant Palestinians in Gaza. The group aims at creating an Islamic state in historic Palestine, including Israel. PIJ has conducted numerous armed and rocket attacks on Israeli civilian and military targets, including large-scale suicide bombings.

Recent activity: During a large Israeli offensive in Gaza finishing in January 2009, there were numerous reports of suspected PIJ attacks and Israeli counterattacks.

Popular Front for the Liberation of Palestine (PFLP)

Other names: Halhul Gang, Halhul Squad, Palestinian Popular Resistance Forces, PPRF, Red Eagle Gang, Red Eagle Group, Red Eagles.

Background: PFLP is a Marxist-oriented group that broke away from the Arab Nationalist Movement in 1967. PFLP is a leading faction within the

Palestinian Liberation Organization that does not approach the Palestinian struggle religiously. The group has long accepted the concept of a two-state solution between Israel and Palestine but has opposed specific provisions of various peace initiatives.

Recent activity: At the end of December 2008, Ahmed Saadat, leader of PFLP, was sentenced to 30 years in prison by an Israeli military court. During the large Israeli offensive in Gaza finishing in January 2009, PFLP joined the fighting.

Popular Front for the Liberation of Palestine—General Command (PFLP-GC)

Background: PFLP-GC split from PFLP in 1968. Ahmad Jibril, a former captain in the Syrian Army, has led the group since its formation. PFLP-GC maintains an armed presence in several Palestinian refugee camps, has military bases in Lebanon, and maintains strong links to Syria and Iran.

Recent activity: PFLP-GC was implicated by Lebanese security officials in several rocket attacks on Israel in 2007. On May 14, 2008, a rocket fired from Gaza hit a shopping mall in Ashkelon, wounding about a dozen people. PFLP-GC claimed responsibility for the attack.

Real IRA (RIRA)

Other names: 32 County Sovereignty Committee, 32 County Sovereignty Movement, Continuity IRA, Irish Republican Prisoners Welfare Association, Real Irish Republican Army, Real Oglaigh Na Heireann.

Background: RIRA, formed in 1997, is an armed wing of the 32 County Sovereignty Movement, which seeks the removal of British forces from Northern Ireland and the unification of Northern Ireland (part of the UK) with Ireland (the country: Éire in Irish). RIRA also seeks to disrupt the Northern Ireland peace process. The worst act of terrorism RIRA has committed so far was the detonation of a massive car bomb in Omagh town on August 15, 1998, which resulted in 29 killed and about 300 injured.

Recent activity: On March 7, 2009, two British soldiers were gunned down at the gates of the Massereene Army base in Northern Ireland. RIRA was also blamed for civil disturbances in north Belfast on May 14, 2009.

Revolutionary Armed Forces of Colombia (FARC)

Other names: Fuerzas Armadas Revolucionarias de Colombia.

Background: FARC, of Marxist orientation, was formed in the early 1960s in Colombia. The group represents Latin America's oldest, largest, most capable, and best-equipped insurgency. FARC is governed by a general secretariat led by its co-founder Pedro Antonio Marín (also known as Manuel Maru-landa Velez or "Tirofijo") and is organized along military lines. The FARC has carried out numerous assassinations, bombings, mortar attacks, hijack-ings, and kidnappings aimed at political, military, and economic targets.

Recent activity: Battles between FARC rebels and Colombian security forces continue. In April 2009, the extradition of three FARC members to the United States was announced. FARC, for its part, announced the release of a soldier it had kept for 11 years. Ingrid Betancourt, a former Colombian presidential candidate abducted in February 2002, was rescued together with 14 hostages by Colombian forces on July 2, 2008. Operatives from the Israeli firm Global CST played a role in the planning of the operation.

Revolutionary Nuclei (RN)

Other names: Revolutionary Cells, ELA, Epanastatiki Pirines, Epanastatikos Laikos Agonas, June 78, Liberation Struggle, Organization of Revolutionary Internationalist Solidarity, Popular Revolutionary Struggle, Revolutionary People's Struggle, Revolutionary Popular Struggle.

Background: RN was formed from a broad range of leftist and antiestab-lishment (anti-United States, anti-NATO, and anti-EU) factions active in Greece between 1995 and 1998. The group is believed to be an offshoot of or the successor to the Revolutionary People's Struggle, which has not claimed responsibility for attacks since January 1995. The modus operandi of RN in-cludes calls warning of impending attacks, attacks targeting property instead of individuals, use of rudimentary timing devices, and strikes taking place from the late evening to early morning hours.

Recent activity: The last confirmed RN attack on American interests in Greece apparently occurred in November 2000, when the Athens offices of Citigroup and the studio of a Greek-American sculptor were targeted.

Revolutionary Organization 17 November (17N)

Other names: Epanastatiki Organosi 17 Noemvri, 17 November.

Background: 17N was formed in Greece in 1975. Its name derives from the November 1973 student uprising in protest against the Greek military junta (1967–1974). It is an antiestablishment group seeking the severing of Greece's ties to NATO and the EU, the removal of U.S. military bases from Greece, and the withdrawal of Turkish military forces from Cyprus. 17N's ini-tial attacks were assassinations of senior American officials and Greek public figures. Five American diplomatic employees have been murdered since 17N began its terrorist activities in 1975. The group began bombings in the 1980s. In the 1990s, improvised rocket attacks were added and the targets expanded to include Turkish diplomats, EU facilities, and foreign firms.

Recent activity: Greece authorities claim that 17N was dismantled in the run-up to the 2004 Olympics, when its leader and several key figures were convicted.

Revolutionary People's Liberation Party/Front (DHKP/C)

Other names: Dev Sol, Dev Sol Armed Revolutionary Units, Dev Sol Silahli Devrimci Birlikleri, Dev Sol SDB, Devrimci Halk Kurtulus Partisi-Cephesi, Devrimci Sol, Revolutionary Left.

Background: DHKP/C was formed in 1978 in Turkey as a splinter faction of Dev Genc (Revolutionary Youth) and was originally called Devrimci Sol or Dev Sol. It was renamed DHKP/C in 1994. The group, inspired by Marxist ideology, is anti-United States, anti-NATO, and anti-Turkish establishment. Its goals include the creation of a socialist state in Turkey. The group has targeted current and retired Turkish security and military officials, as well as U.S. military and diplomatic personnel and facilities. It is believed that DHKP/C has training facilities or offices in Lebanon and Syria and a large support network throughout Europe.

Recent activity: An intensification of operations against DHKP/C and arrests of members over the last few years has weakened its capabilities.

Revolutionary Struggle (RS)

Background: RS publicly emerged in 2003, when it detonated bombs at the Evelpidon Court of Law in central Athens where 17N members were on trial. The group appears to have added antiglobalization to 17N's aims as a leftist antiestablishment and anti-American group. In May 2004, before the Athens Olympics, bombs were exploded outside a police station and a bank in Athens; messages that were left stated that "rich Western Olympic tourists" were not welcome. On January 12, 2007, the U.S. Embassy in Athens was hit by a rocket. Similar attacks have followed. However, it is not certain to what extent RS is a centralized organization or a disperse system of anarchist cells using copy-cat tactics and similar far-left slogans. RS was designated a terrorist organization by DOS only on April 22, 2009.

Recent activity: In January 2009, semiautomatic weapons were used in attacks on police officers. On June 22, 2009, RS claimed responsibility for the murder of Nektarios Savas, a police officer guarding a witness in a far-left militant's trial. RS militants were also suspected of being behind bomb attacks on a tax office and a McDonald's restaurant in Athens in July 2009.

Shining Path (SL)

Other names: Sendero Luminoso, Ejército Guerrillero Popular (People's Guerrilla Army), Ejército Popular de Liberacion (People's Liberation Army),

Partido Comunista del Peru (Communist Party of Peru), Partido Comunista del Peru en el Sendero Luminoso de José Carlos Mariátegui (Communist Party of Peru on the Shining Path of Jose Carlos Mariategui), Socorro Popular del Peru (People's Aid of Peru).

Background: SL, inspired by a Maoist ideology, was formed in Peru in the late 1960s by former university professor Abimael Guzmán. The group's stated goal is to destroy existing Peruvian institutions and replace them with a communist peasant revolutionary regime. In the past, particularly during the 1980s, SL carried out indiscriminate bombing campaigns, ambushes, and assassinations. In the 1990s, the Peruvian government made important gains against the group. Remnants of SL now focus on drug-trafficking activities as means to obtain funds for further attacks.

Recent activity: Early in April 2009, SL guerillas killed 14 soldiers on patrol in ambush attacks. The attacks, preceded by a dozen similar ambushes since the beginning of the year, took place in the remote cocaine-growing region of Ayacucho.

United Self-Defense Forces of Colombia (AUC)

Other names: Autodefensas Unidas de Colombia, Los Paramilitares.

Background: AUC was formed in Colombia in 1997 as an umbrella structure bringing together paramilitary groups fighting leftist guerillas. AUC is sometimes referred to in Colombia simply as Los Paramilitares. The allusion originates in the various paramilitary groups formed since the 1980s to retaliate against kidnappings and extortion by guerillas. However, AUC progressively shifted its focus from counter-guerrilla to drug- and crime-related activities. Over 30,000 paramilitary members and support personnel were demobilized between 2003 and 2006 as part of a peace deal. Colombia now faces criminal groups formed by demobilized paramilitaries, those who refused to demobilize, and new recruits.

Recent activity: On April 15, 2009, Daniel Rendón (alias Don Mario) was arrested. While he was one of the most wanted drug lords in Colombia, he was also one of the AUC paramilitaries who refused to demobilize. In July 2009, the Colombian press reported that prosecutors have obtained confessions with regard to some 21,000 crimes committed by over 600 demobilized AUC members between 1987 and 2005.

Mexican Drug-Trafficking Organizations

Drug-trafficking organizations are found wherever the drug trade meets demand or supply. They vary in size and sophistication. However, historically the most powerful organizations have originated in South America, particularly Colombia. In the 1980s and 1990s, the Cali and Medellin cartels controlled the traffic into the United States. They were dismantled in the 1990s. Mexico became the key transit hub for drugs bound for the North American market and Mexican drug-trafficking organizations came of age. There is ongoing fighting between Mexican security forces and drug cartels, as well as between and within cartels for control of turf and the trade. Mexican drug-trafficking organizations are likely to dominate the headlines over the next decade. Therefore, it seems relevant to profile the main cartels in order to understand what they are and what is at stake. While Mexican authorities identify eight cartels as being behind drug-trafficking in Mexico (Colima, La Familia, Gulf, Juarez, Oaxaca, Sinaloa, Tijuana, and Valencia), other reports detail other organizations. The list below, compiled from information available as of July 2009, covers those eight cartels in addition to the Beltran Leyva Organization and the Zambada Cartel.

Beltran Leyva Organization

Other names: Organización de Beltrán Leyva, Beltran Leyva Cartel, Cartel de Beltrán Leyva, Grupo de Beltrán Leyva, Beltran Leyva Brothers' Organization, Beltran Leyva Brothers' Cartel, Organización de los Hermanos Beltrán Leyva, Grupo de los Hermanos Beltrán Leyva, Cartel de los Hermanos Beltrán Leyva (also spelled Beltrán-Leyva).

Background: The Beltran Leyva Organization can be approached either as a paramilitary force or, more recently, as a drug-trafficking organization. Either way, it largely involves a group based in the northwestern state of Sinaloa and led by the brothers Marco Arturo, Hector Alfredo, Mario Alberto, and Carlos Beltrán Leyva.

The paramilitary force is commonly associated with Marco Arturo and Hector Alfredo. The force, called the Negros and led by Edgar Valdez Villarreal from Laredo, Texas, was created to help the Sinaloa Cartel counteract the advances of the Gulf Cartel and its paramilitary force, the Zetas. The Sinaloa and the Gulf cartels are in an ongoing fight for control of the border region as well as turf in inner Mexico in alliance with other drug-trafficking organizations.

Hector Alfredo, "El Mochomo," was arrested in January 2008. On May 30, 2008, the Beltran Leyva Organization and Marcos Arturo, the presumed head of the organization, were designated under the Foreign Narcotics Kingpin Designation Act (the Kingpin Act). Kingpin Act designations work by freezing the identifiable assets of the designated persons and cutting them off from the financial system within the U.S.'s area of jurisdiction.

The designation followed the apparent splitting off of the Beltran Leyva Organization from the Sinaloa Cartel and its possible emergence as an independent operation. However, other reports suggest that an alliance with the Gulf Cartel might have been forged.

Colima Cartel

Other names: Cartel de Colima, Amezcua Contreras Organization, Amezcua Contreras Cartel, Organización de Amezcua Contreras, Grupo de Amezcua Contreras, Cartel de Amezcua Contreras, Amezcua Contreras Brothers' Organization, Amezcua Contreras Brothers' Cartel, Organización de los Hermanos Amezcua Contreras, Cartel de los Hermanos Amezcua Contreras (sometimes spelled Amezcua-Contreras).

Background: The Colima Cartel was established in the late 1980s by the brothers José de Jesús, Adán, and Luis Ignacio Amezcua Contreras. It was based in Colima, a coastal state in the western part of Mexico, and focused on the traffic in methamphetamine The fact that the focus of the Colima Cartel did not interfere with the cocaine trade exploited by most Mexican trafficking organizations at the time facilitated its consolidation.

José de Jesús, the presumed head of the Colima Cartel, and Luis Ignacio were arrested in June 1998. Adán became the new leader, but he was arrested in May 2001. The Colima Cartel appears to continue controlling the methamphetamine traffic in Western Mexico and the largest cities (Mexico City, Guadalajara, and Monterrey), as well as controlling the supply of methamphetamine to international networks.

La Familia

Other names: The Family, La Familia Michoacana, The Michoacana Family. The group was previously known as La Empresa or The Enterprise.

Background: La Familia is a drug-trafficking organization that has had a meteoric rise since 2006.

The best way to describe its origins is by establishing a parallel with the United Self-Defense Forces of Colombia (AUC), a designated international terrorist organization profiled above. AUC emerged in 1997 and brought together paramilitary factions targeting leftist guerrillas in Colombia. Some of these factions evolved into drug-trafficking organizations and their leaders into drug lords.

Likewise, La Familia surfaced under the guise of a vigilante force seemingly targeting the trafficking organizations engaged in the production and trafficking of methamphetamine in Michoacan, particularly the Sinaloa Cartel, the Beltran Leyva Organization, the Gulf Cartel, and the Zetas. However, La Familia has also added to its operations religious fanaticism, far-right and antipoverty rhetoric, and borrowing from the conflict in Iraq, gruesome decapitations that are sometimes broadcast on the Internet.

Three of the leading figures behind La Familia are believed to be Nazario "El Chayo" Moreno, José de Jesús "El Chango" Mendez Vargas, and Servando "La Tuta" Gómez Martínez.

There is currently intense fighting for the control of the drug trade in the state of Michoacan by various trafficking organizations, with La Familia and the Zetas dominating the violent upsurge. At the same time, La Familia appears to be spreading its mantle throughout central Mexico, including the state of Guanajuato and parts of Mexico City. It is uncertain whether the growing numbers of killings in various parts of Mexico attributed to a force called the Mata Zetas (Kill Zetas) represent another facet of La Familia or a new paramilitary force. Either way, vigilante violence linked to drug-trafficking, in fact or as a propaganda tool, is new to the Mexican experience.

Gulf Cartel

Other names: Cartel del Golfo, Osiel Cardenas Guillen Organization, Osiel Cardenas Cartel, Grupo de Osiel Cárdenas Guillén, Organización de Osiel Cárdenas Guillén, Cartel de Osiel Cárdenas Guillén, Cardenas Guillen Organization, Cardenas Guillen Cartel, Organización Cárdenas Guillén, Grupo Cárdenas Guillén, Cartel Cárdenas Guillén, Cardenas Guillen Brothers' Organization, Cardenas Guillen Brothers' Cartel, Organización de los Hermanos Cárdenas Guillén, Grupo de los Hermanos Cárdenas Guillén, Cartel de los Hermanos Cárdenas Guillén (also spelled Cardenas-Guillen).

Background: The origins of the Gulf Cartel appear to be found in the smuggling operations into the United States (mostly spirits) run by Juan Nepomuceno Guerra from the 1930s or 1940s onward. In the 1970s, he entered drug-trafficking, mostly focusing on marijuana. He started trading in Colombian cocaine in the 1980s, when the organization now known as the Gulf Cartel emerged. Nepomuceno Guerra died in 2001, though his nephew Juan García Abrego had taken control of the Cartel sometime in the 1980s.

García Abrego was arrested and extradited to the United States in 1996. The last major leader of the cartel was Osiel Cárdenas Guillén, who was arrested in 2003. With assistance from his brother Ezequiel Cárdenas Guillen, he continued running operations from prison in Mexico until he was extradited to the United States in 2007. Meanwhile, turf competition between the Gulf and Sinaloa cartels intensified, which persuaded the Cárdenas Guillén brothers to form a paramilitary force called the Zetas. The Zetas comprise former elite Mexican soldiers as well as recruits from Centro America, particularly Guatemala.

The historical base of operations of the Gulf Cartel is Matamoros, a border town that is the neighbor of Brownsville, Texas. However, the cartel exerts control over the border strip across Texas, which covers the cities of Reynosa (opposite McAllen, Texas) and Nuevo Laredo (opposite Laredo, Texas). In addition, the cartel controls traffic across the Gulf of Mexico and parts of central Mexico. In Central Mexico, a turf war with La Familia has been escalating since 2008.

From Colombia to Europe, the Gulf Cartel has established a vast international trafficking network. The Cartel and the Zetas also engage in kidnappings and extortion. On September 15, 2008, they escalated their violent campaign by throwing grenades into a crowd gathered to celebrate Independence Day in Morelia, Michoacan's capital; eight people were killed and several injured. However, the Gulf Cartel blames La Familia for the attack.

Juarez Cartel

Other names: Cartel de Juarez, Amado Carrillo Fuentes Organization, Amado Carrillo Fuentes Cartel, Organización de Amado Carrillo Fuentes, Cartel de Amado Carrillo Fuentes, Grupo de Amado Carrillo Fuentes, Carrillo Fuentes Organization, Carrillo Fuentes Cartel, Organización Carrillo Fuentes, Grupo Carrillo Fuentes, Cartel Carrillo Fuentes (also spelled Carrillo-Fuentes), La Alianza Triángulo de Oro, Golden Triangle Alliance.

Background: The Juarez Cartel surfaced in the 1980s and was established by Amado Carrillo Fuentes, who died while undergoing plastic surgery in 1997. He had extensive links with Colombian drug lords and became known as "El Señor de Los Cielos" (the Lord of the Skies) due to the private air wing the cartel used to transport cocaine.

Upon the death of Amado Carrillo Fuentes, there was infighting within the cartel for control as well as with the competing Sinaloa Cartel for turf. While some factions of the Juarez Cartel defected to the Sinaloa Cartel, Ricardo García Urquiza together with Vicente Carrillo Fuentes, brother of the founder of the cartel, took control. However, other reports argue that Juan Jose Esparragoza "El Azul" Moreno was the leader of the cartel until 2004. Nevertheless, upon the arrest of Ricardo García Urquiza in November 2005, Vicente Carrillo Fuentes became the sole leader of the Juarez Cartel. Vicente Carillo Leyva, son of Amado Carrillo Fuentes, is also at the top of the hierarchy.

In 2007, the chief of the Instituto Nacional para el Combate a las Drogas, the national counter-narcotics law enforcement agency, was arrested for operating as an informant for the Juarez Cartel.

The base of operation of the Juarez Cartel is Ciudad Juarez, Chihuahua. Ciudad Juarez is a border town next to El Paso, Texas, strategically located at the center of the border region and bordering New Mexico. Some analysts estimate that up to 40 percent of the cocaine passing through Mexico is controlled by the Juarez Cartel. In addition, the cartel controls an extensive national network covering roughly two-thirds of Mexico.

Oaxaca Cartel

Other names: Cartel de Oaxaca, Istmo Cartel, Cartel del Istmo, Pedro Diaz Parada Organization, Organización de Pedro Díaz Parada, Parada Brothers' Cartel, Parada Brothers' Organization, Organización de los Hermanos Parada, Grupo de los Hermanos Parada, Cartel de los Hermanos Parada.

Background: The Oaxaca Cartel was established by Pedro Díaz Parada in the 1970s and based around the rural communities of San Pedro Totolapa and Santa Maria Zoquitlan in Oaxaca. The cartel originally exerted control over the cultivation and trade of marijuana in the southwestern states of Oaxaca and Guerrero, and subsequently throughout southern Mexico (covering also Chiapas, Tabasco, and southern Veracruz).

This region encompasses the Istmo of Tehuantepec, the narrowest part of Mexico, hence the organization is sometimes referred to as the Istmo Cartel. There are also some references to the cartel as a brothers' organization. However, it is not clear who the brothers are or which roles they play.

Although the Oaxaca Cartel remains a key supplier of marijuana, like other old Mexican drug-trafficking organizations it diversified into cocaine by the 1990s. It is believed the Oaxaca and the Sinaloa Cartels have been collaborating for a while.

Pedro Díaz Parada was first arrested in April 1985, but he escaped from prison a few months later dressed as a woman. In May 1990, he was rearrested, but he escaped again in January 1992. He was arrested for a third time in 2007 and remains in the custody of the federal authorities. It is not clear what are the names of the current leaders of the cartel, or whether Díaz Parada continues to run it from prison.

Sinaloa Cartel

Other names: Cartel de Sinaloa, Guzman Loera Organization, Guzman Loera Cartel, Organización de Guzmán Loera, Grupo de Guzmán Loera, Cartel de Guzmán Loera, Pacific Cartel, Cartel del Pacífico.

Background: The origins of the Sinaloa Cartel are linked to the disintegration of the Guadalajara Cartel in the early 1990s.

The Guadalajara Cartel was established in the 1980s by Rafael Caro Quintero and Miguel Angel Félix Gallardo. It was perhaps the first Mexican drug-trafficking organization to establish close links with Colombian cartels for the large-scale trafficking of cocaine and heroin. Caro Quintero killed a Drug Enforcement Administration (DEA) agent in November 1984 in Mexico and escaped the country. He was arrested in Costa Rica in April 1985. Félix Gallardo was arrested in 1989. Subsequently, the Guadalajara Cartel split into two factions: the Tijuana Cartel and the Sinaloa Cartel.

In the early 1990s, Héctor Luis Palma Salazar and Joaquín Archivaldo "El Chapo" Guzmán Loera led the Sinaloa Cartel. Palma Salazar was arrested in 1995. Guzmán Loera was arrested in 1993 in Guatemala and was in prison in Mexico from 1995. In 2001, Guzmán Loera escaped from prison, thereby assuming control of the Sinaloa Cartel.

Within the organization, the alliance of the brothers Arturo y Alfredo Beltrán Leyva and their paramilitary force the Negros have also figured. The force has been used to fight the advances of the Gulf Cartel in the border region, particularly around the city of Nuevo Laredo. In Mexico City, the Sinaloa Cartel uses a criminal group called the Pelones for petty crime, kidnappings, and assassinations. There have been also reports linking the Sinaloa Cartel to the activities of the Mara Salvatrucha gang, which operates in the United States, Central America, and increasingly Mexico.

Tijuana Cartel

Other names: Cartel de Tijuana, Felix Arellano Organization, Felix Arellano Cartel, Organización de Félix Arellano, Cartel de Félix Arellano, Arellano Felix Brothers' Organization, Arellano Felix Brothers' Cartel, Organización de los Hermanos Arellano Félix, Grupo de los Hermanos Arellano Félix, Cartel de los Hermanos Arellano Félix.

Background: After the arrest of Miguel Angel Félix Gallardo (the last leader of the Guadalajara Cartel) in 1989, the faction led by his nephew Ramón Eduardo Arellano Félix took control of trafficking into California and established as its base of operations the city of Tijuana, which is a neighbor of San Diego, California.

Ramón Eduardo Arellano Félix is one of a family of seven brothers (Francisco Rafael, Benjamin, Carlos Alberto, Eduardo, Ramón Eduardo, Luis Fernando, and Francisco Javier) and four sisters. All of them have been involved in the running of the Tijuana Cartel.

Ramón Eduardo died in a confrontation with Mexican security forces in Mazatlan in February 2002. Benjamin was arrested in March 2002 (though in July 2009 he was still listed by the DEA, San Diego Division, as a wanted fugitive, with La Palma Federal Penitentiary in Mexico recorded as his last known address). Francisco Javier was arrested by U.S. authorities in August 2006. Francisco Rafael was extradited to the United States in 2006 and released in 2008; he returned to Mexico. Eduardo was arrested in October 2008.

Carlos Alberto and Luis Fernando have evaded capture. In addition, the four Arellano Félix sisters and members of the extended family are involved in the operation of the cartel.

Among other noteworthy reports on the trafficking activities of the Tijuana Cartel is the fact that since the 1990s over 100 underground tunnels running between Mexico and the United States (used to smuggle drugs and people into the United States and arms into Mexico) have been uncovered.

Valencia Cartel

Other names: Cartel de Valencia, The Valencia, Los Valencia, Cartel del Milenio, Millennium Cartel.

Background: The Valencia Cartel was established at the end of the 1990s and is based in the state of Michoacan. Its leader was Armando Valencia Cornelio until his arrest in August 2003. Thereafter, Luis Valencia Valencia assumed control. It appears to be a family-run cartel. However, there are conflicting reports as to its precise leadership structure.

The rural communities of the state of Michoacan have been since the 1980s important areas of production of marijuana and opium poppy plants, and the Michoacan coast is an important transit post for South American cocaine. There are also numerous clandestine laboratories synthesizing methamphetamine and processing opiates. The important port of Lazaro Cardenas also figures in trafficking activities. Zhenli Ye Gon, a man of Chinese origin who became a Mexican in 2002, was arrested in 2007. He was involved in methamphetamine production and imported the chemicals needed through the port.

The importance of Michoacan in the drug trade has put the state at the center of a turf battle between the Valencia and Gulf cartels since the beginning of the 21st century. In 2002, Jorge Luis Valencia Gonzalez, nephew of Armando Valencia, was assassinated by members of the Gulf Cartel's paramilitary force, the Zetas. Apparently an alliance was forged afterward between the Valencia and the Sinaloa cartels to fight the attempts of the Gulf Cartel to dominate the region. The fighting has intensified with the rise of La Familia since 2006.

Zambada Cartel

Other names: Cartel de Zambada, Ismael Zambada Garcia Organization, Organización de Ismael Zambada García, Grupo de Ismael Zambada García.

Background: It is unclear from the information available whether the so-called Zambada Cartel can be approached as a drug-trafficking organization in its own right or whether it is simply a glorified faction within the Sinaloa Cartel.

When Joaquín Archivaldo "El Chapo" Guzmán Loera assumed control of the Sinaloa Cartel in 2001, Ismael "El Mayo" Zambada García started to play a key role in the Sinaloa Cartel. Nevertheless, Zambada García appears to control trafficking operations both in Mexico and in the United States and is said to maintain direct links with Colombian drug lords.

Zambada García continues to collaborate with the Sinaloa Cartel. However, his designation under the Kingpin Act in May 2007, together with the money-laundering organization managed by his daughters, has strengthened the view of his network as a distinctive component in Mexican drug-trafficking.

Notes

1. Ike Skelton, "Letter to the Honorable Donald H. Rumsfeld," Secretary of Defense (Washington, DC, April 2, 2004).

2. Donald H. Rumsfeld, "Letter to the Honorable Ike Skelton, Ranking Minority Member, Committee on Armed Services, U.S. House of Representatives" (Washington, DC, May 4, 2004).

3. See Department of State, *Country Reports on Terrorism 2008* (Washington, DC: Department of State, April 2009); and *Country Reports on Terrorism 2007* (Washington, DC: Department of State, April 2008).

4. Independent Monitoring Commission (UK and Ireland), *Twenty-First Report of the Independent Monitoring Commission* (London: Stationery Office, May 7, 2009), 6.

5. See "Transcript: FT Interview with Deputy Chief of Hizbollah," *Financial Times*, May 12, 2009.

6. Syed Shoaib Hasan, "Banned Pakistani Groups 'expand,'" *BBC*, June 30, 2009.

7. Ibid.

Documents

Arms Export Control Act

The Arms Export Control Act (AECA) comprises Chapter 39 of Title 22, Foreign Relations and Intercourse, of the *United States Code*. The *Code* codifies the permanent laws of the United States. The following excerpts have been compiled from the 2006 edition of the *Code*.

Subchapter III. Military Export Controls

Section 2778: Control of arms exports and imports:

(a) (1)...the President is authorized to control the import and the export of defense articles and defense services and to provide foreign policy guidance to persons of the United States involved in the export and import of such articles and services. The President is authorized to designate those items which shall be considered as defense articles and defense services for the purposes of this section and to promulgate regulations for the import and export of such articles and services. The items so designated shall constitute the United States Munitions List.

(f) (1) The President shall periodically review the items on the United States Munitions List to determine what items, if any, no longer warrant export controls under this section.

(b) (1) (A)(i)...every person (other than an officer or employee of the United States Government acting in an official capacity) who engages in the business of manufacturing, exporting, or importing any defense articles or defense services designated by the President under subsection (a)(1) of this section shall register with the United States Government agency charged with the administration of this section, and shall pay a registration fee which shall be prescribed by such regulations.

(c) Any person who willfully violates any provision of this section or section 2779 [Fees of military sales agents] of this title, or any rule or regulation issued under either section, or who willfully, in a registration or license application or required report, makes any untrue statement of a material fact or omits to state a material fact required to be stated therein or necessary to make the statements therein not misleading, shall upon conviction be fined for each violation not more than $1,000,000 or imprisoned not more than ten years, or both.

Subchapter IV. General, Administrative, and Miscellaneous Provisions

Section 2794. Definitions:
(3) "defense article,"... includes—

(A) any weapon, weapons system, munition, aircraft, vessel, boat, or other implement of war.

(4) "defense service"... includes any service, test, inspection, repair, training, publication, technical or other assistance, or defense information (as defined in section 2403(e) of this title), used for the purposes of making military sales, but does not include design and construction services under section 2769 of this title.

(5) "training" includes formal or informal instruction of foreign students in the United States or overseas by officers or employees of the United States, contract technicians, or contractors (including instruction at civilian institutions), or by correspondence courses, technical, educational, or information publications and media of all kinds, training aid, orientation, training exercise, and military advice to foreign military units and forces.

International Traffic in Arms Regulations

The International Traffic in Arms Regulations (ITAR) are contained in parts 120 to 130 of title 22, Foreign Relations, of the *Code of Federal Regulations*. The following extracts are from the version last revised in April 2009.

Sec. 120.1 General authorities and eligibility

(a)...The statutory authority of the President to promulgate regulations with respect to exports of defense articles and defense services was delegated to the Secretary of State by

Executive Order 11958, as amended.... By virtue of delegations of authority by the Secretary of State, these regulations are primarily administered by the Deputy Assistant Secretary for Defense Trade Controls and Managing Director of Defense Trade Controls, Bureau of Political-Military Affairs.

(c) Eligibility. Only U.S. persons (as defined in Sec. 120.15) and foreign governmental entities in the United States may be granted licenses or other approvals (other than retransfer approvals sought pursuant to this subchapter). Foreign persons (as defined in Sec. 120.16) other than governments are not eligible.

Sec. 121.1 General. The United States Munitions List

(a)...Changes in designations will be published in the Federal Register. Information and clarifications on whether specific items are defense articles and services under this subchapter may appear periodically through the Internet Web site of the Directorate of Defense Trade Controls.

Sec. 122.1 Registration requirements

(a) Any person who engages in the United States in the business of either manufacturing or exporting defense articles or furnishing defense services is required to register with the Directorate of Defense Trade Controls.

Sec. 122.3 Registration fees

(a) A person who is required to register must do so on an annual basis upon submission of a completed Form DS-2032, transmittal letter, and payment of a fee as follows:

(1) Tier 1: A set fee of $2,250 per year is required for new registrants or registrants for whom the Directorate of Defense Trade Controls has not reviewed, adjudicated or issued a response to any applications during a 12-month period ending 90 days prior to expiration of the current registration.

Sec. 123.1 Requirement for export or temporary import licenses

(a) Any person who intends to export or to import temporarily a defense article must obtain the approval of the Directorate of Defense Trade Controls prior to the export or temporary import, unless the export or temporary import qualifies for an exemption under the provisions of this subchapter.

Sec.127.1 Violations

(a) It is unlawful: (1) To export or attempt to export from the United States, or to reexport or retransfer or attempt to reexport or retransfer from one foreign destination to another foreign destination by a U.S. person of any defense article or technical data or by anyone of any U.S. origin defense article or technical data or to furnish any defense service for which a license or written approval is required by this subchapter without first obtaining the required license or written approval from the Directorate of Defense Trade Controls.

Uniformed Code of Military Justice

The Uniformed Code of Military Justice (UCMJ) is contained in Title 10, Armed Forces, Chapter 47 of the *United States Code*. UCMJ, effective since 1951, applies to all branches of the forces and is administered by military authorities through a court martial system. The following excerpts have been compiled from the 2006 edition of the *Code*.

Sec. 101. Definitions

(a) (13) The term "contingency operation" means a military operation that—

(A) is designated by the Secretary of Defense as an operation in which members of the armed forces are or may become involved in military actions, operations, or hostilities against an enemy of the United States or against an opposing military force.

Sec. 802 Art. 2. Persons subject to this chapter

(a) (1) Members of a regular component of the armed forces, including those awaiting discharge after expiration of their terms of enlistment; volunteers from the time of their muster or acceptance into the armed forces; inductees from the time of their actual induction into the armed forces; and other persons lawfully called or ordered into, or to duty in or for training in, the armed forces, from the dates when they are required by the terms of the call or order to obey it.

(10) In time of declared war or a contingency operation, persons serving with or accompanying an armed force in the field.

Sec. 803. Art. 3. Jurisdiction to try certain personnel

(a)...a person who is in a status in which the person is subject to this chapter and who committed an offense against this chapter while formerly in a status in which the person was subject to this chapter is not relieved from amenability to the jurisdiction of this chapter for that offense by reason of a termination of that person's former status.

Sec. 807. Art. 7. Apprehension

(a) Apprehension is the taking of a person into custody.

(b) Any person authorized under regulations governing the armed forces to apprehend persons subject to this chapter or to trial thereunder may do so upon reasonable belief that an offense has been committed and that the person apprehended committed it.

Sec. 814. Art. 14. Delivery of offenders to civil authorities

(a) Under such regulations as the Secretary concerned may prescribe, a member of the armed forces accused of an offense against civil authority may be delivered, upon request, to the civil authority for trial.

Sec. 817. Art. 17. Jurisdiction of courts-martial in general

(a) Each armed force has court-martial jurisdiction over all persons subject to this chapter. The exercise of jurisdiction by one armed force over personnel of another armed force shall be in accordance with regulations prescribed by the President.

Sec. 825. Art. 25. Who may serve on courts-martial

(a) Any commissioned officer on active duty is eligible to serve on all courts-martial for the trial of any person who may lawfully be brought before such courts for trial.

Sec. 832. Art. 32. Investigation

(a) No charge or specification may be referred to a general court-martial for trial until a thorough and impartial investigation of all the matters set forth therein has been made. This investigation shall include inquiry as to the truth of the matter set forth in the charges, consideration of the form of charges, and a recommendation as to the disposition which should be made of the case in the interest of justice and discipline.

Sec. 877. Art. 77. Principals

Any person punishable under this chapter who—

(1) commits an offense punishable by this chapter, or aids, abets, counsels, commands, or procures its commission; or
(2) causes an act to be done which if directly performed by him would be punishable by this chapter.

Military Extraterritorial Jurisdiction Act

The Military Extraterritorial Jurisdiction Act (MEJA) of 2000 is contained in Title 18, Crimes and Criminal Procedure, Part II, Criminal Procedure, Chapter 212 of the *United States Code*. The following excerpts have been compiled from the 2006 edition of the *Code*.

Sec. 3261. Criminal offenses committed by certain members of the Armed Forces and by persons employed by or accompanying the Armed Forces outside the United States

(a) Whoever engages in conduct outside the United States that would constitute an offense punishable by imprisonment for more than 1 year if the conduct had been engaged in within the special maritime and territorial jurisdiction of the United States—

  (1) while employed by or accompanying the Armed Forces outside the United States; or

  (2) while a member of the Armed Forces subject to chapter 47 of title 10 (the Uniform Code of Military Justice),

Sec. 3267. Definitions

   ...(1) The term "employed by the Armed Forces outside the United States" means—

(A) employed as—

  (i) a civilian employee of—

    (I) the Department of Defense (including a nonappropriated fund instrumentality of the Department); or

    (II) any other Federal agency, or any provisional authority, to the extent such employment relates to supporting the mission of the Department of Defense overseas;

  (ii) a contractor (including a subcontractor at any tier) of—

    (I) the Department of Defense (including a nonappropriated fund instrumentality of the Department); or

    (II) any other Federal agency, or any provisional authority, to the extent such employment relates to supporting the mission of the Department of Defense overseas; or

  (iii) an employee of a contractor (or subcontractor at any tier) of—

    (I) the Department of Defense (including a nonappropriated fund instrumentality of the Department); or (II) any other Federal agency, or any provisional authority, to the extent such employment relates to supporting the mission of the Department of Defense overseas;

(B) present or residing outside the United States in connection with such employment; and

(C) not a national of or ordinarily resident in the host nation.

Sec. 3265. Initial proceedings

(a)(1) In the case of any person arrested for or charged with a violation of section 3261(a) who is not delivered to authorities of a foreign country under section 3263, the initial appearance of that person under the Federal Rules of Criminal Procedure—

(A) shall be conducted by a Federal magistrate judge; and
(B) may be carried out by telephony or such other means that enables voice communication among the participants, including any counsel representing the person.

International Convention against the Recruitment, Use, Financing and Training of Mercenaries

The *International Convention against the Recruitment, Use, Financing and Training of Mercenaries* was opened for signature and ratification or for accession on December 4, 1989, and in accordance with UN General Assembly Resolution 44/34. The following are excerpts based on the Annex attached to that resolution.

Article 1 ...

1. A mercenary is any person who:
   (a) Is specially recruited locally or abroad in order to fight in an armed conflict;
   (b) Is motivated to take part in the hostilities essentially by the desire for private gain and, in fact, is promised, by or on behalf of a party to the conflict, material compensation substantially in excess of that promised or paid to combatants of similar rank and functions in the armed forces of that party;
   (c) Is neither a national of a party to the conflict nor a resident of territory controlled by a party to the conflict;
   (d) Is not a member of the armed forces of a party to the conflict; and
   (e) Has not been sent by a State which is not a party to the conflict on official duty as a member of its armed forces.
2. A mercenary is also any person who, in any other situation:
   (a) Is specially recruited locally or abroad for the purpose of participating in a concerted act of violence aimed at:
      (i) Overthrowing a Government or otherwise undermining the constitutional order of a State; or
      (ii) Undermining the territorial integrity of a State;
   (b) Is motivated to take part therein essentially by the desire for significant private gain and is prompted by the promise or payment of material compensation;

(c) Is neither a national nor a resident of the State against which such an act is directed;

(d) Has not been sent by a State on official duty; and

(e) Is not a member of the armed forces of the State on whose territory the act is undertaken.

Article 5

1. States Parties shall not recruit, use, finance or train mercenaries and shall prohibit such activities in accordance with the provisions of the present Convention.

Article 6

States Parties shall co-operate in the prevention of the offences set forth in the present Convention, particularly by:

(a) Taking all practicable measures to prevent preparations in their respective territories for the commission of those offences within or outside their territories, including the prohibition of illegal activities of persons, groups and organizations that encourage, instigate, organize or engage in the perpetration of such offences;

Article 12

The State Party in whose territory the alleged offender is found shall, if it does not extradite him, be obliged, without exception whatsoever and whether or not the offence was committed in its territory, to submit the case to its competent authorities for the purpose of prosecution, through proceedings in accordance with the laws of that State. Those authorities shall take their decision in the same manner as in the case of any other offence of a grave nature under the law of that State.

Article 16

The present Convention shall be applied without prejudice to:

...(b) The law of armed conflict and international humanitarian law, including the provisions relating to the status of combatant or of prisoner of war.

Montreux Document

The *Montreux Document on Pertinent International Legal Obligations and Good Practices for States Related to Operations of Private Military and Security Companies during Armed Conflict* was finalized on September 17, 2008. It is an initiative of the Government of Switzerland (Federal Department of Foreign Affairs) and the International Committee of the Red Cross endorsed by several states, including the United States. It aims at creating global standards of operation for private military and security companies (PMSCs) that are respectful of international humanitarian law. The following are excerpts from the *Montreux Document*.

Part One: Pertinent International Legal Obligations Relating to Private Military and Security Companies

E. PMSCs and Their Personnel

22. PMSCs are obliged to comply with international humanitarian law or human rights law imposed upon them by applicable national law, as well as other applicable national law such as criminal law, tax law, immigration law, labour law, and specific regulations on private military or security services.

25. If they are civilians under international humanitarian law, the personnel of PMSCs may not be the object of attack, unless and for such time as they directly participate in hostilities.

F. Superior Responsibility

27. Superiors of PMSC personnel, such as

a) governmental officials, whether they are military commanders or civilian superiors, or
b) directors or managers of PMSCs,may be liable for crimes under international law committed by PMSC personnel under their effective authority and control, as a result of their failure to properly exercise control over them, in accordance with the rules of international law. Superior responsibility is not engaged solely by virtue of a contract.

Part Two: Good Practices Relating to Private Military and Security Companies

A. Good practices for Contracting States

IV. Terms of Contract with PMSCs

14. To include contractual clauses and performance requirements that ensure respect for relevant national law, international humanitarian law and human rights law by the contracted PMSC. Such clauses, reflecting and

implementing the quality indicators referred to above as selection criteria, may include:

a) past conduct (good practice 6);
b) financial and economic capacity (good practice 7);
c) possession of required registration, licenses or authorisations (good practice 8);
d) personnel and property records (good practice 9);
e) training (good practice 10);
f) lawful acquisition and use of equipment, in particular weapons (good practice 11);
g) internal organisation and regulation and accountability (good practice 12);
h) welfare of personnel (good practice 13);

V. Monitoring compliance and ensuring accountability
19. To provide for criminal jurisdiction in their national legislation over crimes under international law and their national law committed by PMSCs and their personnel and, in addition, to consider establishing:

a) corporate criminal responsibility for crimes committed by the PMSC, consistent with the Contracting State's national legal system;
b) criminal jurisdiction over serious crimes committed by PMSC personnel abroad.

B. Good practices for Territorial States
IV. Criteria for granting an authorisation
35. To take into account that the PMSC's personnel are sufficiently trained, both prior to any deployment and on an ongoing basis, to respect relevant national law, international humanitarian law and human rights law; and to establish goals to facilitate uniformity and standardisation of training requirements.

C. Good practices for Home States
VI. Monitoring compliance and ensuring accountability
68. To monitor compliance with the terms of the authorisation, in particular by establishing close links between its authorities granting authorisations and its representatives abroad and/or with the authorities of the Contracting or Territorial State.

IPOA Code of Conduct

Members of the International Peace Operations Association (IPOA) are required to observe the *IPOA Code of Conduct*. The Code has gone through several revisions since its adoption on April 1, 2001. The following excerpts are from version 12, adopted on February 11, 2009.

.

1. Human Rights

1.1. Signatories shall...adhere to all applicable international humanitarian and human rights laws.

3. Accountability

3.3. Signatories shall take firm and definitive action if their personnel engage in unlawful activities. For serious infractions, such as grave breaches of international humanitarian and human rights laws, Signatories should report such offences to the relevant authorities.

4. Clients

4.1. Signatories shall only work for legitimate, recognized governments, international organizations, non-governmental organizations and lawful private companies.

6. Personnel

6.3. Signatories shall utilize adequately trained and prepared personnel in all their operations in accordance with clearly defined company standards that are appropriate and specific to their duties undertaken and the environment of operations.
6.7. Signatories shall, where appropriate, seek personnel that are broadly representative of the local population.

7. Insurance

7.1. Foreign and local personnel shall be provided with health and life insurance policies appropriate to their wage structure and the level of risk of their service as required by law.

8. Control

8.1. Signatories shall endorse the use of detailed contracts specifying the mandate, restrictions, goals, benchmarks, criteria for withdrawal and accountability for the operation.

9. Ethics

9.2.1. Signatories that could potentially become involved in armed hostilities shall have appropriate Rules for the Use of Force established with their clients before deployment, and shall work with their clients to make any necessary modifications should threat levels or the political situation merit change.

9.2.2. All Rules for the Use of Force shall be in compliance with international humanitarian and human rights laws...while preserving a person's inherent right of self-defense.

9.4. Arms Control

9.4.1. Signatories using weapons shall put the highest emphasis on accounting for and controlling all weapons and ammunition utilized during an operation and for ensuring their legal and proper accounting and disposal at the end of a contract.

11. Application and Enforcement

11.4. Signatories shall have an effective mechanism for personnel to internally report suspected breaches of international humanitarian and human rights laws and violations of other applicable laws or the IPOA Code of Conduct.

International Counterterrorism Instruments

The following 16 conventions and protocols are regarded as the key legal instruments available to criminalize acts of international terrorism. The place and date in parentheses correspond to the place in which and the date when the corresponding convention or protocol was agreed. The date an instrument entered into force does not necessarily reflect its universal application, as there are states that have not yet ratified particular conventions or protocols. The summaries offered have been compiled from each particular instrument as well as from information available from the United Nations as of July 2009. While certain key terms and legal phrases are preserved, these summaries do not incorporate verbatim extracts from each convention or protocol.

1. Convention on Offences and Certain Other Acts Committed on Board Aircraft (Tokyo, September 14, 1963)

Also known as: Aircraft Convention
Entry into force: December 4, 1969

Summary: The Aircraft Convention authorizes the commander of an aircraft to impose reasonable measures, including restraint, on any person who the commander judges has committed or is about to commit acts affecting inflight safety. An aircraft should be considered "in flight" at any moment from the time its external doors are closed upon embarkation up until the time the doors reopen for disembarkation.

2. Convention for the Suppression of Unlawful Seizure of Aircraft (The Hague, December 16, 1970)

Also known as: Unlawful Seizure Convention
Entry into force: October 14, 1971
Summary: The Unlawful Seizure Convention makes it an offense for any person onboard an aircraft to seize or exercise control of the aircraft, or to attempt to do so by force, threat to use it, or any other form of intimidation. States that are party to the convention shall either extradite or prosecute the offender(s), and make hijacking punishable by severe penalties. The convention does not apply to aircraft used in military, customs, or police services.

3. Convention for the Suppression of Unlawful Acts against the Safety of Civil Aviation (Montreal, September 23, 1971)

Also known as: Civil Aviation Convention
Entry into force: January 26, 1973
Summary: The Civil Aviation Convention makes it an offense for any person to place an explosive device on an aircraft, to attempt such acts, or to be an accomplice of a person who performs or attempts to perform such acts. The convention also makes it an offense to perform an act of violence against a person on board an aircraft in flight, if that act is likely to endanger the safety of the aircraft. States that are party to the convention shall either extradite or prosecute the offender(s), and make the offense punishable by severe penalties. The convention does not apply to aircraft used in military, customs, or police services.

4. Protocol for the Suppression of Unlawful Acts of Violence at Airports Serving International Civil Aviation, Supplementary to the Convention of 23 September 1971 for the Suppression of Unlawful Acts against the Safety of Civil Aviation (Montreal, February 24, 1988)

Also known as: Airport Protocol
Entry into force: August 6, 1989
Summary: The Airport Protocol extends the provisions set forth in the Civil Aviation Convention to cover airports serving international civil aviation.

5. Convention on the Prevention and Punishment of Crimes against Internationally Protected Persons, including Diplomatic Agents (New York, December 14, 1973)

Also known as: Diplomatic Agents Convention
Entry into force: February 20, 1977
Summary: The Diplomatic Agents Convention requires states making punishable by appropriate penalties the murder, kidnapping, other attack, or threat to commit such attacks against the person or the liberty of internationally protected persons. Internationally protected persons are heads of state or of government, ministers for foreign affairs, representatives or officials of a state or international organization who are entitled to special protection, as well as their accompanying family. States should also take all practicable measures to prevent the commission of such crimes.

6. International Convention against the Taking of Hostages (New York, December 17, 1979)

Also known as: Hostage Taking Convention
Entry into force: June 3, 1983
Summary: The Hostage Taking Convention makes it an offense for any person to commit or attempt to commit an act of "hostage-taking," or participates as an accomplice to the act. An act of hostage-taking is committed when any person seizes or detains or threatens to kill, to injure, or to continue to detain another person in order to compel a third party to do or abstain from doing any act as a condition for the release of the hostage. The third party can be a state, an international organization, a natural or juridical person, or a group of persons.

7. Convention on the Physical Protection of Nuclear Material (Vienna, October 26, 1979)

Also known as: Nuclear Materials Convention
Entry into force: February 8, 1987
Summary: The Nuclear Materials Convention applies to nuclear material used for peaceful purposes while in international nuclear transport. It requires states to make punishable by appropriate penalties the unlawful receipt, possession, use, transfer, alternation, disposal, or dispersal of nuclear material which causes or is likely to cause death or serious injury to any person, or substantial damage to property. Also punishable offenses are the theft or robbery of nuclear material, its embezzlement or fraudulent obtaining, or the demand for it by threat or use of force.

8. Amendments to the Convention on the Physical Protection of Nuclear Material (Vienna, July 8, 2005)

Also known as: Amendments to the Nuclear Materials Convention

Status: As of April, 30, 2009, the Amendments to the Nuclear Materials Convention have not entered into force.

Summary: While continuing to stress the right of states to develop and apply nuclear energy for peaceful purposes, the Amendments to the Nuclear Materials Convention aim to strengthen the legal regime by making it binding for states to protect national nuclear facilities (including associated buildings and equipment), as well as nuclear material in peaceful domestic use, storage, and transport. The Amendments do not apply to nuclear materials used or retained for military purposes, or to nuclear facilities containing such material.

9. Convention for the Suppression of Unlawful Acts against the Safety of Maritime Navigation (Rome, March 10, 1988)

Also known as: Maritime Convention; SUA 1988
Entry into force: March 1, 1992
Summary: The Maritime Convention makes it an offense for any person to seize or exercise control over a ship (any type of vessel not permanently attached to the sea-bed) by force, threat to use force, or any form of intimidation. If likely to engender the safe navigation of a ship, it is also considered an offense to perform an act of violence against a person on board; to destroy or cause damage to a ship or its cargo; to place a device or substance that is likely to destroy or cause damage to a ship or its cargo; to destroy or seriously damage navigational facilities or interferes with their operation; and to communicate information known to be false. The convention does not apply to warships, as well as ships owned or operated by states when used as naval auxiliaries or for customs or police purposes.

10. Protocol to the Convention of 10 March 1988 for the Suppression of Unlawful Acts against the Safety of Fixed Platforms Located on the Continental Shelf (Rome, March 10, 1988)

Also known as: Fixed Platform Protocol; SUA PROT 1988
Entry into force: March 1, 1992
Summary: Extends the legal regime and offenses stipulated in the Maritime Convention to cover also fixed platforms, which are defined as any artificial islands, installations, or structures permanently attached to the sea-bed for the purpose of exploration or exploitation of resources, or other economic purposes.

11. Protocol to the Convention of 10 March 1988 for the Suppression of Unlawful Acts against the Safety of Maritime Navigation (London, October 14, 2005)

Also known as: Protocol to the Maritime Convention; SUA PROT 2005
Status: As of April, 30, 2009, the Protocol to the Maritime Convention has not entered into force.

Summary: Further elaborating on the Maritime Convention's legal regime and offenses, this Protocol criminalizes the use of a ship as a device to conduct an act of terrorism; the transport on board a ship of materials likely to be used to cause death or serious injury or damage in furtherance of an act of terrorism; and the transporting on board a ship of persons who have committed an act of terrorism.

12. Protocol to the Protocol for the Suppression of Unlawful Acts against the Safety of Fixed Platforms Located on the Continental Shelf (London, October 14, 2005)

Status: As of April, 30, 2009, the Protocol of 2005 to the Fixed Platform Protocol has not entered into force.

Summary: Adapts the changes introduced by the Protocol to the Maritime Convention (SUA PROT 2005) to cover also fixed platforms. Among other stipulations, this Protocol makes it an offense for any person to discharge oil, liquefied natural gas, or other hazardous or noxious substance in such quantities or concentrations as to cause or intend to cause death or serious injury or damage.

13. Convention on the Marking of Plastic Explosives for the Purpose of Detection (Montreal, March 1, 1991)

Also known as: Plastic Explosives Convention
Entry into force: June 21, 1998
Summary: In light of the use of plastic explosives in terrorist acts involving the destruction of aircraft, other means of transportation, and other targets, the Plastic Explosives Convention introduces a legal regime to control and limit their use. Parties to the convention are obliged to ensure effective control over unmarked and undetectable plastic explosives within the national territory; as well as to take necessary measures to ensure that those held by the military or police are destroyed, consumed, marked, or rendered permanently ineffective within fifteen years after the date of entry into force of the convention in each signatory state.

14. International Convention for the Suppression of Terrorist Bombings (New York, December 15, 1997)

Also known as: Terrorist Bombing Convention
Entry into force: May 23, 2001
Summary: The Terrorist Bombing Convention makes it an offense for any person to deliver, place, discharge, or detonate explosives or other lethal devices in, into or against a place of public use, a government facility, a public

transportation system, or an infrastructure facility. The intention of the act should be to cause death or seriously bodily injury, or extensive destruction. It is also an offense for any person to participate as an accomplice or to organize or direct such acts.

15. International Convention for the Suppression of the Financing of Terrorism (New York, December 9, 1999)

Also known as: Terrorist Financing Convention
Entry into force: April 10, 2002
Summary: The Terrorist Financing Convention makes it an offense for any person to provide or collect funds to be used in full or in part to carry out acts of terrorism; as well as with the intention to cause death or serious bodily injury to a civilian, or to any other person not taking an active part in the hostilities in a situation of armed conflict. The convention also draws attention to persons engaged in the financing of terrorism through organizations which also have or claim to have charitable, social, or cultural goals, which nevertheless engage in illicit activities such as drug-trafficking or gun running.

16. International Convention for the Suppression of Acts of Nuclear Terrorism (New York, April 13, 2005)

Also known as: Nuclear Terrorism Convention
Entry into force: July 7, 2007
Summary: The Nuclear Terrorism Convention makes it an offense for any person to unlawfully and intentionally possess radioactive materials, or make or possess a device with the intention to cause death or seriously bodily injury, or substantial damage to property or the environment. The convention also criminalizes the use of or damage to a nuclear facility in a manner that releases or risks the release of radioactive material. It is also an offense for any person to participate as an accomplice or to organize or direct such acts.

Selected Bibliography

Aaron, Patrick. "Ex-Army Officer Helped Paper Get Sensitive Information." *Wall Street Journal*, May 15, 2009.

Arnold, Guy. *Mercenaries: The Scourge of the Third World*. London: Macmillan Press, 1999.

Assistant Deputy Under Secretary of Defense for Program Support. "Contractor Support of U.S. Operations in USCENTCOM AOR, Iraq, and Afghanistan." Washington, DC, February 2009.

Atwood, Rodney. *The Hessians: Mercenaries from Hessen-Kassel in the American Revolution*. Cambridge: Cambridge University Press, 1980.

Avant, Deborah D. *The Market for Force: The Consequences of Privatizing Security*. Cambridge: Cambridge University Press, 2005.

Baigell, Matthew. "'The Mercenaries': An Interview with Leon Golub." *Arts Magazine*, May 1981, 167–69.

Baker, Bruce. "Uneasy Partners: Democratisation and New Public Management," in *Contesting Public Sector Reforms: Critical Perspectives, International Debates*, ed. Pauline Dibben, Ian Roper, and Geoffrey Wood, 38–53. Basingstoke, UK: Palgrave Macmillan, 2004.

Barlow, Eeben. *Executive Outcomes: Against all Odds*. Alberton, South Africa: Galago Books, 2007.

BBC. "Profile: Idriss Deby." *BBC News*, February 2, 2008.

Block, Robert, and Daniel Pearl. "Much-Smuggled Gem Aids al-Qaida." *Wall Street Journal*, November 16, 2001.

Brooks, Doug. "From Humble Beginnings in Freetown: The Origins of the IPOA Code of Conduct." *Journal of International Peace Operations*, 3, no. 5 (March–April 2008): 9–10.

Callahan, Raymond. "The Company's Army, 1757–1798," in *The East India Company: 1600–1858*. Vol. 5, *Warfare, Expansion and Resistance*, ed. Patrick Tuck, 21–31. London: Routledge, 1998.

Carbonnier, Gilles. "The Carrot and the Stick: Reconsidering the Conditions Imposed on Aid." *Forum* 2 (February 2000): 12–19.

Carlton, David, and Carlo Schaerf, eds., *International Terrorism and World Security*. London: Croom Helm, 1975.

Center for Systemic Peace. "Global Trends in Armed Conflict, 1946–2008." Severn, MD, http://www.systemicpeace.org/conflict.htm (accessed June 1, 2009).

Center for the Study of Democracy. *Crime without Punishment: Countering Corruption and Organized Crime in Bulgaria*. Sofia, Bulgaria: CSD, January 2009.

Channel 4. "Aegis Close Down Website." *Channel 4 News*, April 7, 2006.

Chatterjee, Pratap. *Iraq, Inc.: A Profitable Occupation*. New York: Seven Stories Press, 2004.

Chauvet, Lisa, Paul Collier, and Anke Hoeffler. "The Cost of Failing States and the Limits of Sovereignty." Paper prepared for the World Institute for Development Economics Research of the United Nations University. Center for the Study of African Economies, University of Oxford, February 2007.

Childs, John. *Warfare in the Seventeenth Century*. London: Cassell & Co., 2001.

Clarke, Richard A. "Memorandum from Richard A. Clarke to Condoleezza Rice, January 25, 2001—Subject: Presidential Policy Initiative/Review—The Al-Qida Network." National Security Archive, George Washington University, http://www.gwu.edu/~nsarchiv/.

Clayton, Anthony. *Frontiersmen: Warfare in Africa since 1950*. London: UCL Press, 1999.

Committee on Oversight and Government Reform. "Hearing on Private Security Contracting in Iraq and Afghanistan." Washington, DC, October 2, 2007.

Confesercenti. *Le mani della criminalità sulle imprese. XI Rapporto SOS Impresa—Confesercenti*. Rome: Confesercenti, November 11, 2008.

Congressional Budget Office. *Contractor Support of U.S. Operations in Iraq*. Washington, DC: Congress of the United States, August 2008.

Congressional Research Service. *Private Security Contractors in Iraq: Background, Legal Status, and Other Issues*. Washington, DC: Congress of the United States, August 25, 2008.

Control Risks Group. "RiskMap 2004: International Political and Security Risks: What Can We Expect in 2004." Press Release, November 11, 2003.

Cotton, Evan, *East Indiamen: The East India Company Maritime Service*, ed. Charles Fawcett. London: Batchworth Press, 1949.

Cotula, Lorenzo, Sonja Vermeulen, Rebeca Leonard, and James Keeley. *Land Grab or Development Opportunity? Agricultural Investment and International Land Deals in Africa*. London/Rome: IIED/FAO/IFAD, 2009.

Davis, James R. *Fortune's Warriors: Private Armies and the New World Order*. Vancouver, BC: Douglas & McIntire, 2000.

Defense Science Board Task Force on Defense Biometrics. *Report of the Defense Science Board Task Force on Defense Biometrics*. Washington, DC: Office of the Under Secretary of Defense for Acquisition, Technology, and Logistics, March 2007.

Department of Defence (Australia). *Defence 2000: Our Future Defence Force*. Canberra: Defence Publishing Service, 2000.

Department of Defence (Australia). "Defence and Industry: Strategic Policy Statement." Canberra, June 2, 1998.

Department of Defense. *2006 Quadrennial Defense Review Report.* Washington, DC: Department of Defense, February 6, 2006.

Department of Defense. *Annual Report to the President and the Congress.* Washington, DC: Department of Defense, February 1995.

Department of Defense. "Defense Budget Recommendation Statement. As Prepared for Delivery by Secretary of Defense Robert M. Gates." Arlington, VA, April 6, 2009.

Department of Defense. *Directions for Defense. Report of the Commission on Roles and Missions of the Armed Forces.* Washington, DC: Department of Defense, May 24, 1995.

Department of Energy. "Order DOE O 470.1." Washington, DC, September 28, 1995.

Department of National Defence (Canada). *1994 Defence White Paper.* Ottawa, ON: Ministry of Supply and Services, 1994.

Department of State. *Country Reports on Terrorism 2007.* Washington, DC: Department of State, April 2008.

Department of State. *Country Reports on Terrorism 2008.* Washington, DC: Department of State, April 2009.

Department of State. "Overview of Civilian Police and Rule of Law Programs: General Information Fact Sheet." Washington, DC: Bureau of International Narcotics and Law Enforcement Affairs, Office of Civilian Police and Rule of Law, January 20, 2009.

Department of the Army. *Contractors on the Battlefield: Field Manual* (FM 3–100.21). Washington, DC: Department of the Army, January 2003.

Diplock Committee. *Report of the Committee of Privy Counsellors Appointed to Inquire into the Recruitment of Mercenaries* Cmnd 6569. London: Stationery Office, August 1976.

Duffield, Mark. *Global Governance and the New Wars: The Merging of Development and Security.* London: Zed Books, 2002.

Energy Information Administration. "September 2009 International Petroleum Monthly." Washington, DC, November 10, 2009, http://www.eia.doe.gov/emeu/ipsr/t21.xls.

European Commission. "Annex to the Proposal for a Directive of the European Parliament and of the Council on the Coordination of Procedures for the Award of Certain Public Works Contracts, Public Supply Contracts and Public Service Contracts in the Fields of Defence and Security." Brussels, Belgium, December 5, 2007.

Federal Department of Foreign Affairs (Switzerland) and the International Committee of the Red Cross. *Montreux Document on Pertinent International Legal Obligations and Good Practices for States Related to Operations of Private Military and Security Companies during Armed Conflict.* Montreux, Switzerland: The Directorate of International Law and the International Committee of the Red Cross, September 17, 2008.

Food and Agriculture Organization. "1.02 Billion People Hungry." Rome, *FAO Newsroom,* June 19, 2009.

Forbes. "The Global 200." New York, April 8, 2009, http://www.forbes.com/lists/2009/18/global-09_The-Global-2000_Rank.html.

Foreign and Commonwealth Office (UK). *Consultation on Promoting High Standards of Conduct by Private Military and Security Companies (PMSCs) Internationally.* London: Stationery Office, April 2009.

Foreign and Commonwealth Office (UK). *Private Military Companies: Options for Regulation.* London: Stationery Office, February 2002.

Fowler, Kenneth. *Medieval Mercenaries.* Vol. 1, *The Great Companies.* Oxford: Blackwell, 2001.

Fukuyama, Francis. "The End of History?" *The National Interest,* 16 (Summer 1989): 3–18.

Gaastra, F.S., and J. R. Bruijn. "The Dutch East India Company's Shipping, 1602–1795, in a Comparative Perspective." In *Ships, Sailors and Spices: East India Companies and Their Shipping in the 16th, 17th and 18th Centuries,* ed. Jaap R. Bruijn and Femme S. Gaastra, 177–208. Amsterdam: NEHA, 1993.

Government Accountability Office. *High-Level DOD Coordination Is Needed to Further Improve the Management of the Army's LOGCAP Contract.* Washington, DC: Government Accountability Office, 2005.

Government Accountability Office. *Rebuilding Iraq: Actions Still Needed to Improve the Use of Private Security Providers.* Washington, DC: Government Accountability Office, 2006.

Government Accountability Office. *Rebuilding Iraq: Fiscal Year 2003 Contract Award Procedures and Management Challenges.* Washington DC: Government Accountability Office, 2004.

Halliday, Fred. *Mercenaries.* Nottingham, UK: Russell Press, 1977.

"The Heart of Darkness." *Time,* December 22, 1961, 16–21.

Hoffman, Bruce. *Inside Terrorism.* New York: Columbia University Press, 2006.

Howard, Michael. "The Springtime of Nations." *Foreign Affairs* 69, no. 1 (1990): 17–32.

Howard, Michael. *War in European History.* Oxford: Oxford University Press, 1977.

Howe, Herbert M. "Private Security Forces and African Stability: The Case of Executive Outcomes." *Journal of Modern African Studies,* 36, no. 2 (1998): 307–31.

Huntington, Samuel P. *The Soldier and the State: The Theory and Politics of Civil-Military Relations.* Cambridge, MA: Belknap Press, 2002.

Independent Monitoring Commission (UK and Ireland). *Twenty-First Report of the Independent Monitoring Commission.* London: Stationery Office, May 7, 2009.

International Atomic Energy Agency. "Amendments to the Convention on the Physical Protection of Nuclear Material." Vienna, July 8, 2005.

International Atomic Energy Agency. *Convention on the Physical Protection of Nuclear Material,* in *United Nations Treaty Series* 1456, no. I-24631 (February 23, 1987): 124–60.

International Business Leaders Forum and BSR. "Voluntary Principles on Security and Human Rights," http://www.voluntaryprinciples.org/ (accessed January 1, 2008).

International Campaign to Ban Landmines. *Landmine Monitor Report: Toward a Mine-Free World. Executive Summary 2008.* Concord, Canada: St. Joseph Communications, 2008.

International Civil Aviation Organization. *Convention on Offences and Certain Other Acts Committed On Board Aircraft,* in *United Nations Treaty Series* 704, no. I-10106 (December 22, 1969): 220–54.

International Civil Aviation Organization. *Convention on the Marking of Plastic Explosives for the Purpose of Detection,* in *United Nations Treaty Series* 2122, no. I-36984 (October 25, 2000): 359.

International Cocoa Organization. "Assessment of the Movements of Global Supply and Demand." Berlin, Germany: April 3, 2008.

International Committee of the Red Cross. *Code of Conduct for the International Red Cross and Red Crescent Movement and Non-Governmental Organizations (NGOs) in Disaster Relief.* Geneva: ICRC/International Federation, 1994.

International Institute for Strategic Studies. *The Military Balance 1989–1990.* London: Brassey's, 1989.

International Institute for Strategic Studies. *The Military Balance 1995–1996.* Oxford: Oxford University Press, 1995.

International Institute for Strategic Studies. *The Military Balance 1998–1999.* Oxford: Oxford University Press, 1998.

International Institute for Strategic Studies. *The Military Balance 2009.* London: Routledge, 2009.

International Labour Organisation. *Minimum Age Convention.* Geneva: International Labour Office, June 26, 1973.

International Maritime Organization. *Convention for the Suppression of Unlawful Acts against the Safety of Maritime Navigation,* in *United Nations Treaty Series* 1678, no. I–29004 (June 26, 1992): 221–34.

International Maritime Organization. *Protocol to the Convention of 10 March 1988 for the Suppression of Unlawful Acts against the Safety of Fixed Platforms Located on the Continental Shelf,* in *United Nations Treaty Series* 1678, no. A-29004 (June 26, 1992): 201.

International Maritime Organization. "Protocol to the Convention of 10 March 1988 for the Suppression of Unlawful Acts against the Safety of Maritime Navigation." London, October 14, 2005.

International Maritime Organization. "Protocol to the Protocol for the Suppression of Unlawful Acts against the Safety of Fixed Platforms Located on the Continental Shelf." London, October 14, 2005.

International Maritime Organization. *Reports on Acts of Piracy and Armed Robbery against Ships: Acts Reported during April 2009.* London: International Maritime Organization, May 5, 2009.

International Maritime Organization. *Reports on Acts of Piracy and Armed Robbery against Ships: Annual Report 2008.* London: International Maritime Organization, March 19, 2009.

International Maritime Organization. *Resolution A.922(22): Code of Practice for the Investigation of the Crimes of Piracy and Armed Robbery against Ships.* London: International Maritime Organization, January 22, 2001.

International Peace Operations Association. *IPOA Code of Conduct.* Washington, DC: International Peace Operations Association, February 11, 2009.

Isenberg, David. *Shadow Force: Private Security Contractors in Iraq*. Westport, CT: Praeger, 2008.

Jackson, Robert H. *Quasi-States: Sovereignty, International Relations, and the Third World*. Cambridge: Cambridge University Press, 1990.

Janowitz, Morris. *The Professional Soldier: A Social and Political Portrait*. New York: Free Press, 1971.

Jones, Colin. "The Military Revolution and the Professionalisation of the French Army." In *The Military Revolution Debate: Readings on the Military Transformation of Early Modern Europe*, ed. Clifford J. Rogers, 149–67. Boulder, CO: Westview Press, 1995.

Krahmann, Elke "Private Military Services in the UK and Germany: Between Partnership and Regulation." *European Security*, 14, no. 2 (2005): 277–95.

Lane, Jan-Erik. *New Public Management*. London: Routledge, 2000.

Lindemann, Marc. "Civilian Contractors under Military Law." *Parameters* 37, no. 3 (Autumn 2007): 83–94.

Lukach, T. "Installations Transforming to Support Joint Warfighting Needs." American Forces Press Service, April 12, 2005.

Maclay, Edgar Stanton. *A History of American Privateers*. Morristown, NJ: Digital Antiquaria, 2004.

Maitland, Alison. "Big Business Starts to Scratch the Surface." *Financial Times*, September 13, 2005.

Mallet, Michael. *Mercenaries and Their Masters: Warfare in Renaissance Italy*. Totowa, NJ: Rowman and Littlefield, 1974.

Mandel, Robert. *Armies without States: The Privatization of Security*. Boulder, CO: Lynne Rienner, 2002.

Marshall, Donnie R. "Statement before the U.S. House of Representatives Committee on the Judiciary Subcommittee on Crime." Washington, DC, March 29, 2001.

McCormack, John. *One Million Mercenaries: Swiss Soldiers in the Armies of the World*. London: Leo Cooper, 1993.

McDowell, R. B., ed. *The Writings and Speeches of Edmund Burke*. Vol. 9, *The Revolutionary War, 1794–1797, and Ireland*. Oxford: Oxford University Press, 1991.

Millennium Challenge Corporation. "Factsheet on the Millennium Challenge Corporation: Reducing Poverty through Growth." Arlington, VA, February 2, 2004.

Ministry of Defence (UK). *The Strategic Defence Review—1998*. London: Stationery Office, 1998.

National Commission on Terrorist Attacks upon the United States. *The 9/11 Commission Report: Final Report of the National Commission on Terrorist Attacks upon the United States*. New York: W.W. Norton & Co, 2004.

National Counterterrorism Center. *2007 Report on Terrorism*. Washington, DC: National Counterterrorism Center, April 30, 2008.

National Counterterrorism Center. *2008 Report on Terrorism*. Washington, DC: National Counterterrorism Center, April 30, 2009.

National Intelligence Council. *Global Trends 2025: A Transformed World*. Washington, DC: U.S. Government Printing Office, November 2008.

Office of Management and Budget. "Circular No. A-76, Revised." Washington, DC, May 29, 2003.

O'Neill, Bard E., *Insurgency and Terrorism: From Revolution to Apocalypse.* 2nd ed. Washington, DC: Potomac Books, 2005.

Organisation for Economic Co-operation and Development. *Emerging Risks in the 21st Century: An Agenda for Action.* Paris: OECD Publications Service, 2003.

Organization of African Unity. *Convention for the Elimination of Mercenarism in Africa.*I In *United Nations Treaty Series* 1490, no. I-25573 (January 15, 1988): 96–103.

Ortiz, Carlos. "Private Military Contracting in Weak States: Permeation or Transgression of the New Public Management of Security?" *Review of African Security* 17, no. 2 (June 2008): 2–14.

Ortiz, Carlos. "Overseas Trade in Early Modernity and the Emergence of Private Military Companies."I In *Private Military and Security Companies: Chances, Problems, Pitfalls and Prospects*, ed. Thomas Jäger and Gerhard Kümmel, 11–22. Wiesbaden, Germany: VS Verlag, 2007.

Ortiz, Carlos. "The New Public Management of Security. The Contracting and Managerial State and the Private Military Industry." *Public Money and Management* 30, no. 1 (January 2010): 35–41.

Ortiz, Carlos. "The Private Military Company: An Entity at the Centre of Overlapping Spheres of Commercial Activity and Responsibility." In *Private Military and Security Companies: Chances, Problems, Pitfalls and Prospects*, ed. Thomas Jäger and Gerhard Kümmel, 55–68. Wiesbaden, Germany: VS Verlag, 2007.

Pardew Jr., James W. "Briefing on Train-and-Equip program for the Bosnian Federation. Briefing by Ambassador James W. Pardew, Jr. to the U.S. Department of State." Washington, DC, July 24, 1996.

Pelton, Robert Young. *License to Kill: Hired Guns in the War on Terror.* New York: Random House, 2006.

People's Bank of China. "Gold and Foreign Exchange Reserves." Beijing, China, September 2009.

Peters, Guy. *The Future of Governing: Four Emerging Models.* Lawrence: University Press of Kansas, 1996.

Piracy Reporting Centre. "Pirate Attacks off Somalia Already Surpass 2008 Figures." London, International Maritime Bureau, May 12, 2009.

President's Commission on Law Enforcement and Administration of Justice. "Task Force Report: Organized Crime." Washington, DC, 1967.

Rainey, Hal. G. *Understanding and Managing Public Organizations.* 4th ed. San Francisco: Jossey-Bass, 2009.

Rashid, Ahmed. *Taliban: The Story of the Afghan Warlords.* London: Pan Books, 2001.

"Ratendra's Lifetime Mission." *The Sun* (Fiji), September 14, 2003.

Redlich, Fritz. *The German Military Enterpriser and His Work Force: A Study in European Economic and Social History.* Vol. 1.Wiesbaden, Germany: Franz Steiner Verlag, 2004.

Reno, William. "African Weak States and Commercial Alliances." *African Affairs* 96, no. 383 (April 1997): 165–85.

Republic of Angola and the Union for the Total Independence of Angola. "Lusaka Protocol." Lusaka, Zambia, November 15, 1994.

Republic of Angola and the Union for the Total Independence of Angola. "Peace Accords for Angola," (the Bicesse Accords). Lisbon, May 31, 1991.

Republic of Bosnia and Herzegovina, Republic of Croatia and Federal Republic of Yugoslavia. "General Framework Agreement for Peace in Bosnia and Herzegovina" (the Dayton Peace Accords). Paris, December 14, 1995.

Republic of South Africa. *Prohibition of Mercenary Activity and Prohibition and Regulation of Certain Activities in an Area of Armed Conflict Bill.* Cape Town, Government Gazette, October 24, 2005.

Republic of South Africa. *Regulation of Foreign Military Assistance Act.* Cape Town: Government Gazette, May 20, 1998.

Roberts, Adam, and Richard Guelff. *Documents on the Laws of War.* 3rd ed. Oxford: Oxford University Press, 2000.

Rosenbloom, David H., and Robert S. Kravchuck. *Public Administration: Understanding Management, Politics, and Law in the Public Sector.* 5th ed. New York: McGraw-Hill, 2002.

Rubin, Elizabeth, "An Army of One's Own: In Africa, Nations Hire a Corporation to Wage War." *Harper's Magazine* (February 1997): 44–55.

Rumsfeld, Donald. H. "Letter to the Honorable Ike Skelton, Ranking Minority Member, Committee on Armed Services, U.S. House of Representatives." Washington, DC, May 4, 2004.

Seal, Patrick, and Maureen McConville. *The Hilton Assignment.* London: Trinity Press, 1973.

Shearer, David "Private Armies and Military Intervention." *Adelphi Paper* 316 (1998).

Shoaib Hasan, Syed. "Banned Pakistani Groups 'expand.'" *BBC,* June 30, 2009.

SIEDO (Subprocuraduría de Investigación Especializada contra la Delincuencia Organizada, Mexico). "México y Eastados Unidos Trabajan Coordinamente Para Combatir El Lavado De Dinero Provenienete Del Narcotráfico," Press Release 025/05. Mexico City, January 13, 2005.

Singer, Peter W. *Corporate Warriors: The Rise of the Privatized Military Industry.* New York: Cornell University Press, 2003.

Skelton, Ike. "Letter to the Honorable Donald H. Rumsfeld," Secretary of Defense. Washington, DC, April 2, 2004.

Smith, Adam. *An Inquiry into the Nature and Causes of the Wealth of Nations.* Hamburg: Management Laboratory Press, 2008.

Solis, William M. *Testimony before the Subcommittee on National Security, Emerging Threats, and International Relations.* Washington, DC: Government Accountability Office, June 13, 2006.

Special Inspector General for Iraq Reconstruction. *Cost, Outcome, and Oversight of Iraq Oil Reconstruction Contract with Kellogg Brown & Root Services, Inc.* Arlington, VA: Office of the Special Inspector General for Iraq Reconstruction, January 13, 2009.

Special Inspector General for Iraq Reconstruction. *Quarterly Report to the United States Congress.* Arlington, VA, April 30, 2007.

Steensgaard, Niels."The Companies as a Specific Institution in the History of European Expansion." In *Companies and Trade: Essays on Overseas Trading Companies during the Ancien Régime*, ed. Leonard Blussé and Femme Gaastra, 245–64. Leiden, Netherlands: Leiden University Press, 1981.

Stockholm Peace Research Institute. *SIPRI Yearbook 1998: Armaments, Disarmament and International Security.* Oxford: Oxford University Press, 1998.

Stockholm Peace Research Institute. *SIPRI Yearbook 2006: Armaments, Disarmament and International Security.* Oxford: Oxford University Press, 2006.

Subcommittee on Investigations and Oversight. "Memorandum from Subcommittee Staff to Chairman Brad Miller, Subcommittee on Investigations and Oversight, Committee of Science and Technology." Washington, DC, August 21, 2008.

Suez Canal Authority. "2008 Report." Ismailia, Egypt, 2008, http://www.suezcanal. gov.eg/Files/Publications/32.pdf.

Superintendent Government, India. *The Army in India and Its Evolution: Including an Account of the Establishment of the Royal Air Force in India.* Calcutta: Superintendent Government Printing, 1924.

Switzerland. *Protocol Additional to the Geneva Convention of 12 August 1949, and relating to the Protection of Victims of International Armed Conflicts (Protocol 1),* in *United Nations Treaty Series* 1125, no. I-17512 (January 23, 1979): 3.

Syed Shoaib Hasan. "Banned Pakistani Groups "Expand.'" *BBC News,* June 30, 2009.

Taleb, Nassim Nicholas. *The Black Swan: The Impact of the Highly Improbable.* London: Penguin Books, 2007.

Taulbee, James Larry. "The Privatization of Security: Modern Conflict, Globalization and Weak States." *Civil Wars* 5, no. 2 (2002): 1–24.

Thomson, Janice E. *Mercenaries, Pirates, and Sovereigns: State-Building and Extraterritorial Violence in Early Modern Europe.* Princeton, NJ: Princeton University Press, 1994.

Tickler, Peter. *The Modern Mercenary: Dog of War, or Soldier of Honour?* Wellingborough, UK: Patrick Stephens, 1987.

TOTAL. "Angola's Deepwater Girassol Field Comes on Stream," Press Release. Courbevoie, France, December 4, 2001.

TOTAL. *Girassol: A Stepping Stone for the Industry.* Courbevoie, France: TOTAL, September 19, 2008.

"Transcript: FT Interview with Deputy Chief of Hizbollah." *Financial Times,* May 12, 2009.

United Kingdom, "Defence (Options for Change): Statement by the Secretary of State for Defence (Mr. Tom King) to the House of Commons." *Hansard* 177 (July 25, 1990): 468–86.

United Kingdom. *Drug Trafficking Act 1994.* London: Stationery Office, 1994.

United Kingdom. *Terrorism Act 2000.* London: Stationery Office, 2000.

United Nations. "50 Years of United Nations Peacekeeping Operations, 1948–1998." New York, October 1998, http://www.un.org/en/peacekeeping/sites/50years/.

United Nations. *Convention on the Control of Transboundary Movement of Hazardous Wastes and Their Disposal (Basel Convention),* in *United Nations Treaty Series* 1673, no. 28911 (May 5, 1992): 57.

United Nations. *Convention on the Law of the Sea,* in *United Nations Treaty Series* 1833, no. 31363 (November 16, 1994): 3.

United Nations. *Convention on the Prevention and Punishment of Crimes against Internationally Protected Persons, including Diplomatic Agents,* A/Res/3166 (XXVIII), annex. New York: United Nations, December 14, 1973.

United Nations. *Convention on the Rights of the Child,* in *United Nations Treaty Series* 1577, no. 27531 (September 2, 1990): 3.

United Nations. *International Convention against the Recruitment, Use, Financing and Training of Mercenaries,* A/Res/44/34, annex. New York: United Nations, December 4, 1989.

United Nations. *International Convention against the Taking of Hostages,* in *United Nations Treaty Series* 1316, no. 21931 (June 3, 1983): 205.

United Nations. *International Convention for the Suppression of Acts of Nuclear Terrorism,* A/Res/59/290, annex. New York: United Nations, April 13, 2005.

United Nations. *International Convention for the Suppression of Terrorist Bombings,* A/Res/52/164, annex. New York: United Nations, December 15, 1997.

United Nations. "General Assembly Resolution A/Res/3034(XXVII)." New York, December 18, 1972.

United Nations. *International Convention for the Suppression of the Financing of Terrorism,* A/Res/54/109, annex. New York: United Nations, December 9, 1999.

United Nations. "Security Council Resolution S/RES/1373 (2001)." New York, September 28, 2001.

United Nations. "Security Council Resolution S/RES/733 (2007)." New York, February 20, 2007.

United Nations. "United Nations Global Compact:" New York, http://www.unglobalcompact.org/ (accessed June 1, 2009).

United Nations. "United Nations Peacekeeping: Questions and Answers." New York, September 1998, http://www.un.org/Depts/dpko/dpko/question/faq.htm.

United Nations Children's Fund (UNICEF). "The Paris Principles: Principles and Guidelines on Children Associated with Armed Forces or Armed Group." Paris, January 30, 2007.

United Nations Conference on Trade and Development. *Capital Flows and Growth in Africa.* New York: United Nations, 2000.

United Nations Department of Peacekeeping Operations. "United Nations Peacekeeping Fact Sheet." New York, June 2009.

United Nations Development Programme. "UNDP: Frequently Asked Questions" New York, http://www.un.org/depts/ptd/ (accessed September 1, 2007).

United Nations Development Programme. *Human Development Indices: A Statistical Update 2008.* New York: Human Development Report Office, 2008.

United Nations General Assembly. "Approved resources for peacekeeping operations for the period from 1 July 2008 to 30 June 2009." New York, May 1, 2009.

United Nations Mine Action Service. "International Mine Action Standards." New York, http://www.mineactionstandards.org/ (accessed February 27, 2009).

United Nations Office on Drugs and Crime. *World Drug Report 2008.* New York: United Nations, June 2008.

United Nations Office on Drugs and Crime. *World Drug Report 2009*. New York: United Nations, June 2009.

United States. *Code of Federal Regulations*. Washington, DC, http://www.gpoaccess.gov/cfr/.

United States. *Competition in Contracting Act of 1984*. Public Law 98-369, 98 Stat. 1175. Washington, DC: Government Printing Office, 1984.

United States. *Federal Register*. Washington, DC, http://www.gpoaccess.gov/fr/.

United States. *Foreign Corrupt Practices Act of 1977*. Public Law 95-213, 91 Stat. 1494. Washington, DC: Government Printing Office, 1977.

United States. *FY2008 National Defense Authorization Act*. Public Law 110–181. Washington, DC: Government Printing Office, 2008.

United States. *Homeland Security Act of 2002*. Public Law 107–296. Washington, DC: Government Printing Office, 2002.

United States. *Security and Accountability for Every Port Act of 2006*. Public Law 109–347. Washington, DC: Government Printing Office, 2006.

United States. *United States Code*. Washington, DC, http://www.gpoaccess.gov/uscode/.

United States. *Uniting and Strengthening America by Providing Appropriate Tools Required to Intercept and Obstruct Terrorism Act of 2001*. Public Law 107-56, 115 Stat. 272. Washington, DC: Government Printing Office, 2001.

United States Sentencing Commission. *2008 Federal Sentencing Guidelines Manual*. Washington, DC: United States Sentencing Commission, November 1, 2008, http://www.ussc.gov/2008guid/.

United States, United Kingdom, and the International Civil Aviation Organization. *Protocol for the Suppression of Unlawful Acts of Violence at Airports Serving International Civil Aviation, Supplementary to the Convention of 23 September 1971 for the Suppression of Unlawful Acts against the Safety of Civil Aviation*, in *United Nations Treaty Series* 1589, no. A–14118 (December 22, 1990): 474–78.

United States, United Kingdom, and the Union of Soviet Socialist Republics. *Convention for the Suppression of Unlawful Acts against the Safety of Civil Aviation*, in *United Nations Treaty Series* 974, no. I–14118 (July 18, 1975): 177.

United States, United Kingdom, and the Union of Soviet Socialist Republics. *Convention for the Suppression of Unlawful Seizure of Aircraft*, in *United Nations Treaty Series* 860, no. I-12325 (March 3, 1973): 105.

Van Creveld, Martin *The Transformation of War*. New York: Free Press, 1991.

Weber, Max. "Bureaucracy." In *From Max Weber: Essays in Sociology*, eds. and trans Gerth, H. H., and C. Wright Mills, 196–244. London: Routledge, 1997.

Weber, Max. "Politics as a Vocation." in *From Max Weber: Essays in Sociology*, eds. and trans Gerth, H. H., and C. Wright Mills, 77–129. London: Routledge, 1997, 1997.

White House. "Farewell Radio and Television Address to the American People by President Dwight D. Eisenhower." Washington, DC, January 17, 1961.

White House. "Inaugural Address By President Barack Hussein Obama." Washington, DC, January 21, 2009.

White House. "President Clinton: Training and Equipping the Bosnian Federation." Washington, DC, July 9, 1996.

White House. "Remarks Announcing America's Economic Bill of Rights." Washington, DC, July 3, 1987.

White House. "Remarks by President Clinton Announcing the Initiative to Streamline Government." Washington, DC, March 3, 1993.

White House. "White House Fact Sheet: Training and Equipping the Bosnian Federation." Washington, DC, July 9, 1996.

White, Leonard D. "Introduction to the Study of Public Administration." In *Classics of Public Administration*, ed. Jay M. Shafritz, Albert C. Hyde, and Sandra J. Parkes, 5th ed., 56–63. Belmont, CA: Wadsworth, 2004.

Wilson, Peter. "Warfare in the Old Regime 1648–1789." In *European Warfare 1453–1815*, ed. Jeremy Black, 69–95. London: Macmillan Press, 1999.

Wilson, Woodrow. "The Study of Administration." In *Classics of Public Administration*, ed. Jay M. Shafritz, Albert C. Hyde, and Sandra J. Parkes, 5th ed., 22–55. Belmont, CA: Wadsworth, 2004.

Wool, Harold. *The Military Specialist: Skilled Manpower for the Armed Forces.* Baltimore: Johns Hopkins University Press, 1968.

World Bank Independent Evaluation Group. *Engaging with Fragile States: An IEG Review of World Bank Support to Low-Income Countries under Stress. 2006.* Washington, DC: World Bank, 2006.

Young, Adam J. *Contemporary Maritime Piracy in Southeast Asia: History, Causes and Remedies.* Singapore: ISEAS Publishing, 2007.

Zamparelli, Steven J. "Contractors on the Battlefield: What Have We Signed Up For." *Air Force Journal of Logistics* 23, no. 3 (Fall 1999): 11–9.

Index

About the Author

CARLOS ORTIZ is a visiting research fellow at the Centre for Global Political Economy at the University of Sussex in the United Kingdom, from which he was awarded a PhD in international relations. Since the mid-1990s, he has conducted extensive research into the history and organization of private military companies, as well as the public management strategies and regulations involving their use. He has published various articles and lectured in these areas. His work has also been oriented toward the dissemination of scholarly resources on security contracting worldwide.